TOO LONG A SACRIFICE

TOO LONG A SACRIFICE

Life and Death in Northern Ireland Since 1969

JACK HOLLAND

DODD, MEAD & COMPANY
NEW YORK

Acknowledgement is made to the following:

Anvil Books for quotation from *Paisley, Man of Wrath* by Patrick Marrinan, 1973.

Commonweal for some material in chapter 5 that appeared in a different form in the August 31, 1979 issue.

Faber and Faber for four lines from poem "February Afternoon" by Edward Thomas.

Granada Publishing Ltd. for two lines beginning "Which of us can forgive himself?" from *The Doors of Stone, Poems 1938–1962* by F. T. Prince.

Harcourt Brace Jovanovich, Inc. and Faber and Faber Ltd. for excerpt from "Gerontion" from *Collected Poems 1909–1962* by T. S. Eliot.

A. M. Heath & Company, Ltd. and Mrs. Sonia Brownell Orwell for excerpt from *Homage to Catalonia* by George Orwell.

Lines from "Easter, 1916" are reprinted by permission of Macmillan Publishing Co., Inc. from *Collected Poems* of W. B. Yeats. Copyright 1924 by Macmillan Publishing Co., Inc., renewed 1952 by Bertha Georgie Yeats.

Magill magazine, Dublin, for quote of interview with a member of the Provisional IRA, 1978.

The Nation for excerpts from "Letter from a Belfast Ghetto," March 24, 1979, and "Inside the IRA," October 27, 1979, by Jack Holland.

Excerpts from "Ulster Bloody Ulster" by Jack Holland appeared in *The New York Times Magazine*, July 15, 1979. Copyright © 1979 by The New York Times Company. Reprinted by permission.

Excerpt from Derek Mahon's *Poems 1962–1978* copyright © 1979 Derek Mahon. Reprinted by permission of Oxford University Press.

One line of a poem by Isaac Rosenberg is from *The Collected Works of Isaac Rosenberg*, edited by Ian Parsons. Poems, plays and letters of Isaac Rosenberg © The Literary Executors of Mrs. A. Wynick 1937 and 1979. Reprinted by permission of Oxford University Press, Inc. and Chatto and Windus Ltd.

Pluto Press for quotation from *Northern Ireland: The Orange State* by Michael Farrell, 1976.

Random House, Inc. for four lines of W. H. Auden poem, "Those Who Will Not Reason," from *The English Auden: Poems, Essays and Dramatic Writings*, edited by Edward Mendelson. Copyright © 1977 by Edward Mendelson, William Meredith, and Monroe Spears, Executors of the Estate of W. H. Auden.

Rolling Stone for quote from article by John Hamill, November 29, 1979.

The Student Christian Journal for quote from *Estranged Relations: A Brief Guide to Anglo Irish History*, edited by Mary Condren and Garreth Byrne, published by SCM Publications, 40 Moat Lane, Birmingham B5 5BE, England, 1979.

1   2   3   4   5   6   7   8   9   10

Library of Congress Cataloging in Publication Data

Holland, Jack, 1947–
    Too long a sacrifice.

    Includes index.
    1. Northern Ireland—History—1969–   I.   Title.
DA990.U46H64   941.60824   80-27267
ISBN 0-396-07934-2

For my mother and father

Contents

List of Illustrations

Preface

This book arises out of a series of articles I wrote on Northern Ireland for a variety of American magazines over the last two or three years. It is an attempt to give as full a perspective as possible on certain aspects of the situation which I feel are crucial to an understanding of it but which have not been commonly dealt with in American writing.

It is a personal account, and a critical one, but it is not a polemic: there has already been much sloganeering, much crying and much sermonizing about Northern Ireland. I should be well satisfied if the following pages should instead induce some thinking about it.

The Northern Ireland problem came to the attention of the world in the 1960s; during the 1970s its violent scenes became familiar to many; as we go into a new decade my hope is that, when it ends, another book like this will not need to be written.

The situation being what it is in Northern Ireland, I have found it necessary to give several of the people mentioned in this book false names. I am thinking of "Sean O'Neill," the young Provisional IRA member mentioned in chapters 2 and 6; "Sammy," the Ulster Defence Association assassin interviewed in chapter 4; and "Detective Sergeant Miller," the policeman whose work I describe in chapter 7. I would also like to point out that the description of the murder in chapter 4 is based on immediate sources which, again for obvious as well as ethical reasons, cannot be attributed.

There are many people who assisted me in gathering the material for this book who will have to remain anonymous. They did so under often trying circumstances. To them I offer my thanks.

My thanks are also due to David McKittrick, the Northern Editor of the *Irish Times*, whose knowledge of the Northern Ireland situation proved invaluable. I would particularly like to acknowledge his cooperation in the use of material in chapter 4 from our joint manuscript, *The Assassins: A History of the Ulster Defence Association*, which will appear later in the year from Mercier Press, Cork.

I would like to thank the members of my family, particularly my mother, for the many interesting letters they wrote me over the years, and my aunt Cissy for her information concerning the Belfast mills and much else.

Finally, to my wife, Mary Hudson, my thanks for all her help in many different ways, which made the completion of this book much less of a task than it might have been.

J. H.

Too long a sacrifice
Can make a stone of the heart.
O when may it suffice?

WILLIAM BUTLER YEATS, "EASTER, 1916"

General Glossary

*(A fuller glossary of organizations
appears at the end of the text.)*

REPUBLICANS: Those who want a United Ireland. Overwhelmingly Catholic.

LOYALISTS: Those loyal to the British crown. Overwhelmingly Protestant.

ULSTER: One of the original four provinces of Ireland. Six of its nine counties (those with a Protestant majority) were formed into Northern Ireland in 1921 by British government decree.

NORTHERN IRELAND: Part of the United Kingdom but with its own parliament until 1972. Population one and a half million, of which one-third are Catholic.

UNIONIST PARTY: The main Protestant political grouping in Northern Ireland. Now split.

ROYAL ULSTER CONSTABULARY: Northern Ireland's police force, mostly Protestant.

B-SPECIALS: An all-Protestant militia recruited to support the police. The British government abolished it in 1969.

ULSTER DEFENCE REGIMENT: A locally recruited regiment of the British army meant to replace the B-Specials. Mostly Protestant.

ULSTER VOLUNTEER FORCE (1): Protestant militia formed to oppose Irish Home Rule in 1912.

ULSTER VOLUNTEER FORCE (2): An illegal Protestant terrorist group formed in 1965.

ORANGE ORDER. 200-year-old religious Protestant organization with strong links to the Unionist Party.

REPUBLIC OF IRELAND (formerly the FREE STATE): Independent of Britain since 1921. Population approximately three million. Mostly Catholic.

IRISH REPUBLICAN ARMY (IRA). Irish nationalist guerrilla group, mostly Catholic, formed to fight the British in the 1919–21 War of Independence and currently split into:

PROVISIONAL IRA: responsible for most of the recent violence, and

OFFICIAL IRA: a Stalinist Communist organization on cease-fire since 1972.

SINN FEIN (Pronounced "Shin Fane"—Gaelic for "Ourselves Alone"). Political wing of the IRA. Now split into Provisional and Official factions.

TOO LONG A SACRIFICE

1

Ghosts

Patiently endured so long as it seemed beyond redress, a grievance comes to appear intolerable once the possibility of removing it crosses men's minds. For the mere fact that certain abuses have been remedied draws attention to others and they now appear more galling....
—ALEXIS DE TOCQUEVILLE

In the street outside our house was the ghost of a dead policeman. He had been a member of the Northern Ireland Royal Ulster Constabulary (RUC), a Protestant paramilitary force set up to defend a beleaguered state. He was killed in a conflict that my grandparents, with whom I lived, recalled vividly. To me it seemed an age away. A Catholic Irish Republican Army (IRA) sniper felled him in the confused and bloody fighting that followed the birth of Northern Ireland, a state made up of Ireland's Protestant-dominated six northeastern counties. The Catholic Irish majority, under the leadership of the IRA, were fighting throughout the rest of Ireland for an independent republic. But in Belfast they were fighting to defend the city's Catholic population against angry Protestant loyalists determined to stay out of an Irish republic and loyal to the British crown. The British offered the compromise of partition, giv-

1

ing the northeast its own parliament under British rule, and the rest of Ireland dominion status within the Commonwealth.

The compromise was accepted; the Catholics of the new state of Northern Ireland, born in 1921, were stranded. They were besieged by a two-thirds larger loyalist population, who were themselves besieged by nationalist Irish beyond their erratic, crazy border. Between July 1920 and July 1922, 453 people were killed in Belfast alone, 257 of them Catholics. The RUC man was one of the many members of the crown forces to die at the hands of the IRA, which during the years after the creation of Northern Ireland has struck at army and police, as well as occasionally taking retaliatory action against Protestant civilians. His death did not affect the outcome. Northern Ireland survived, but at a terrible cost. Blood had been spilled, and a large minority was alienated from the state within which they found themselves.

My Catholic grandmother, Kate Murphy, did not call his killing murder. When still very young, I became aware of the moral limbo in which acts of war could be perpetrated. I became vaguely conscious that the police—the Royal Ulster Constabulary—were forces fighting in an old war, a war not yet lost or won. On the other side were those who pulled the trigger that cut down the constable in our gateway: the shadowy army of the IRA.

The policeman's ghost was there as one reminder of the price paid for Northern Ireland's existence. To me it was real enough. Hovering in the gas-lit street in the deep shadows cast by the gently humming street lamps, it would appear with every unexpected noise and disappear with every dawn.

Soon it was to be joined by other ghosts, other reminders that I was a citizen of a state stained with the blood of old animosities, old hatreds—a state with a frightening legacy.

Divided states produce unusual families. I had the fortune to be part of one. It was unusual because, during a time when sectarian passions were virtually unchecked, a Catholic, Kate Murphy, my grandmother, married a Protestant, William Henry Holland, my grandfather. I lived with them until I was six—they shared their home with three of their children, including my father, who lived with them long after his marriage and long after I was born.

It was a large old house in a shabbily genteel section of a Catholic area in downtown Belfast called "the Markets." My grandfather, a big-boned, handsome veteran of World War I with a strong back and fine mustache, was a stablekeeper for a Belfast carting firm. We lived on their premises, next door to the stables where the big dray horses were kept. My grandfather had a way with horses. He'd been a coach driver at the turn of the century, and during the First World War he drove a supply wagon team through the mud of many battlefields. I would go to the stables with him, watch him fondle and stroke the big animals with a rare tenderness.

The state of which we were citizens—and the Catholics were for the most part reluctant citizens—was set up to ensure privileges would be accorded to "loyalists." And loyalists were Protestants. By definition, a Catholic was a rebel.

In the unlikely event that Catholics had any doubts, the government, composed entirely of Protestant Unionists, spelled this out quite clearly. In the words of a man who was to reign as Northern Ireland's Prime Minister for twenty years, Lord Brookeborough: "I recommend those people who are loyalists not to employ Roman Catholics, 99% of whom are disloyal; I want you to remember one point in regard to the employment of people who are disloyal . . . you are disenfranchising yourselves in that way. . . ."

My grandfather, though by no means a loyalist politically, ensured that his privilege as a Protestant kept the family immune to the poverty and deprivation which afflicted the poorer sections of the Markets, where some of the oldest slums in Belfast housed a large Catholic population. We lived near the "better half"; the houses there were three stories high, with front-room parlors and luxuries unheard of in the other streets, such as bathrooms. In this section years before, the music hall artistes who came to Belfast had rented rooms. This gave even the Markets' more privileged section a rather unsavory reputation in what was a dour, puritanical city.

My mother came from the poorer area. During the thirties her parents were so indigent that a sister and brother were placed in a foster home. When the boy died, his parents were forced to bury him in a paupers' grave—a common, unmarked pit for those who even in death were not accorded their private space. Her father was a baker. Most Market people who had jobs worked as laborers, or had little stalls in the weekly vegetable market held in the area and from which it derived its name. But there was also a lucrative smuggling business. After World War II goods which were scarce in Northern Ireland were often plentiful in the Irish Free State, as it was called then. To avoid paying customs duties, people resorted to smuggling—sometimes on a large scale. It added to the Markets' already dubious reputation.

My father was the youngest of a family of seven: three girls and four boys. He was the only one baptized a Catholic. The hospital where he was born was run by nuns, who more or less kidnapped him when they discovered his mother was a Catholic. Once bap-tized, his mother decided to rear the last of her children in the faith from which she herself had lapsed. My aunt Martha, his sister, was converted at the age of twenty-one. So on Sundays I was perplexed to see my parents, my grandmother, and my aunt go off to mass while my grandfather and my favorite uncle, Tom, stayed mysteri-ously at home.

When I went to visit my Uncle Willy, who was and is a Protes-tant, I noticed the walls of his house were decorated with pictures of a pallid-looking gentleman in a splendid uniform. He was "The King." Across the back of his armchairs I observed covers that came from somewhere called Canada; they were pictures of men with sharp-pointed hats riding horses, and they were dressed in red jackets.

At home in the Markets, my parents' room was hung with pic-tures of Jesus Christ and the Sacred Heart, as well as those of a sweet-faced lady in a blue mantle. She was "The Queen"—of heav-en. When my mother talked of a better place in this world—which she often did—it was not Canada, but the United States. So we had our contending royal families—earthly and unearthly—and our ri-val utopias. By the age of six, I'd made these rough equations in my mind.

There were a few other, minor mysteries that caught my atten-tion. We had an old radio, which sat in the corner of our living room. Its speakers were like the ribs of a big horse. When the local Northern Ireland radio station was closing down for the night it broadcast the British national anthem, "God Save the King" (later "Queen"). Or so I believed, for I rarely had the chance to hear this piece of music, dreary and somber as it is. My grandmother, true to her maiden name of Murphy, would switch to the station of the Irish Free State (known as the Republic of Ireland after 1948), broadcasting from Athlone in central Ireland. After eleven P.M. she would huddle up against the speakers, turn to Athlone, and listen intently as the Irish national anthem, "The Soldier's Song," was broadcast. Musically, I think, we were better off for it—it was a livelier tune altogether. The words had a nice, defiant ring that was decidedly more appealing:

> *Soldiers are we, whose lives are pledged to Ireland;*
> *Some have come from a land beyond the wave,*
> *Sworn to be free, no more our ancient sireland*
> *Shall shelter the despot or the slave.*

Still, I had to strain my ears to hear it. My grandmother insisted on keeping it low lest a passing RUC man catch its rebellious strains, even though that was most unlikely—the street was separated from us by fifty yards and a stout gate. Perhaps she was thinking of the ghost, who if he heard "The Soldier's Song" would come banging on our door. For her the simple act of changing stations was tantamount to an act of rebellion. (Northern Ireland's Catholics still show the same dislike of the British anthem. The televisions are all switched off in Catholic homes just before the closedown of the British stations. In cinemas in Catholic areas, when the anthem is being played, the audience rises in a body and walks out. When I went occasionally into a loyalist ghetto to go to the movies, I always had to be very careful to remember where I was and not bolt for the door when "The Queen" came on.)

As I grew older I realized my grandmother's caution was founded on past experience. Before coming to live in the Markets, her family had lived in a loyalist area of the city around the Crumlin Road, which runs northwest towards the basalt hills of the nearby countryside. When Northern Ireland was receiving its bloody baptism between 1921 and 1924, she was forced to take her children out of the city, back to the safety of the South Down Mountains of Mourne, the Catholic enclave where she grew up. These evacuations came with every crisis the Northern state suffered; she, a Catholic living among loyalists, was a hostage for the behavior of Catholics elsewhere.

The early twenties produced a crop of horror stories that became the repertoire of my grandmother. As a child I sat fascinated on her knee when she told me them. Her own experiences were rarely mentioned. To her they were of no consequence—she had survived. She thought only of those who had not. She repeated one story again and again. Huddled against her warm bosom and her apron, which smelled of baked bread, I listened to the story of the McMahon murders.

Owen McMahon was a publican, one of the few trades for Northern Ireland's Catholics that opened a way into the middle class. He and his family lived on the Antrim Road, a quiet, tree-lined thoroughfare of large, comfortable homes and substantial gardens. As she told it, on the early hours of a cold March morning in 1922, a group of armed militiamen known as the B-Specials, an organization formed to reinforce the police, broke into the McMahon home. They lined up Owen McMahon, his five sons, and a barman who worked for him and lived in his house, and shot them in the living room. Though seriously wounded, two of the sons survived. According to my grandmother, a young boy who had hid under the couch escaped. It was an image of ultimate terror for me—at night I would see the terrified boy crouching beneath the couch listening to the shootings and the heavy thuds of his brothers and father as they slumped to the floor.

In later years I discovered that the McMahons were killed in reprisal for the IRA's shooting two B-Specials the day before. It was a pattern that established itself early on in the history of the state: The guerrillas attack the forces of the state, and the loyalists reply by striking at those who they believe support them—the ordinary Catholics. Contemporary loyalist terrorist groups, such as the Ulster Defence Association (UDA) and the Ulster Volunteer Force (UVF), regularly kill innocent Catholics in response to IRA actions. Their assumption, one which they've been brought up to accept without question, is that Catholics are by nature "disloyal."

By the end of the 1920s, the state of Northern Ireland seemed stable. The recalcitrant Catholics were beaten into submission; the threat from the IRA diminished as that organization split again and again over political developments in the South. My grandmother's flights to the Mourne Mountains became a thing of the past. Northern Ireland's Unionist government ruled a one-party state with an extraordinary battery of legal powers, assembled under its Civil Authority (Special Powers) Act, passed in the local parliament in 1922. This act allowed the government to intern its citizens without trial, to arrest without warrant, to prohibit inquests, and to impose the death penalty for a variety of small firearms and explosives offenses. It had a catchall provision, which read: "If any person does any act of such a nature as to be calculated to be prejudicial to the preservation of the peace or maintenance of order in Northern Ireland and not specifically provided for in the regulations, he shall be deemed to be guilty of an offense against the regulations."

Though intended only to be operational for one year, the act soon became permanent. It was an outrage against civil liberties, and a standing condemnation of the government that felt such powers necessary for its preservation. Westminster, the sovereign parliament, kept it quiet as a kind of dirty secret. After all, Northern Ireland was supposed to be part of the United Kingdom. Most people outside Northern Ireland did not realize at what cost it would remain so. The act did find admirers, however. In 1963, Mr. Vorster, Prime Minister of South Africa, was speaking for passage of the Coercion Bill in the South African parliament. He said he "would be willing to exchange all the legislation of that sort for one clause of the Northern Ireland Special Powers Act." Northern Ireland loyalists were rather taken with the implied comparison: Were not they, like the white South Africans, defending civilization against the depredations of the natives?

The existence of the Special Powers Act did little to make my grandmother feel secure. She was rearing a Catholic boy, my father, the only one of her children to be brought up a Catholic. Living as they did in the middle of a loyalist ghetto meant he was constantly being attacked and threatened. To defend himself, he took up boxing. (By the age of seventeen he had won the Ulster bantamweight title.)

In the 1930s the state underwent another crisis, provoked by the world economic slump. Belfast's major industries were then the linen mills and the shipbuilding works. The latter employed twenty thousand men in the 1920s. By 1933 the figure was nearer two thousand. The vast majority affected were Protestant. For a brief and remarkable period they joined with the Catholic unemployed to march and protest in demand for higher relief rates. The Unionists replied by fanning the flames of sectarian hatred again. Loyalist spokesmen cajoled the protesting Protestants by telling them they were the victims of a Catholic-Republican-Communist conspiracy to destroy Northern Ireland. The RUC was sent into Catholic areas to break up demonstrations, and soon the unity of the two sides was smashed as the crisis deteriorated into Catholic and police confrontations.

Before long, bands of loyalist assassins were back on the streets, and Catholics—once more seen in their old role as disloyal rebels—were being murdered. For my family, the crisis of the state took on its old familiar form. This time, they were more vulnerable because of my father, and because his sister Martha had become a Catholic. My grandmother packed her bags and bundled her son and daughter into a train for the safety of the South Down hills. They left just in time. A day or so afterwards a gang of armed men came to the door looking for my father. They regarded his flight to safety as a minor triumph—they'd forced another "Fenian," as the loyalists describe Catholics, to leave the city.

My aunt Martha returned home shortly afterwards. She had worked since she was fourteen in a linen mill near home. At seven one morning she walked into her workplace in the winding room and was about to begin when the other workers, all Protestants, walked out. She was told they would not work with her because Catholics had attacked some British soldiers in another part of Belfast. Since she was now a Catholic, she was somehow held responsible for the actions of her coreligionists. She was forced to leave. When sectarian tensions died down, Martha went back. But soon she found herself another job in a different mill.

What few Catholic workers there were in the shipyards were expelled, as they had been in the twenties, when several of them were thrown into the water and pelted with "Belfast confetti"—screws and bolts—as they tried to struggle ashore. By the time this particular outbreak of sectarian violence had tapered off, hundreds of Catholics had lost their jobs, and over two thousand had been driven from their homes by intimidatory mobs.

Partition had created a state in which the Catholics were hostages to loyalist fears, to be bullied, threatened, and evicted whenever the Unionist government and its followers perceived a challenge to its rule. Loyalist violence, inflicted as it was with racist fury, was a reminder to Catholics of their second-class status within Northern Ireland. Not surprisingly, thousands of Catholics emigrated every year.

Loyalist attitudes were starkly revealed during the trial of two Protestants accused of murdering a Catholic publican in Belfast in 1935. A Unionist member of parliament, A. P. Babington, appearing on behalf of the accused men, said of the victim, "The man was a publican and a Roman Catholic and therefore liable to assassination." The logic was impeccable.

In moving to the Markets area, my grandparents left the fears of sectarian harassment behind them. By the time I was old enough to understand my grandmother's stories, Northern Ireland was comparatively tranquil. Rummaging around in my grandfather's wardrobe, I soon came across the trappings of other wars, which for me took precedence over the animosities of almost forgotten days.

Once I found a frightening contraption of tubes and straps with a glass front. It was his gas mask from the trenches, he explained. He told me with grim humor how he was forced to catch rats once and eat them. That, I learned, was World War I. And then there was World War II, represented for me by a large wasteground directly behind our house and stableyard. My father told me that it was once a street, until it was flattened by a German bomb during the Belfast blitz in 1941. He was an auxiliary fireman during World War II and dug the corpses out of the rubble. He said they were like burned toast, stiff and black.

Yet even in the midst of these titanic global conflicts, the Irish issue, with its ghosts of old rebellions and its echoes of old battles, made itself felt. My father, I learned, refused to join the British army in 1940—he was a Catholic, and the Irish Free State to which he felt allegiance was neutral. His brother Willy, whose cover slips from Canada I used to peruse, was a Protestant and volunteered. He took part in the D-Day invasion in 1944. I concluded there must be something profoundly important here after all, since it cut across the behavior of people otherwise so close and made them diverge suddenly, drastically, and in unexpected ways.

When I was six my grandfather died. Neither my father nor my uncle Tom wanted to run the stables, so a big move was planned. The extended family was breaking up. My parents found a house to rent in a new working-class development, or "estate," on the northwestern outskirts of the city, at the foot of the bleak slopes of Divis Mountain. My grandmother, my aunt Martha, and Tom went off to life in a little side street on the fringe of the Falls Road Catholic ghetto, the biggest nationalist enclave in Belfast. As events turned out, I was soon to rejoin them.

I had never lived in a new house before, and I found it an exceedingly depressing experience. It felt bare, cold, un-lived in; it seemed to reflect the nature of the development outside, which was windswept, bleak, and unfinished. The houses had been thrown up so quickly that the builders had left pyramids of sand and cement in the mucky back gardens. The streets were pot-holed, and in the wet winter days turned into lakes. The winds from the nearby mountains shook the fragile homes, in which the doors and windows banged and the drafts whistled. The much-heralded amenities then new to the Belfast working class, such as indoor toilets and bathtubs, were forgotten beside the discomforts of spending winters in such an exposed place. Overriding all of this, however, was the fact that the estate was almost entirely Protestant. Because of acute housing shortage, which affected Northern Ireland Catholics most of all, we were forced to take a house wherever we could get it. By 1953 some of the older slum areas had been cleared and their inhabitants rehoused in the estates, which followed the sectarian lines of the districts they replaced.

Given the history of Belfast and my own family's experience, it seems like folly for my parents to have moved into a loyalist area. But by 1953 the pogroms, the street battles, the bloodshed, and evictions that had characterized Northern Ireland's early years were receding into the dim past. Certain political and social changes had occurred as well, which helped bring it more on a par with the rest of the United Kingdom.

In the aftermath of World War II, a Westminster Labour government had introduced a series of acts creating a national health scheme and social security insurance; there had already been an education bill enacted by the wartime coalition government at Westminster. That provided free secondary education and a chance for working-class children to go to university.

The Unionist government, now settled in new parliamentary buildings at Stormont near Belfast, was forced to follow suit. Though it went strongly against their conservative instincts, the Unionists did not want to risk alienating the Protestant working class by refusing to implement the reforms. By the early fifties Northern Ireland had a welfare state as in the rest of Britain; citizens had access to a university education.

These social changes had a profound effect on Northern Ireland. At one level they placed Catholics on a par with Protestants for the first time in the history of the state. This in turn would make the still-prevalent sectarian discrimination even more intolerable to the rising generation of the minority population—and seemingly more anachronistic.

In spite of the postwar social progress, loyalist politicians still felt free to express their old sectarian sentiments. As late as 1954 a Unionist declared in Stormont, "Ulster is a Protestant country, and this is a Protestant parliament for a Protestant people." There were other reminders of the underlying problems: the IRA was still splitting, and one of its factions conducted a sporadic campaign in the rural areas. In England meanwhile, there were signs of things to come. A man called John Stephenson was arrested with two others after they had raided a British arsenal for arms for the IRA, which was planning another "war" against Northern Ireland. Some years later Mr. Stephenson, his name gaelicized to Sean MacStiofain, would emerge as the chief of staff of the Provisional IRA.

These were signs that my parents could not be expected to read and few could interpret. We settled in our new home among our loyalist neighbors, finding them friendly and helpful, and forgot about the past and its hints as to the course the future might take.

I went to a Catholic school in an area between the Protestant Shankill Road and the Catholic Falls Road. It was a long journey, a large part of it along the Shankill Road. Unlike my father, my mother had never lived in a Protestant area before, so was not quite so confident or at home as he was. She insisted on meeting me after school and escorting me home. I was glad of her company; as we walked up the Shankill toward our bus stop I was unnerved to read the anti-Catholic graffiti splashed across the walls: "NO POPE HERE," "FUCK THE POPE," "FUCK THE IRA," as well as slogans like "GOD SAVE THE QUEEN," and "UP KING BILLY"—in support of King William of Orange, who defeated the Catholic pretender to the English throne in a battle fought on Irish soil in the late seventeenth century. I found him at least more colorful, as he was often depicted on huge wall paintings, bewigged, riding his white charger across the River Boyne.

For a child brought up in the Markets it was all very intimidating. I'd heard about the Shankill and the loyalist gangs based there from my family; and there I was, standing on the road at the heart of Protestant Belfast, waiting for a bus! Surely, I thought, they'd easily recognize this nervous little boy as a Fenian, a rebel, a Popehead. But when it became clear that they could not merely by looking at me distinguish me from a Protestant boy, I was somewhat reassured.

My reassurance was soon dispelled. One afternoon I made the journey home alone. When the bus reached the terminus not far from my house I got off to find a greeting party of boys about my age with some older youths. Just beyond the terminus was a stony lane running up to the base of Divis Mountain, past disused farms and fallen-down cottages. The gang grabbed me and marched me up the lane to a big field. The grass was wet with the day's rain. One of the older boys took a dirty handkerchief out of his pocket and tied it around my eyes, then pushed me onto my knees while another tied my hands behind my back.

"You're a fuckin' Fenian," they said. I had never been called that before. (It is roughly the equivalent of "nigger.") I remembered the MacMahons, the child hiding under the couch listening to the men being murdered; I saw the Catholic swimming as he was battered by bolts and screws; and it all became real to me then. I was beaten with sticks across the back and whipped on the face with the thick roots of torn-up weeds. I was made to mumble a few prayers—the loyalists, in spite of their anti-Catholic feelings, regard the powers of the Roman liturgy as somewhat akin to magic. Then I was released and warned to be quiet—which I was.

A few days later, I saw one of the boys. He came up to me near the lane and asked me if I wanted to see something. I said yes. He held out his hand. In his palm were the bodies of two baby birds, their heads cut off. He had killed them with an axe. Perhaps I was being given to understand I had gotten off lightly.

I was so upset by my experience that shortly after the beating I returned to my grandmother's house. She had just moved into Drew Street near the Falls Road. My mother, who was pregnant with her second child, was unhappy living where she was. It took her four years to find another house. She became desperate after her home was attacked one night by a loyalist gang—the windows were stoned and the gate kicked in. Finally, she found a smaller house in Andersonstown, a Catholic development then being built, and moved there when my sister was about three.

It was no surprise to me that during the 1970s the estate from which we fled became a base for loyalist assassination squads. One group, who earned the name of the Shankill Road Butchers because they used to cut up their victims with long knives and broken glass, dumped the body of a murdered Catholic not far from our old house.

I was greatly relieved to be living in the Falls area. I felt at home, snug in my grandmother's tiny two-bedroom house in Catholic nationalist territory. Moving from ghetto to ghetto in Belfast has the

same effect on one as moving from nation to nation. I'd been an ex-
ile in Northern Ireland, the United Kingdom. Now in the Falls, I
felt as if I were back in Ireland again.

The story of Northern Ireland is in many ways the story of Belfast. And the heart of Belfast's story is the Falls, the district comprising the road by that name and the warren of narrow streets and
red-bricked workers' homes of which it is the spine.

Four centuries ago, when the Elizabethan conquerors were beginning their destruction of Irish Celtic society, Walter Devereux, the
Earl of Essex, mentioned the small trading post of Belfast (from the
Gaelic "Beal Feirste," "Mouth of the Fiord") in one of his dis-
patches to Queen Elizabeth I. He referred to a mill, a brewhouse,
and a stonehouse. The mill ground meal for English troops. The
buildings were located near the western boundary of the small settlement (population then 600) near where the Falls Road begins today.

Beyond the gates of the seventeenth-century town the native
Celts, forbidden by law to dwell within the town itself, huddled in
wattle huts. The area around which they gathered became known
as the Falls Road (from the Gaelic "tour na faille," "district of the
hedges"). During periods of unrest the native Irish would use this
track through the scrublands as an escape route to the nearby
mountains. Travellers in the late seventeenth century also refer to
a holy well in the area. Its water reputedly "looked like white wine
on the lees and had not the taste of ordinary water." Even at this
date, the Falls was very much a Catholic, Celtic enclave.

Built on the banks of the slow-moving River Lagan, with easy access to the sea through Belfast Lough, the city flourished as a trading port with a small shipbuilding industry in the eighteenth
century. It was not until the nineteenth century, however, that it became a boom town. A large part of the increasing population was
Catholic peasants fleeing the famine-devastated lands of the south.
Between 1841 and 1861 the city's population jumped from 75,000
to 120,000; the population of the Falls area increased from 20,000
to 40,000.

The vast majority of the new Falls residents were illiterate peasants. They came to the city seeking food, shelter, and work. Belfast
had then something to offer them: the linen mills were flourishing,
and a large percentage of the Falls population worked in the district's mills. Belfast's other major industry, its shipbuilding works,

was then—as it is now—almost entirely manned by Protestants. The city was still a Protestant city, and the poorer ones feared and resented the influx of Catholics. It meant increased competition for jobs; it meant overcrowding and disease. Sectarian riots were ever more frequent as the nineteenth century came to a close. By then the Falls Road had taken on the characteristics it had when I was a young boy. The maze of narrow streets formed a crazy pattern, one which evolved from older field boundaries on the property of Lord Donegal, who had sold his estate in the area to industrial developers. The streets and their little houses were dominated by the tall, slim mill chimneys and by the spires of chapels. Life on the Falls revolved around the structures of work and worship.

The nineteenth-century houses were built in rows, two stories high. They were so small that local children used to celebrate their lack of space sardonically in song:

> *Dan, Dan, the funny wee man*
> *Washed his face in the frying pan,*
> *Combed his hair with the leg of a chair,*
> *Dan, Dan, the funny wee man.*

The plight of Dan, the funny wee man, was only a slight exaggeration. Space was a privilege the poor could not afford. Because there were no bathrooms in the old working-class houses, we were forced to perform our ablutions in the dark, narrow kitchens, in many of the houses awkwardly placed under the stairway to the bedrooms. In our home in Drew Street, it was possible to stand by the gas stove, cook dinner, wash clothes, and scrub one's feet and face without moving from where one was.

Our toilet facilities were restricted to a drafty hut in a corner of the small backyard just beyond the kitchen. The backyard opened out on to an alleyway, or "entry" as it is known in Belfast. This was where the garbage bins were left out; it was a festering, narrow passageway, full of refuse and sometimes dead cats, rats, and occasionally dogs. Teen-agers used it for courting purposes—it was dark, private, and very narrow. "Love *had* pitched his mansion in the place of excrement."

Apart from the kitchen there were two rooms downstairs, the living room, with one window looking out onto the street, and the "wee room" just off it, used either as an eating place or as an extra bedroom.

Drew Street, near the Catholic Falls Road, Belfast, where the author grew up. A typical nineteenth-century working-class street of small red-brick houses. In 1969 the mill warehouse at the end of the street was converted by the army into a base.

Of the two upstairs bedrooms, the one at the front of the house had space for a double bed, two wardrobes, a dressing table, and a commode. The last was a small, decorated chair on top of a chamber pot; it was used mostly by the very old who did not want to sit in the cold of a drafty hut on a winter night. (The first task in the house every morning was to empty it.) The small bedroom at the back facing toward the yard and entry had space only for one double bed. One stepped out of bed in the morning straight into the landing at the top of the tiny staircase.

Work in the Falls was dominated by the linen mills. They were situated in this area originally because they needed the water flowing down from the basalt-domed mountains nearby that surfaced in gushing streams just above the Falls Road. When my aunt Martha, along with my uncle Tom and my grandmother, moved to Drew Street, she was already working in a nearby mill. She'd begun work on her fourteenth birthday as a winder, and she remained one for nearly fifty years. She wound the fine linen thread, which had already gone through a process of preparing and spinning, onto a reel and then on to a spool or bobbin; from the winding room the linen went to the weavers. Martha was fortunate in that the winders' workplace was the only comparatively healthy spot in the mill. Elsewhere the temperature was uncomfortably hot and the air kept very damp in order to prevent the brittle flax from breaking. Lung disease was common. Tuberculosis was a frequent cause of early death among mill workers who inhaled dust particles all day long in these humid conditions.

As was fairly typical in those days, Martha never married (in spite of her great beauty and vivacity) in order to take care of her mother. She was called to work every morning by the screech of the millhorn.

> *Five o'clock the horn does blow,*
> *Half past five we all must go.*
> *If you be a minute late,*
> *Oul Jack Horn will shut the gate*
> *So early in the morning.*

It was a harsh, penetrating blast. In her first years as a millgirl, Martha began work at six in the morning and worked without a break until one in the afternoon. She returned at two and worked until as late as nine in the evening sometimes, again with no break. Her first pay was 9 shillings and 45 pence—less than two dollars per week.

Later her work in the local mill near Drew Street was less arduous. There, she began work at seven; a tea break was allowed at ten. She could go home for lunch, and work finished at nine, if not earlier. Her wages went up to four pounds a week (by then the pound was worth about three dollars). I remember when I was struggling over my school books she would come in on a Friday night with her pay packet proudly open. She'd show me her earnings—six pounds! And once, during a very good week she brought home nine pounds. "And I had no education," she'd say, disdainfully looking at the stack of books by my chair.

A lot of the street songs of the district were about mills and mill workers. One the girls sang harked back to the days of child labor. It began:

> Wall flower, wall flower, growing up so high,
> All the little children are all going to die,
> All except for Kathy McKay, she is the only one,
> She can dance, she can sing,
> She can show her wedding ring.

Kathy McKay was saved from a lifetime of mill work by marriage. When I was a boy it was still the only way a mill girl could escape spending the rest of her life in the mill as my aunt did. Marriage would take her out of the overcrowded conditions of her own home. For a short time she would have to share her bed with only one other person, her husband. When the family began to grow and the cares of bringing up a lot of children in a little space began to press upon her, she'd look back on her moment of comparative privacy and realize, perhaps, how brief it was.

One of the mill songs collected by a local folklorist and school teacher in the 1940s, Hugh Quinn, celebrates the virtues and vitality of the mill girls, or "doffers" as they were known in the city:

> You might easily know a doffer when she comes into town,
> With her long, yellow hair and her ringlets hanging down,
> With her rubber tied before her and her picker in her hand.
> You might easily know a doffer for she'll always get a man.

The next verse contrasts the mill girls with teachers, who represented a stuffy, priggish middle class despised by the workers:

> *You might easily know a teacher when she comes into town,*
> *With her bustle stuck behind her and upon her face a frown,*
> *And the children stand around her and her cane right in her*
>   *hand;*
> *You might easily know a teacher for she'll never get a man.*

The girls living and working together formed strong bonds of friendship. In the early morning I'd lie in bed listening to them clatter down the street, linked arm in arm, three or four abreast. In a society where adults rarely touched in public, they were physically close and affectionate with each other.

Physical contact between men and women was generally clumsy and awkward, and frequently brutal. According to popular standards, a happy marriage was one in which the man provided for his family and did not beat his wife. For women to expect sexual pleasure from marriage was unheard of: marriage meant a house, a man to work to earn the wages to support the family, and children to bring up. A woman did not expect friendship or companionship from her man—that she got from the relationships formed with her girlfriends. These gave her warmth and a certain amount of emotional sustenance.

Another mill song collected by Hugh Quinn tells of the sadness of the doffers when their mistress leaves them to get married:

> *Oh do you know or do you not*
> *This new doffin mistress we have got?*
> *And Jane Brady it is her name,*
> *And she hangs her clothes up on the highest frame.*
> *Rady right full ra-rady, right full ree.*
>
> *On Monday morning when she comes in*
> *She hangs her clothes up on the highest pin,*
> *Then turns around for to view her girls*
> *Saying, dang you doffers, lay up your ends.*
>
> *Lay up our ends we will surely do,*
> *Our hands are steady and our touch is true,*

Lay up our ends we will do,
All for Lizzie Murphy and not for you.

Oh Lizzie Murphy are you going away?
Is it tomorrow or is it today?
You'll leave us then with a broken heart,
For there's no one left now will take our part.

Oh Lizzie Murphy, when you've gone away,
Every night it's for you we'll pray,
We'll send for you when you're far away
And we'll bring you back and we'll make you stay.

Marriage brought with it large families. The average number of children per household was eight. They were reared on a diet of boiled potatoes, herring, beef sausages, tea, and a variety of different breads. We had wheat breads, soda breads, and potato breads as well as a score of different kinds of rolls or "scones." During weekdays the main meal was eaten at one in the afternoon, when the workers came in from the mills. In the evenings we had tea about six, accompanied by a fry-up of soda bread and sausage. And usually, before bedtime, there would be another pot of tea boiled and maybe a little sandwich. Tea and buttermilk were the staple drinks.

The education of the children was run along sectarian lines. Catholics went to Catholic schools, and Protestants went to state (*ipso facto* Protestant) schools. Catholics were taught Irish history—the story, basically, of Ireland's long struggle for freedom. Protestants received a British view of the world—of how the Empire bestowed the virtues of its civilization on various native cultures, including the Irish. At the Christian Brothers school I attended, St. Gall's, I was strapped once for calling the town of Derry "Londonderry." The brother pointed out that the prefix "London" was a recent (seventeenth-century) invention, and that the real Irish name was Derry, "oak grove" in Gaelic. Unfortunately, it was Londonderry in my atlas; being a stubborn child I insisted, much to his annoyance, on pointing out this anomaly. He walloped me and, with great contempt in his voice, dismissed the atlas as a mere English map.

Catholic children learned Gaelic, were expected to play Gaelic football and hurling, while our Protestant contemporaries played soccer. Gaelic football, which I never played and never understood, is more akin to American football than to soccer. Players are allowed to handle and run with the ball. Among Irish fanatics, playing soccer was regarded as almost treasonous.

Sport and education took on political significance, as did reading comic books. Young Protestants were fed a diet of British comics depicting jolly air force heroes and terribly polite British army captains obliterating the "Huns." Catholic children generally found such comics very stuffy. We preferred comics from America when we could get them. When I was young, for some reason or other they were only to be had in the Free State. This strengthened our identification of the United States with the cause of Ireland.

On good summer days we would walk up one of the several mountain lanes—"lonins," we called them—with sandwiches and bottles of soda. The range of hills that lies to the west of the city is really the end of the Antrim Plateau, a mass of basalt-covered limestone running south from the Atlantic Ocean. Belfast, in spite of its Victorian industrial drabness, was never without a fresh mountain breeze; on a clear day, even from the city center, it was possible to see the small farms hugging the bulge of the Divis Mountain where the fields merged into bare green slopes sprinkled with sheep.

From the mountain itself we could see right across the Lagan Valley to the beautiful patchwork of fields on the gentle drumlins of east County Down, a Protestant area of rich farmlands. Farther east a gleaming white building was clearly visible: Stormont, Northern Ireland's parliament. In an act revealing their deep insecurity, the Unionists made sure their parliament building was as far away from the capital city as they could decently put it. In itself that says something about the nature of the state it ruled.

We whiled away the summer afternoons lounging on the short hill grass drinking soda, eating sandwiches. Whatever went on in that distant, gleaming white building, my friends and I had an overwhelming feeling that it had little to do with us.

The Stormont parliament was modelled on Westminster's, with a House of Commons, seating fifty-two representatives (members of parliament), a Senate equivalent to the House of Lords, and a Prime Minister, who was responsible for selecting his cabinet. But the resemblance ended there. Unlike real democracies which produce real governments, Northern Ireland, established as a Protestant, Unionist state, produced only the replica of a democratic government;

rule by the Unionists only required a part-time government because it had no real opposition. Gerrymandering made most Unionist constituencies safe from electoral upsets; many Unionist MPs never had to fight an election in their political lives. They were returned automatically. It is not surprising that the prevailing feeling in the Unionist government was "why bother?"

The ministers in the government were required to spend but one afternoon a week at their ministerial duties—duties for which they received a nice salary as well as other privileges. Until Terence O'Neill became Prime Minister in 1963, nothing was thought of ministers holding directorships in as many private companies as they wished. O'Neill's predecessor, Lord Brookeborough, who was Prime Minister for twenty years, spent six months of every year sailing to Australia and back with his wife. Even when he was in the country, members of his cabinet often could not find him.

O'Neill, who wanted desperately to make the Unionist government into a real government instead of an imitation one, wrote scathingly of Brookeborough: "A man of limited intelligence, his strong suits were shooting and fishing in Fermanagh and when he came up [to Belfast] on a Monday night or Tuesday morning it was difficult to shake him from some of his more idiotic ideas." O'Neill pointed out that "He was good company and a good raconteur and those who met him imagined that he was relaxing away from his desk. What they didn't realise was that there was no desk!"

The sense of unreality we felt about the Stormont government as we gazed through the summer's haze at the white building far beyond us was obviously not unjustified.

For most of the time we Catholics were not even represented there. There was a Catholic "Nationalist Party"; in the early 1920s proindependence Catholic candidates had even won control in local and parliamentary elections of two of the six counties. But subsequent gerrymandering by the Unionists had whittled away our representatives to a mere rump. The role of the remaining Nationalists as the "loyal opposition" was half-hearted at best. For long periods of time they did not even attend the parliament. (They were hardly encouraged to by the behavior of some Unionists, who would habitually leave the chamber whenever any Nationalist MP rose to address the House.)

There was a feeling among Catholics that whether the Nationalists attended parliament or not made little difference. There would always be the massive, immovable Unionist bloc; its one-party state

Stormont, near Belfast, until 1972 the seat of Northern Ireland's Parliament, set up by the British government in 1921. It was rejected by most of Northern Ireland's Catholics as a Protestant institution. Catholics looked south to Dublin to give their allegiance to an Irish Parliament.

seemed secure. The redrawing of electoral boundaries had ensured that even in cities with a Catholic majority, such as Derry, more Unionists were elected than Nationalists. Gerrymandering secured Unionist control over district councils, which in turn controlled local housing allocation and the filling of local government jobs. Thus Unionists controlled the economic, political, and social structures and ensured the privileges of their Protestant supporters.

Catholic frustration kept breaking out into violence. The Irish Republican Army still existed as a channel for that frustration. The organization had shrunk from being the main arm of the Irish struggle against the British between 1919 and 1921 into a withered stump of a guerrilla group—increasingly irrelevant, it seemed, to the needs of modern Ireland. But in 1956, after much preparation, it launched a campaign against the Unionist state in the hope that the Catholics would rise up and support them. The Catholics did not respond as expected. After six years of intermittent violence during which six RUC men were killed, as well as nine members of the IRA—most of them from premature explosions—the campaign was called off. In a statement marking the end of the campaign, the IRA leadership spoke of its disappointment at having to suspend operations because of the apathy of the local Catholics: "Foremost among the factors motivating this course of action has been the attitude of the general public whose minds have deliberately been distracted from the supreme issue facing the Irish people—the unity and freedom of Ireland."

By 1962 most Catholics in Belfast had indeed been "distracted" from pondering the issue of partition. Unemployment was rising; the traditional industries on which the economy was based, linen and shipbuilding, were failing. Linen could not compete with artificial fabrics, and the mills were closing. Then–Finance Minister Captain Terence O'Neill was determined to attract new industries to the province. This required some dismantling of the old sectarian apparatus that had grown up around the traditional industries, owned as they were by the big Unionist families. When O'Neill became Prime Minister in 1963, he began a modest policy of reform. Few people, including the disgruntled leadership of the IRA, could have realized that within six years O'Neill's liberalism would provoke a loyalist backlash strong enough to bring Northern Ireland to the verge of civil war.

From one of the oldest aristocratic families in the British Isles,

O'Neill rather disdained the trappings and the symbols of loyalist supremacy, finding it all rather provincial. A rather dreary individual, with a sad, drooping face capable of mustering only the most fatuous of smiles, his attitude towards Catholics was well-meaning and paternalistic. He painfully tried to explain the rationale behind his reforms like this: "It is frightfully hard to explain to Protestants that if you give Roman Catholics a good job and a good house they will live like Protestants because they will see neighbours with cars and television sets. They will refuse to have eighteen children, but if a Roman Catholic is jobless and lives in the most ghastly hovel, he will rear eighteen children on the National Assistance. . . . If you treat Roman Catholics with due consideration and kindness, they will live like Protestants, in spite of the authoritative nature of their church."

O'Neill talked about "building bridges" between Catholics and Protestants. He visited Catholic schools and had well-publicized meetings with nuns. But it was not going to be that easy to undo the effects of fifty years of sectarian rule. He had to reckon with the *institutions* of sectarian rule, one of which was the Orange Order.

To maintain the religious apartheid of the state, the Unionists depended on the power of the Orange Order, an organization unique in Western Europe—though it bears some resemblance to the Ku Klux Klan. It was founded in 1795 to counter growing Catholic unrest in Ireland. As a secret society, it terrorized the Catholic community. By the beginning of the twentieth century, the Orange Order had become an organization which united Protestants, regardless of class or social distinction, in their opposition to Irish nationalism. The Orange leadership was the landed aristocracy and ministers of the Protestant churches. After the foundation of the six-county state, Unionist government ministers as well as party members were required to be members of the Order. It became a means of bestowing privilege and of protecting the economic interests of Protestants—from farm laborers and shipyard workers to small businessmen and the landed gentry. To get a job, a house, or to get to be Prime Minister of the country, you had to be a member of the Order. Needless to say, it was virulently anti-Catholic.

The Order celebrates on various days during the year. The big marching day is July 12th, supposed date of King William of Orange's victory over the Catholic King James at the Battle of the Boyne. (The fact that the Pope at the time supported King William was and is conveniently ignored.) All day throughout Northern Ireland the sounds of the lambeg drums reverberate. These enormous drums are five feet in diameter and carried on the marchers' chests. They are beaten with canes strapped to the drummer's wrist rather than with drumsticks. Warmup contests are held before the 12th to see who can beat the lambeg drum for the longest time. A few drummers, in a fury of playing, will keep going into the small hours of the morning, their hands dripping with blood as the canes scrape through their skin.

The Orange Order has lodges, or branches, all over the world. On the 12th they assemble in Northern Ireland. Each lodge has its own banner, but all the men proudly wear the same bright orange sash. The biggest parade is always in Belfast. With their sashes, their bowler hats, and carrying their walking sticks, the Orangemen march beneath the brilliant banners of their lodge to a large field on the southern outskirts of the city. It is a celebration of Protestant supremacy, of the triumph of the north of Ireland over popery, republicanism, and later, communism. The most famous of their marching songs is "The Sash":

> It is old but it is beautiful
> Its colours they are fine.
> It was worn at Derry, Aughrim,
> Enniskillen and the Boyne.
> My father wore it when a youth
> In bygone days of yore,
> On the 12th I proudly wear
> The Sash my father wore.

Their songs are full of the bravado and gusto of the victor. "Croppies [i.e., Catholics] Lie Down" begins:

> Poor Croppies, ye know that your sentence was come
> When you heard the dread sound of the Protestant drum
> In memory of William we hoisted his flag
> And soon the bright Orange put down the Green rag.

In the past the platform that the Order provided for Unionist politicians has been used every 12th as an opportunity to spell out the abiding truths of Unionism, which differed little from the contents of the Orange marching songs.

The outside world might look with skepticism upon this extraordinary anachronism, but, along with the Unionist Party, it controlled Protestant life at all levels with almost totalitarian efficiency. The state was identified with the Unionist Party, and it in turn was absorbed into the Orange Order. Any attempt to reform Northern Ireland was confronted by this monolith.

Part of O'Neill's modernization plans involved the expansion of trade with the Irish Republic. Political relations would have to be improved. At the beginning of 1965, O'Neill arranged for Irish Prime Minister Sean Lemass to come north to meet him. Lemass was the leader of the Fianna Fail party, at one time the bearer of parliamentary republicanism. But by 1965 the Lemass government, like O'Neill's in the North, was trying to attract British and American industry, abandoning old economic and political doctrines that had tended towards economic isolationism.

The meeting was, in many ways, a success. Agreement was reached to pursue economic matters of joint interest to the neighboring states. It was a success with the Catholics, who sensed something new in the stagnant air of local politics. My grandmother, then in her mid-eighties, could hardly believe her eyes—she witnessed the Irish Prime Minister shaking hands with O'Neill with something akin to the awe Americans were to feel when Colonel Armstrong set foot on the moon. She muttered sagely that "the Orangemen won't like this." (She had previously blamed the Orange Order for the assassination of President Kennedy.)

At least as concerns the Lemass-O'Neill meeting, she was right. The loyalists were restless. Already on the Unionist Party's right wing the sectarian war drum was beating. The Lemass visit, a rather ordinary act of diplomacy between two states whose capitals are only one hundred miles from each other, was seen as treachery by right-wing Unionists. There were calls for O'Neill's resignation. On the extreme fringe of Unionism, the noise was more threatening, and it had a familiar ring to it. A divine by the name of the Reverend Ian Kyle Paisley was summoning loyal Protestants to war.

Paisley is a big, bellowing bull-like man with a gift for demagogic oratory. The founder in 1951 of the Free Presbyterian Church, he was the latest in a long line of fundamentalist fire-breathing Protestant preachers to become involved in Northern Irish politics. Until the mid-sixties his notoriety derived mainly from his opposition to ecumenism. He led a protest to object to the lowering of the flag at Belfast City Hall when Pope John XXIII died. He organized a mock mass in a Belfast meeting hall; he visited Rome to protest against a meeting of the Ecumenical Council. The outside world might behold this historical hangover with amazement, but in Northern Ireland he became a real political force.

From the Reverend Thomas Drew of the 1850s to the Paisleys of the 1960s and 1970s, the rhetoric of summons to battle is the same:

Of old time lords of high degree, with their hands strained on the rack the limbs of delicate Protestant women, prelates dabbled in the gore of their helpless victims. The cells of the Pope's prison were paved with the calcined bones of men and cemented with human gore and human hair. . . . (the Reverend Thomas Drew, 1857)

And from Mr. Paisley, circa 1957:

Go into any Roman Church in this city and what do you see? It's like Madame Tussaud's in London. Legions of graven images! Gaudy and vulgar, and an abomination in the sight of God. Equally rank in the nostrils and nauseating are the sanctuary lamps and candelabras placed before sickly prints of the Virgin and other saints. These are the trappings of the great whore of Babylon and the Scarlet Woman. This is what the World Council of Churches is seeking to reconcile with, to unite with, and by doing so betray its Protestant trusteeship. Are you prepared to be a party to this base surrender, to be Lundies and Papists?

(Lundy was a seventeenth-century traitor to the loyalist cause.)

It was with this language that extreme loyalists confronted O'Neill's "bridge building" liberalism. When it came to verbal vigor, undoubtedly Paisley won the day. But it was more than just a quaint anachronistic turn of phrase. In the strange, isolated world of the Northern Ireland loyalist, these words of Paisley's inspired action.

Several forces were now converging to affect the increasingly paranoid state of the loyalists. In England, for the first time in almost twenty years, there was a Labour government, led by Harold Wilson. Labour was regarded with deep suspicion by the ultraconservative Unionist Party, and Wilson was known to regard the Unionists as a tiresome nuisance. (He once referred to the loyalists as "quasi-fascists.") In Ireland the fiftieth anniversary of the 1916

Easter Rising, the event which sparked off the Irish independence struggle, was looming. Loyalists were sure the IRA would mark this occasion by an all-out assault on the border.

Then, of course, there was O'Neill, whom Paisley and his followers regarded as a fifth column bent on betraying Unionism from within. His role as the "enemy within the gates" appealed very much to the loyalists' siege mentality. While Captain O'Neill spoke of modernization with limp phraseology and in his hesitant, upper-class English drawl, disturbed men in the back rooms of dingy little bars off the Shankill Road were locked in old conspiracies. The language of modernization meant "sell-out" to them.

Among those who decided to save Northern Ireland from the multiple demons of loyalist fantasy was Augustus Spence, nicknamed Gusty. He was an ex-military policeman who had served with the British Army in Cyprus, and a steel-fitter by trade. He nourished dreams of reviving the old Ulster Volunteer Force, a Protestant militia which had defied the threat of home rule for Ireland in 1911.

Spence's UVF numbered no more than a dozen men. It became the first of the loyalist terrorist groups, which in recent years have caused so much death and suffering throughout Northern Ireland. 1966 was to be the year of Northern Ireland's Armageddon, when the IRA would launch its all-out attack. The UVF of Gusty Spence would be there to meet it. The assault, the final bloodbath, did not occur. Little did Spence realize, but the IRA in 1966, with only about seventy volunteers in the whole of Northern Ireland, was hardly an organization at all. It was in the midst of a deep crisis caused by the failure of its last campaign; many activists, disillusioned with violent methods, had turned to left-wing politics, while others left the movement altogether. (It would not emerge as a threat for another four years.)

The only military effort the IRA could muster was the attempted destruction of one telephone booth—hardly Armageddon. But that did not matter. Reality was not going to discourage the demented nightmares of the UVF. They declared war on the IRA. "Known IRA men will be executed mercilessly and without hesitation," they said in a statement.

They followed this up with a clumsy, incompetent, but brutal campaign of violence, which, within two months, took the lives of three people, the first of them an old Protestant lady. She was burned to death when a UVF petrol bomb, intended for a Catholic bar, missed and landed in her home instead. The next to die was a drunk man caught by the UVF as he was staggering home one night in May singing Irish songs. That was enough to convince the UVF squad that here they indeed had an IRA man. They shot Martin Scullion, and he crawled home to die, not far from his doorway. Finally, their brief reign of terror came to an end in June after an ambush that left one young Catholic barman dead and two seriously wounded. The police picked up Spence and two of his henchmen shortly afterwards. One of them, Hugh McClean, said when he was charged, "I am terribly sorry I ever heard of that man Paisley or decided to follow him."

Spence was associated with a Paisley organization called the Ulster Protestant Action, formed in the late fifties to "keep Protestants and loyal workers in employment in times of depression in preference to their fellow Catholic workers." They all mingled in the obscure underworld of the Protestant paramilitary groups from which the leaders of the contemporary loyalist terrorist gangs would later emerge.

The three UVF men, Spence, McClean, and Robert Williamson, went to jail for life, and the organization was banned under the Special Powers Act. At the time most Protestants ignored Gusty Spence or even derided him. But within three years, as Northern Ireland headed into another crisis, he had become a loyalist folk hero. The rise of the Catholic civil rights movement was received with anger and confusion among Protestants, many of whom began saying "Gusty was right."

O'Neill had unwittingly stirred up the old ghosts of sectarian hatreds still haunting Northern Ireland. He had also raised the expectations of local Catholics, who were anxious to see an end to those sectarian hatreds, which still blocked their progress towards equality with their fellow citizens. O'Neill was shocked by the ugly apparition of Spence's UVF; he was to be equally shocked and offended by the sight of Catholics disregarding his snail's pace paternalism and demanding immediate reforms.

In February 1967 the Northern Ireland Civil Rights Association (NICRA) was born. It described itself as a nonpolitical, nonsectarian body with members from both sides of the community. Its aim was to end the prevalent discrimination against Catholics in the job market and in housing allocation; to remedy the gerrymandering of constituencies, which gave Protestants unfair representation; to repeal the Special Powers Act; and to abolish the restricted franchise in local government elections, which gave property owners up to six votes each and deprived those who did not pay rates (property taxes) of any vote at all.

The Northern Ireland Civil Rights Association was a product of the frustrations of the rising Catholic middle class combined with the discontent of the poorer Catholics and the new-found radicalism of local university students. The discontent and frustration had only been exacerbated by O'Neill's promises of change. By 1967 he had been in power for almost four years, and though successful in attracting some new industries, the old political abuses still remained. Middle-class Catholics were restricted from jobs in local and central government by discrimination. By the mid-sixties, only 12 percent of those employed in the former, and 6 percent in the latter, were Catholics. At the same time, because of the post–World War II Education Act, more and more Catholics were getting a university education and graduating with higher expectations. (O'Neill's maiden speech in Stormont was in support of the education bill. Little did he realize that twenty years later, when Prime Minister, he would have to deal with some of the consequences of that act.) But the rigidity of the state's sectarian apparatus held Catholics back. By 1966 only 4 percent of those earning two thousand pounds (about five thousand dollars) a year were Catholics. Catholics who belonged to professions were entirely restricted to their own community by the religious apartheid. Previously their political allegiance had gone to the Nationalist Party, but when not abstaining altogether from the Stormont parliament, its opposition proved ineffective. It could not further the ambitions of this new, expanding section of the minority population, eager to break up the fossilized divisions of the one-party government.

The situation of the working-class Catholics was always ripe for revolt. O'Neill's new economic policies often resulted in British-based and American-based industries being placed in areas that were overwhelmingly Protestant. So unemployment among Catholics remained disproportionately high.

In 1967 many Catholics were weary of the unfulfilled promise that sectarian pressures would be relaxed. They did not rise up in armed revolt, but they took to the streets in peaceful protest. In the eyes of the Paisleyites it amounted to the same thing.

The Northern Ireland Civil Rights Association organized its first march in August 1968 in the Catholic town of Dungannon. A young, unmarried Protestant woman had been given a house in preference to many Catholics with big families. The local rural council, controlled by Protestants, had already evicted Catholic families from council houses after they had squatted in them demanding that their housing needs be met. When it was learned that the council had given a house to a woman without a family, a local Nationalist MP, Austin Currie, occupied the house. When he was evicted, the NICRA, after much debate, decided to take to the streets.

The Reverend Ian Paisley immediately announced he would mount a counter-demonstration of the Ulster Protestant Volunteers, the latest in a line of paramilitary groups with which he was associated. The NICRA march was prevented from getting into the center of Dungannon by the presence of loyalist demonstrators. There was a brief scuffle with the RUC before the marchers broke up.

The Paisleyite intervention had set off a sectarian chain reaction that would lead to a conflagration in August 1969. At the time of the Dungannon march, no one in the civil rights movement seemed aware of the nature of that chain reaction. Participants were mostly moderate, middle-class people, with a sprinkling of earnest, radical young students and some republicans who were eager to get away from the failed politics of violence. All were determined to avoid raising the old Catholic nationalist slogans for a united Ireland. They did not want to reduce their campaign for basic civil rights to the slogans of the antipartitionists. There was a desire to reassure Protestants that Catholics were prepared to work within Northern Ireland to achieve a more democratic state.

O'Neill was now under pressure from three different quarters. Moderate Catholics were on the streets demanding reform. On the loyalist fringes, the Paisleyites were threatening violence and disruption if reforms went ahead. Within O'Neill's party the extremists had some support. But within his own government there was a more dangerous threat. Several of his ministers were staunch right-wingers, and very unhappy with the way things were developing. The most serious challenge was from Minister of Home Affairs William Craig, the man who controlled internal security.

Craig openly sneered at the civil rights movement. When it was proposed to hold a second demonstration in Derry on October 5th, a group within the Orange Order, the Apprentice Boys, announced its intention to march at the same time. Craig banned all marches that day. It seemed that loyalist intervention had once more frustrated genuine peaceful protest. But the civil rights movement took the momentous decision to go ahead and defy the ban.

The marchers included the usual amalgam: There were Catholic politicians like Gerry Fitt, a Westminster MP; there were young student radicals under a grouping called the Young Socialist Alliance; and there were representatives of the Derry Catholic middle class—men like John Hume, a thirty-one-year-old school teacher soon to become one of Northern Ireland's leading political figures; there were, as well, some old republicans pushing ahead with their program of involvement in democratic politics, in an effort to turn the IRA away from the gun. Michael Farrell, a member of the Young Socialists from Belfast's Queens University, described what happened in his book, *The Orange State:*

> Two thousand marchers set off from the Waterside station and got about two hundred yards. They were met by a solid wall of RUC, who batoned Gerry Fitt, at the head of the march. Crushed in the narrow street most of the marchers didn't even see this, and the organisers tried to hold a meeting.
>
> The Young Socialists made a determined effort to get through however and the RUC baton-charged. The marchers were caught between two lines of police, batoned savagely and hosed with water cannon. . . .
>
> Scattered fighting broke out throughout the city as the RUC charged groups of marchers and ended up in the Bogside [the city's large Catholic ghetto] where barricades were put up that night and petrol bombs used for the first time in Derry.

A British-appointed inquiry into the outbreak of violence in Northern Ireland stated in its report, "There is a body of evidence, which we accept, that these police also used their batons indiscriminately." They left seventy-seven civilians injured. But whatever any official inquiry said about that afternoon in Derry, it could not match the sight of police violence witnessed on millions of television screens throughout the United Kingdom and Ireland. The TV cameras gave the citizens of the United Kingdom a glimpse of the Northern Ireland police in action. They were shocked, and the Labour government of Harold Wilson was furious.

O'Neill met with Wilson at the beginning of November. The British Prime Minister insisted that the necessary reforms go ahead, and he warned the intransigent Unionists that their opposition to O'Neill would cause Westminster to make a "very fundamental reappraisal" of the position of Northern Ireland within the United Kingdom. O'Neill returned to Belfast. Shortly afterwards Craig was dismissed from his cabinet. The Prime Minister made a desperate and effective television plea for peace and cooperation. The civil rights marches were suspended voluntarily to give him a chance to get his reforms through.

It was already too late. Other elements were now forcing the pace. On the Catholic side, a student group, the People's Democracy, went ahead with another march at the beginning of January 1969. It provoked the most violent response so far—the marchers were ambushed by hordes of Paisleyites and B-Specials. Many were clubbed senseless; one woman was almost drowned in a stream.

On the loyalist side, the extremists took to a more serious form of protest against O'Neill's liberalism. Several members of Paisley's Ulster Protestant Volunteers began a bombing campaign aimed at vital installations and Catholic churches. By the middle of the spring of 1969, the Prime Minister was at the end of his tether. He came close to losing a vital election in his own constituency to Paisley himself. His weakly held cabinet was breaking up under the pressure from the Unionist right wing. At the end of April he resigned.

The torch of liberal Unionism was passed to James Chichester-Clarke, a cousin of the former Prime Minister. But the attempt to reform Northern Ireland had failed, destroyed by the sectarian forces that had once been marshalled by the Unionist Party to bring the state into existence.

Chichester-Clarke did push through the one-man, one-vote reform. Other reforms, including placing the housing allocation system on a fairer basis and replacement of the gerrymandered Derry city administration by a commission, went ahead. But by the time these reforms had begun to take effect, they were irrelevant. By then the very existence of the Unionist government, which had needed these abuses to guarantee its survival, was at stake.

Like the liberal policies of O'Neill, those of the Civil Rights Association did not achieve their aim of building a nonsectarian democratic movement for reform. Its coy attempt to avoid the national question—to keep to broad democratic demands—was to no avail.

Though the civil rights movement did not want to talk about a united Ireland, the loyalists did. What Catholic liberals did not realize was that the discriminatory practices could not be challenged without challenging the state itself. The right-wing loyalists and Unionists immediately saw every demand for reform as an attack upon the whole structure of the state. It was paranoia, but it was the paranoia on which Northern Ireland was founded.

Paranoia has its own dialectic. By squeezing the issue of a united Ireland out of demands for civil rights, the loyalists distilled the essential problem facing Northern Ireland: partition. Protestant loyalist opposition to civil rights on the basis that it was just a disguise for Catholic nationalist ambitions forced Catholics once more to see the existence of a partitioned state as the root cause of all their woes, and to regard civil rights reforms as mere tinkering. Ironically enough, it was loyalist intransigence rather than Catholic militancy which laid the basis for the beginning of the Provisional IRA, the most powerful threat Northern Ireland has ever faced.

However, though the political and social conditions necessary for the birth of the Provisionals were rapidly developing throughout 1969, one thing more was needed: a total breakdown of Catholic confidence in the state and its forces of law and order. Such alienation was required to give moral authority to those within the IRA who wanted to return to the gun.

The breakdown happened on August 14, 1969. It began in Derry, the Catholic city where the civil rights marchers had previously been bloodied by William Craig's police. On August 12th, the Orange Order's Apprentice Boys section held an annual parade second only in splendor and color to the 12th of July itself, and second only to it in the amount of provocation it directed at the nationalist community. After the events of the previous year, the march could with justification have been banned. But Chichester-Clarke was not strong enough to outface his right wing, which would have interpreted such a ban as a complete betrayal of Unionism; so with many pleas for calm he allowed it to go ahead. As was their custom, when the Apprentice Boys passed near the Catholic slum of the Bogside the marchers jeered and threw pennies, an act of contempt which in 1969 the Catholics were in no mood to accept. They replied with stones. The loyalists advanced on the Bogside, and the police intervened, throwing up a cordon. Catholic barricades were erected, stones were piled high, and a petrol bomb production line went into full gear.

At 7:15 P.M. the RUC moved against the barricades and a full-scale riot began. As news of the "Battle of the Bogside" spread to Catholic ghettos in other areas of Northern Ireland, people came out onto the streets. In Belfast, Catholic crowds stoned police stations on the Falls Road. Soon, mobs of Catholics and loyalists were battling each other in the narrow streets running between the Falls Road and the Shankill. There were incendiary attacks on vulnerable Catholic homes led, according to witnesses, by members of the B-Specials. A loyalist mob marched on Divis Street at the foot of the Falls Road. It was only stopped when one of the Protestant crowd, Herbert Roy, was shot dead by a Catholic gunman.

The RUC roared into the Falls Road riot in Shorland armored cars armed with heavy-caliber Browning machine guns—for many years the standard machine gun of the United States army. The police were not exactly equipped for crowd control. But then, the RUC was not expecting a riot, but a revolution. They blasted a Catholic block of flats with the Brownings, blowing the head off a nine-year-old boy, Patrick Rooney, as he sat up in bed, disturbed by the noise. They also killed an off-duty British soldier visiting his Catholic parents.

In other Belfast Catholic ghettos, the RUC fired into Catholic mobs and killed two men. Another Catholic was killed trying to prevent a loyalist mob from burning down Bombay Street, where he lived, which was burned to the ground. There was trouble in Armagh, Dungannon, and in the Catholic town of Dungiven in south County Derry. There the B-Specials fired into a crowd of Catholics, killing one man.

On August 14th, after continued pressure from Stormont, the British government put its troops on the streets of Derry. The following day they took up position between the two communities in Belfast. For the first time in decades the British army had been called out to support the civil authorities.

Of the eight fatalities in Belfast, six were Catholics. The two Protestant deaths, one of which occurred when a shotgun blast hit a Protestant vigilante near a barricade in north Belfast, were proof to the loyalists that the IRA was once more rampant in Northern Ireland. The following weeks saw thousands of loyalists patrolling their streets, getting ready for the IRA onslaught that more and more of them now felt was coming. Loyalist vigilante groups began springing up in the Protestant areas.

On the Catholic side, the August violence left people with a feeling of helplessness. Like the Protestants, they formed vigilante groups or "defense committees," which became coordinated under the Central Citizens Defence Committee. But contrary to loyalist fears, the dreaded IRA took little part in the violence. When those Catholics who wanted more militant action sought it out in the aftermath of the riots, they found a small, disorganized group, riven with factions. The IRA was taken aback by the violence of that August, which only deepened the crisis it had been undergoing since the failure of its last campaign. The new situation, with Catholics clamoring for action, would shortly lead to a complete split in the organization, out of which came the Provisional IRA.

The ghosts of Ireland's old conflicts were haunting the streets of Belfast again.

2

A Desperate City

Those who will not reason
Perish in the act.
Those who will not act
Perish for that reason.

—W. H. AUDEN

While Northern Ireland hovered on the brink of civil war, Aunt Martha sat securely and proudly in her new armchair. A short woman grown stout, with small arms and fine features, she seemed the very image of immobility. She held a delicate delft cup of strong brown tea. Outside, Drew Street was still in tumult after the conflagration of two weeks before. Many residents had left; others were still talking about evacuation, worried that Protestant gangs or the hated B-Specials would advance on them from the nearby Donegal Road, a loyalist district just south of the Falls area.

Aunt Martha seemed unconcerned about that. She was calm, confident in the midst of her new possessions. She'd redecorated the house so completely that I hardly recognized it as the home I grew up in. I'd been away at university for almost three years and was on a visit to Belfast for a few days toward the end of August 1969.

There was wall-to-wall carpeting in the front room; there was a new soft couch, as well as a china cabinet full of delft cups and saucers and bowls. The house was now Martha's, and she had put the stamp of her character upon it. Her mother and brother, with whom she'd lived all her life and whom she had looked after when she'd finished a hard day's work in the mill, had both died some years before. She was fifty-nine years old and proud of her modest comfort. Martha, who had lived through other periods of civil war, riot, and unrest, had made a cozy, snug little nest for herself. She now had the privacy that she had never known before. The outside world of burnings and murder and British intervention seemed suddenly remote.

Not far from where we sat talking and drinking tea, the ashes still smoldered from the burned-out homes and factories; the victims of the violence were still being mourned. On the streets puzzled British soldiers watched and waited, rather bemused as they took tea from local Catholics who saw them as their saviors. At the top of every street was a barricade, and behind the barricades the people waited. No one knew what would happen next or who would make the next move.

"Aunt Martha," I said, "what do you make of all this?" She looked at me rather regretfully and shook her head. Behind that look were years of hardship, years of work and sacrifice. She replied, "It will never be the same again." Some of her neighbors had told her she should evacuate, but Martha refused.

"They thought they'd be burnt out," she went on, "they wanted me to go too. I told them to catch themselves on—I stayed where I was. No one was going to put me out of my wee house. I didn't move in the thirties, and I'm not moving now."

Aunt Martha had become a Catholic at the age of twenty-one; she had turned away from the faith of her father because she'd found it drab. She chose the faith of her mother—then a lapsed Catholic—with no encouragement, except, as she once pointed out to me, the persuasion of the beauty of the Catholic chapel: its stained glass windows, its altars, its statues, the ritual and the mystery of its ceremonies. It appealed to her imagination, which was starved by the esthetically unimpressive mission halls of the various Protestant sects found in every loyalist back street.

Yet, in other ways that had little to do with religion, she remained a Protestant. There were some things she still could not understand about the Catholic nationalist community though she had lived within it for half her life. "The Burnses were over here the other night," she said to me, "all talk about being second-class citizens. I looked at them and said I've never been a second-class citizen. Their head's full of nonsense."

Agnes Burns was Martha's younger sister. She too became a Catholic, but unlike Martha, she married and reared ten children in a two-bedroom house. They grew up in one of the poorest Catholic areas of north Belfast, known cryptically as "the Bone." And bare as bone it was. Martha's nephews were now complaining about the treatment of Catholics in Northern Ireland, and Martha was not sympathetic. She expected Catholics (and Protestants for that matter) to be grateful for what they had: a welfare state; free education; and more lately, courtesy of Terence O'Neill, one-man, one-vote.

Terence O'Neill was Martha's political hero. She lamented that he was not allowed by the civil rights marchers and the Paisleyites to carry out his reforms. "He was a decent man," she said regretfully, "and if they'd have given him a chance, the Catholics would have gotten all they asked for. But not in this place—a man like that hasn't a chance."

Outside, the long summer's twilight was darkening. The sounds of shouting, of youths and children at Drew Street's barricade, distracted her for a moment.

"They're piling up stones all week. That's their ammunition. They've no sense." She got up and peered through the curtains up the street. "Just wee lads—and a few older ones. You'd think men of that age would know better than to be out throwing stones!" When she returned to her seat I asked her if she thought it would get worse.

"Worse! It's just beginning," she exclaimed. "The IRA have been waiting for this for years." Martha looked at me in wonder. "Don't you know that?" she asked. She explained: "Till this happened no one listened to them oul fellas with the rusty revolvers. All they were good for was shooting at policemen in the dark. They were out of date. No one paid attention to them. The young boys were going to university, like you. But mark my word, these last few weeks have changed it all. Paisley and his crowd have played right into their hands." She got up to make another pot of tea.

"Paisley blamed it all on the IRA anyway," I said when she came back.

"That was always the excuse of Paisley and his likes," she replied contemptuously. "They always said that. Sure you would have thought the way they went on that Terence O'Neill was an IRA man. But now oul Paisley will have something to squawk about—the IRA will get more support than it knows what to do with."

Her upbringing had allowed little room for personal feelings or their indulgence; her life had been too tightly run by circumstance to permit divergence into self-pity or self-expression—that was looked down upon as mere bravado. Her generation was expected to accept its lot in life and get on with it. Her lot had been the mill and the care of her mother and her unmarried brother. Her only break in the monotony was worship on a Sunday or occasional nights out to the cinema, and as she got older, she read religious books about other converts.

What she saw in the streets outside was in some ways familiar. She had witnessed barricades before; she'd seen troops on the streets before; and she'd watched the black smoke before, billowing over the ashes where once little homes had stood. But she had not experienced the feeling that was now abroad—the feeling that one's lot in life should not be accepted and that it might be changed. That was the feeling now sweeping the nationalist ghettos, and with it there was anger and determination. But to Martha it was all the overindulgence of a generation who had it too easy, who never had to suffer as she had. She had been reared to sacrifice, not to protest. And to people who accept sacrifice as their lot, the protests of others seem like acts of selfishness.

At 10:30 P.M. twilight still glowed faintly on the horizon. Martha was lamenting the passing of something. Though she rarely permitted herself to show her feelings, now she turned nostalgic.

"It was a good wee town once," she almost whispered. "We had cinemas, theaters, music halls, and Woolworth's was packed on a Saturday. There was plenty of shops for everybody. It used to be great going down the town. It would be all lit up at night. But things will never be the same again." She was aware that within the past few weeks something fundamental had changed in Northern Ireland: A new generation had moved, and the direction in which it seemed to be going frightened her, as change must a woman who had lived her life with little prospect of change.

As I got up to leave she warned me to be careful not to trip over the barricade at the top of the street. She was obviously disdainful of the barrel or two and the few pieces of old furniture that constituted Drew Street's barricade. "They must think the B-Specials are going to come up the road in wheelchairs if they think that'll stop them," she said with a look of skepticism as I walked out the front door.

Outside, all through the ghetto, the prevailing mood was far from skeptical. People were expectant, hopeful that the upheavals of recent weeks had created a momentum able to move everyone towards some overwhelming solution to the Northern Ireland problem. They spoke of a possible invasion of the Irish army from the south, of the British government's abolishing Stormont, even of the possible intervention of U.N. forces to keep the peace. It felt as if the old molds were broken, and the people were determined that the crust of Unionist sectarianism would not be allowed to harden again.

The streets were ablaze with bonfires. Impromptu *ceilis* were being held, with local musicians playing Irish tunes, and people dancing. The RUC had been expelled from the Catholic streets and was nowhere to be seen; the pubs remained open long after the legal closing time (11:00 P.M.). The drinkers were standing on the pavements outside enjoying the music, the feeling of "liberation."

As I passed through one of the many barricades into a side street off Leeson Street, the very heart of the Falls ghetto, a short-haired youth pulled me aside, recognizing that I was a stranger to the street. "Do you support the PD?" he asked, with a hint of menace. The People's Democracy was one of the Catholic radical student groups that had played an important part in many civil rights protests. Of course I answered yes.

What surprised me was that a working-class youth from the Falls Road should ask me that rather than the more traditional "Do you support the IRA?" Quite clearly the general feeling was that the IRA had let the Catholics down. They had expected its battalions of trench-coated volunteers in black berets to rise from the ground at the first sign of trouble. By 1969, the battalions no longer existed.

In fact, the Catholics of Northern Ireland had turned their backs on the Irish Republican Army a decade before. It no longer seemed relevant to their situation. Many in the IRA itself agreed, and after the debacle of the 1950s border campaign turned to other forms of activity. Led by "Chief of Staff" Cathal Goulding, a stocky, handsome Dubliner, the IRA had forsaken the blowing up of stone bridges straddling the border for organizing "fish-ins" to protest the selling of Irish natural resources to foreign investors. The IRA became involved in all forms of social agitation in Dublin, and in the North its members took part in the civil rights marches.

Goulding was under the influence of Dublin Communists whose policies were aimed at moving the republicans away from their customary, somewhat esoteric attitudes and simple solutions to the problems of Ireland. The IRA's political wing, Sinn Fein, refused to allow its elected members to take their seats in either of the two Irish parliaments. The IRA tradition held that Stormont and the Dublin parliament, the *Dail,* were the illegitimate creations of the British. The only parliament the republicans recognize is that of the first *Dail*—the 1918 parliament outlawed by the British and dominated by Sinn Fein. The 1918 British general election had included Ireland—then still part of the United Kingdom—as one unit. Sinn Fein fought the election in all thirty-two counties on an independence platform, and had won a majority throughout the country. It then proceeded to establish an Irish parliament, which was, of course, illegal.

According to traditional republicans, the leading body of the IRA, the Army Council, was the political inheritor of this parliament. The Communists regarded all this as rather metaphysical, and entirely beside the point. After all, the subsequent partitioning of Ireland had led to the dissolution of the first *Dail.* They wanted the IRA and Sinn Fein to accept the fact of partition and the governments it created. Goulding brought Communists into the leadership of the movement, and a campaign was begun to end the policy of abstention from the parliaments. Many in the IRA balked at this, as they did at other suggested innovations. It was proposed, for instance, that republicans discontinue the saying of the Rosary at republican commemorations. This was hardly received with favor by some members who were daily communicants. More far-reaching changes were planned. The most profound—that the IRA abandon the use of armed force as a means of achieving a united Ireland in the immediate future—would mean the liquidation of the IRA as a guerrilla army.

A Stalinist adaptation of Marx's "three stages" theory of historical development was resurrected from the archives of 1930s Communism to explain to IRA men why armed force was now inappropriate. The use of force would only come at a certain stage in the evolution of the state; Northern Ireland had still to reach that stage; in the meantime armed force being inappropriate, if not downright reactionary, the IRA was to devote itself to helping ordinary democracy develop.

The Northerners raised a skeptical eyebrow at this explanation, which some of them referred to irreverently as the "three Stooges theory." It seemed incredibly naive to them to expect ordinary democracy to develop in a place where the government had organized things specifically to prevent this from happening. Still, that was the new road and the IRA—however reluctantly—took it. Many of the men who had experienced jail and its hardships in the North dropped out of the movement until by 1967 there were only about seventy IRA men in all of Northern Ireland.

Just as the IRA was getting ready to abandon the armed struggle, Northern Ireland was precipitated to the edge of civil war. Its Communist mentors in Dublin had felt that many of the guiding principles of the IRA were so much metaphysics; in the aftermath of August 15th many Catholics in Belfast felt the same about fish-ins. Slogans began appearing in the Catholic nationalist ghettos: "IRA = I RAN AWAY." The old stalwarts, who had through years of neglect argued for armed struggle, winced at first. But then they looked up and saw a specter rising out of the ashes of the gutted houses.

I caught a glimpse of it myself that late August night when I was home. Returning to Drew Street after walking around the area I met a young man standing by the barricade. Sean O'Neill had been a childhood friend. The first time in my life I had gotten drunk was with him, standing up an entry near a pile of rubbish guzzling cheap wine.

Sean had never shown any interest in the IRA; in that he was typical of my generation, which socially and culturally was drifting away from traditional Irish interests and activities. We went to rock and roll dances, not to Irish *ceilis;* our friends went to live and work in the northern English cities of Manchester or Birmingham and not Dublin. Many of them joined the British army. I was surprised therefore to hear him talk about nothing else except what the Irish Republican Army had to do.

Sean was nineteen at the time, with glossy black hair and a boyish face. He'd left school three years before, worked in England for a while, returned to Belfast, and had an assortment of odd jobs. Before, he'd spoken only of going back to England and perhaps getting a job as a merchant seaman. He'd an older brother, a British army marine, who he told me that night was returning to the city because of the "troubles." There was no thought of returning to England now. "We must be ready for the next time," he said to me. Along with several of his friends, he'd already contacted the local IRA commander in the lower Falls district. For the first time in a generation the IRA was getting recruits. When his older brother returned he would bring military skills, which Sean believed the IRA was soon going to need. (The police would later come to know him as "the Wizard" because of his skill in making bombs.) In the meantime, Sean's friends were joining up, getting guns, training, making ready for the onslaught of the civil war he felt was inevitable. Sean hadn't heard about the new-look IRA, but he did think that Dublin had no idea about what was going on in Belfast. "They don't care. We'll have to do it ourselves," he explained.

"Do what?" I asked him.

He paused for a second and shrugged his shoulders. Then he said, "Get rid of Northern Ireland."

"And what about the British army?"

"They'll have to go too," he answered matter-of-factly.

It was simple and clear-cut, the kind of solution produced by anger and frustration. It was the force behind the birth of the Provisional IRA.

The IRA had not long to last as a united organization. The Northern experience was pulling it asunder. In December 1969 a group of IRA men, repudiating the Goulding leadership and its policies, established their own "Provisional" Army Council. They appointed as their new chief of staff Sean MacStiofain, né John Stephenson. He and Goulding were friends; they had been involved in an arms raid in England, and both had spent long terms in prison because of it. But MacStiofain had long opposed the drift away from armed struggle towards the policy of compromise. The Northern crisis gave him the opportunity he needed to rally those who agreed with him. He had strong support among the Belfast stalwarts ("the '40s men" as they were called), who felt themselves abandoned by Dublin. These men had seen a vision of the Holy Grail of Irish unity which would solve all ills; they felt now was the time to reach for it. Compromise was unthinkable. They had already sacrificed too much.

The Provisionals in Belfast chose as a symbol for their organization a phoenix rising out of its ashes. The slogan underneath it read, "Out of the ashes of '69 arose the Provisionals." It distinguished them as "the Provisionals," as if to set them apart from the previous IRA organization. There were many reasons why they should do so.

The IRA of history was a rural-based guerrilla army recruited mostly from poorer farmers, a rather conservative and very Catholic section of the population. The aftermath of the 1969 riots for the first time saw large numbers of urban poor, working-class youths from the ghetto slums of Belfast, waiting to join the IRA. Many of them, like Sean O'Neill, did not come from a republican tradition and had shown little interest in Irish affairs until then. They had grown up on a cultural diet of popular British and imported American television shows. A considerable number of them had been immigrant workers in Liverpool, Manchester, or Birmingham, or had served in the British army. The Belfast working class was, after all, the only industrial working class in Ireland, and inevitably its culture increasingly resembled that of the northern English working class.

The generation that formed the first volunteers of the Provisional IRA came from this background. Their leaders, however, had more conservative, republican origins. In Belfast the men who took over the leadership of the Brigade Staff were IRA veterans from the sporadic campaigns of the 1940s. All had spent long periods in jail. One, Joe Cahill, had been under sentence of death for the murder of a policeman in 1942 and had had his sentence commuted (another IRA man was hanged for the killing). Billy McKee had been the Provisionals' Belfast commanding officer until 1964, when he was edged out by Liam McMillen, a man more sympathetic to the Goulding strategy. McKee had the reputation of being a strict disciplinarian and was supposedly a daily communicant. "The '40s men" in many ways reflected the rural Catholic conservatism of the movement, in spite of their urban background.

These men were middle-aged and jail-hardened. For years they'd felt keenly the scorn of their own people and the failure of their efforts against mounting indifference. They sacrificed the better part of their lives for a vision the new Dublin "intellectual" Communists snubbed as that of simpletons. Soon they would be at the head of an army of angry working-class youths, larger than anything they had dreamed of through their years of isolation. The bitterness of the old, of those who have sacrificed everything, leading the impatience of the young, who were prepared to sacrifice everything, created a force with a frightening potential for destruction.

When an organization like the IRA splits, people are forced to take what may be the most important decision in their lives. In this case, many chose to stay with the leader they knew, Cathal Goulding, rather than begin again with a fragmented organization and another round of bloodshed that might lead to the same debacle as had other IRA campaigns.

Goulding's IRA, known after the split as the "Official" IRA, chose not to act—the time was not right for revolution, they reasoned. To act against Northern Ireland as the Provisionals were planning to do would provoke a sectarian backlash from the loyalists, which, the Officials argued, would set back the cause of a united Ireland for generations. They said, however, that they would "defend" Catholic areas. The Official IRA believed that reason and political organizing would prepare the way for revolution, the time for action. The Provisionals sought through action to create the revolutionary circumstances that would destroy partition and elevate them to political power.

The appeal of the Provisionals in Belfast was strongest in those areas most vulnerable to sectarian attack—the isolated enclaves of north and east Belfast. Here, after the August riots, Catholics had at first set up defense groups organized under a body called the Central Citizens Defence Committee (CCDC) to patrol their streets and man the barricades. The IRA in the city had always been primarily a defense group, and because the Catholic nationalists refused to recognize the RUC as its police force, it had also a policing function. The Provisionals took over both roles, gradually at first, then with increasing effect as the crisis deepened through 1970 and early 1971. The Provisionals recruited many members from the defense groups, eventually absorbing them.

Something of the ruthlessness of the new organization was shown when it claimed its first victim. He was a Belfast man—an informer, or "tout" as it is called in the city. He was suspected of giving information to the police that led to the arrest of one of the Provisionals' leaders. A group of them took him to the banks of a polluted stream which flows through west Belfast and shot him in the mouth, killing him instantly. The Belfast leadership had not "sanctioned" the killing, and it was regarded as a serious breach of republican discipline, for strictly speaking, "executions" had to be approved at a high level of the organization. The men who had carried it out were expelled from the movement and told to leave the country. But a high-ranking Provisional intervened and had their "sentence" commuted. He realized that if he was to keep the army together, then he would have to forego traditional republican procedure and bow to the morality of the ghetto.

The Officials, in spite of their hesitation about launching into a full-scale armed struggle, proved equally ruthless. It soon became clear that there were difficulties involved in pursuing a political course while retaining an illegal army. These were accentuated by many within the movement who expected its revolutionary aspirations to lead to action sooner than the leadership obviously intended. This created tensions which resulted in further fragmenting and bitter feuds. The Officials showed that they had absorbed of Stalinism more than just its three stages theory—they had also acquired with its politics a taste for purges, which often ended in the murder of those who disagreed with the leadership's policy. Because of these feuds and defections, the Official IRA has dwindled to the level of a local gang whose main function is to protect the organization's many drinking clubs.

The same month that the IRA met to decide its future course, another meeting took place which would have equally important consequences for the coming decade. In December 1969 a group of Protestants met in an area of the upper Shankill Road. They were the leaders of the myriad loyalist defense groups, most of which had sprung up in the wake of the August riots. Every area had spawned its "Defence Association." At the meeting were members of the Shankill Road Defence Association, the Woodvale Defence Association, all of them "front-line" groups from areas close to Catholic neighborhoods.

Unlike the IRA, the loyalists had little in the way of ideology to argue about. They were there simply to defend what they had from the depredations of the Catholic nationalist community, led, they were certain, by IRA gunmen.

It was a small gathering, held in a local clubhouse. Most of the men already had long histories of paramilitary involvement. They had been involved with either Gusty Spence's UVF of the mid-sixties—which had declared war against the IRA only to kill three innocent people—or with the Reverend Ian Paisley's organization,

Protestant paramilitary leaders, members of the Woodvale Defence Association (WDA), a local Shankill Road defense group which was instrumental in transforming the Ulster Defence Association (UDA) from an organization of vigilantes into an assassination gang. The man in the center, Sammy McCracken, was one of the few Protestants interned by the British. The security forces believed the WDA group in the UDA was behind many of the assassinations of Catholics in the early and mid-1970s.

the Ulster Protestant Volunteers, then in deep trouble with the police. In the spring of 1969, several of its members had been charged with the bombings that led to the resignation of Terence O'Neill. Others present had been part of obscure Protestant gangs which, like fungi, flourished in the darker corners of the paramilitary underworld.

What brought them together that December was fear. Initially the loyalists regarded the recent bout of burning and rioting as a triumph. They believed they had taught the "Fenians" a lesson. The destruction of Catholic homes and the attack on the Falls were already being celebrated as a victory for loyalism. One of the songs written to commemorate the attack on Bombay Street, where nearly every house was destroyed and a Catholic teen-ager killed, was grandiosely called "The Battle of Bombay Street." The language celebrating the "battle" was expressive of loyalist attitudes. (It later appeared in a collection of loyalist ballads put out by Protestant prisoners.) To the tune of "The Battle of New Orleans," it goes:

> *On the 14th August, we took a*
> *Little trip, up along Bombay Street*
> *And burned out all the shit,*
> *We took a little petrol, and took*
> *A little gun, and we fought the*
> *Bloody Fenians, till we had them*
> *On the run.*
> *Well we fired our guns and the*
> *Fenians started running, there wasn't*
> *As many as there was a while ago,*
> *We fired once more and they began*
> *A running, up along the Falls Road*
> *To get the IRA. . . .*

The men from the defense groups regarded the intervention of the British army as a setback—it stopped them from getting rid of the "Fenians" once and for all. Their resentment at British intervention grew as they became fearful of the Wilson government's intentions—recent moves had filled them with alarm. By December the British had disbanded the B-Specials and set out to "civilianize" the RUC. An English policeman was put in charge of the force with the intention of weeding out its sectarian bias and disarming it. The

B-Specials were regarded as unreformable, particularly after the role they evidently played in the recent riots, when they had sided openly with Protestant mobs. And, adding insult to injury, Wilson sent Jim Callaghan, who as the British Home Secretary was most directly concerned with Northern Ireland affairs, to the North, where he was seen on television talking to known republicans. His attempts to reassure Catholics caused a storm of indignation.

The Protestants were profoundly shocked. The B-Specials were part of their mythology—a force recruited exclusively from the loyalist community to defend them against the IRA. It was being taken from them when they needed it the most. The loyalists saw this as a first step towards forcing them into a united Ireland.

In October there were severe riots in the Shankill, provoked by the news that the police were to be disarmed and the Specials disbanded. Ironically, an RUC constable was shot dead by a Protestant gunman who was there to protest against the disarming of the RUC. It was typical of the contradictory nature of much Protestant violence, and the first of many similar self-defeating actions in which the loyalist paramilitaries got involved. After the riots the British army launched a widespread search for arms in the Shankill. Dozens of people were wounded in gun battles between loyalists and soldiers. Protestants began to see the British as the nationalists had regarded them for centuries—as a threat.

The British proposed replacing the B-Specials with a locally recruited regiment of the British army, to be named the Ulster Defence Regiment. But this was ignored by loyalists in their anger at the British reforms. In any case the UDR would not satisfy them—it was to be under British, not loyalist, control. What the militant Protestants wanted was their own militia.

The vigilantes who met in December proposed that such an organization should be formed from the different defense groups. John McKeague, a lean, fair-haired ex-Paisleyite who, according to a British inquiry, had played an active part in the August turmoil, came forward with the name "Ulster Defence Association." It would act as coordinator for the defense groups throughout Northern Ireland.

In the room were two other leading loyalist paramilitaries, Charles Harding Smith and Andy Tyrie. Both were skeptical about the proposal. Harding Smith was a van driver by trade, Tyrie a gardener *cum* odd-job man. Harding Smith wanted something more than just a collection of defense groups. He was already thinking along the lines of a more militant organization, one that would take the war to the enemy—the IRA and their Catholic supporters, though the loyalists never really distinguished between the two. A plan began to evolve that saw the UDA as merely a front for this other group—the "real" organization. Its business would simply be to kill Catholics.

The UDA's assassins did not emerge for another two years. It took time for the leaders to sort out who was prepared to do what, to get to know them, and to train. But there was another more potent reason concerning British government policy. After the upheaval of late 1969, when Protestants felt the tide of events was running against them, it began turning once more in their favor. The Labour government sent in the army to stop the slide towards civil war and made some dramatic concessions to the minority. But it soon found the troops were being increasingly identified with the Protestant Unionist regime. While this reassured the loyalists and alleviated some of their worst fears, it meant that the relationship between the army and the Catholic population, after the initial euphoria of August to December 1969, deteriorated steadily.

This was almost inevitable, considering the situation into which the troops were sent. Wilson warned Chichester-Clarke in the summer of 1969 that if the army was committed to the streets of Belfast and Derry, then Westminster would have to reconsider its relationship with Stormont. There was a hint that Stormont might be suspended and direct rule from Westminster imposed if the army went in. Many thought this a necessary condition to ensure that the troops would continue to act with impartiality. Some Labour politicians feared that if the Unionists were left in power with the army at their disposal, it would inevitably lead to bloodshed involving the Catholic community and an overall worsening of the crisis. That is exactly what happened.

In the event, the army was introduced without any such political moves. Apart from the reforms made in the police structures and a promise from Chichester-Clarke that the necessary political reforms begun by O'Neill would go ahead unhampered, the British did not interfere with Stormont. But by then the stakes were higher than civil rights. What was in question was the existence of the regime itself.

The previous twelve months showed the Unionists to be increasingly unable to govern Northern Ireland. At the time the British army intervened, the regime was weakened by dissension within and discredited in the eyes of most citizens. Its police force was exhausted, demoralized, and rejected by a large section of the community. The Catholics were even more politically alienated, and the section from which the government drew its support—the Protestants— was becoming more and more hostile. Under these conditions, making such a massive security commitment without drastic political reform in effect shored up the tottering Unionist government.

The intervention of the British army had undoubtedly saved the lives of many Catholics. But the failure of the Wilson government to foresee the consequences of his commitment saved Stormont. In spite of his previous hints, Wilson backed away from direct rule, uncertain as to the reaction it might provoke among loyalists, and unwilling to become too deeply embroiled in a frustrating situation. British intervention was left incomplete, creating a political vacuum the Unionists were all too willing to fill with their drive for a military solution—the last, desperate policy of a politically bankrupt regime. With remarkable ease, the British army was handed over to a government that had proved itself unable to control a police force.

Direct rule was avoided, but only for three years. However, this gave the loyalist paramilitaries ample time to prepare their reaction—the so-called "Protestant backlash" so feared by Wilson.

During those three years the UDA continued to organize on a small scale, contented by the ever more common sight of Catholics battling with British soldiers. As long as they saw the Catholics being "kept in their place" by the authorities, the loyalist militants were relatively happy. Friction between the minority and the army increased throughout 1970 as the Catholic youths began to resent the presence of foreign soldiers in their ghettos.

The tension was heightened in 1970 by the approach of the Orange Order's marching season in the early summer, when the loyalist population again set out to celebrate old victories over the recalcitrant natives. The trouble was, the natives were growing more and more recalcitrant. The Wilson government was forced to face two ugly alternatives: ban the Orange parades in the interests of preserving the peace, but then almost certainly angering the loyalists, or allow the Orangemen to have their fun protected by British troops. If the latter course was taken, the nationalists would see the army performing the old role of the RUC; further bad feeling between them and the troops would then be inevitable. Like so many British governments before and since, Wilson acted to placate the Protestants at the expense of understanding with the Catholic nationalist community.

The only people who were to benefit from this were the Provisional IRA. In Belfast their old leaders, distrustful of the British all along, said "I told you so" as the Catholics saw the army they thought was sent in for their protection marching in step with the Orangemen. It also gave the fledgling phoenix a chance to flap its wings. At the end of June 1970, the nationalist enclave of the Short Strand, in east Belfast, found itself under attack when an Orange parade turned into a running street battle with local Catholics. Protestants attacked the neighborhood Catholic church, attempting to burn it down. The Provisionals appeared as its defenders, led by Billy McKee. Two loyalists and one IRA man were shot dead (the Provisionals' first loss). McKee himself was wounded by Protestant snipers and whisked away across the border to a hospital in Dundalk. A short time later he was back in Belfast.

That same day, June 27th, the Provisionals killed three Protestants in north Belfast during shooting that broke out after another Orange parade passed the Catholic ghetto of Ardoyne. There was severe rioting in the Provisional stronghold of Ballymurphy, a 1950s housing development in west Belfast and one of the most economically depressed areas in Northern Ireland. It too was provoked by an Orange march passing nearby. The army flooded the development with CS gas. Though it badly affected the old, the gas did little to stop those against whom it was aimed. The battling youths simply covered their mouths with wet cloth handkerchiefs and kept on rioting.

By mid-1970 the nationalists saw the army as the military force of the Unionist government. As far as Northern Ireland was concerned, there could not have been a worse time for a British general election. But British domestic concerns dictated otherwise. To the jubilation of Unionists, the election brought a Conservative government led by Edward Heath to power. The Conservatives were regarded by the Unionists as their political allies, more trustworthy than the Labour Party, and more solid in their commitment to supporting the Unionist position.

The new government's Home Secretary, the man most directly concerned with Northern Ireland affairs, was Reginald Maudling.

Unlike his predecessor, Jim Callaghan, he was not particularly interested in what went on in that "bloody awful country" as he reportedly once described it. His tenure as Home Secretary saw a general loosening of control over what the Unionists did and a growing commitment to their drive for a "military" solution.

This became apparent within weeks of the Conservative victory. It involved the UDA in a minor but typical way, as *agents provocateurs.* After the June blood-letting, and with the big Orange celebrations of the 12th of July still to come, the Unionists demanded the British army act resolutely against the Catholic gunmen waiting, they claimed, in the ghettos to strike at the parades.

On July 1, Chichester-Clarke met with his security chiefs and they decided to use maximum force if any further trouble broke out. On July 2nd, two UDA gunmen from the Donegal Road area took up positions in a street bordering the Falls district. Their intention was to shoot at British soldiers—not to hit them, but to make them think they were under attack from the IRA. The loyalists hoped this would lead to more confrontations between the army and the Catholics. They fired at passing foot patrols throughout the afternoon, changing their positions to avoid detection.

The next day the police received information that there were arms in a house in the Leeson Street area. The army moved in and found some guns. The soldiers were jumpy as crowds gathered; after all, they'd heard reports of shooting the previous day. As more people gathered, more troops were sent in until the worst rioting Belfast had yet seen broke out.

Official and then Provisional IRA units were ordered into the area to defend it. The Official IRA sent in a supply of weapons in a commandeered ambulance. These were distributed to its members and to any Provisional who needed a gun. In the subsequent gun battle, fifteen soldiers were wounded and four civilians killed. The British army fired over fifteen hundred rounds of ammunition and were responsible for all the civilian deaths. They also flooded the streets with CS gas, imposed a thirty-six-hour curfew, and began a massive house-to-house search. (It resulted in over five hundred complaints of looting, assault, and bad behavior on the part of the soldiers involved.)

When it was all over, few Catholics had any doubts left as to the course the British were undertaking. The moderates in the Catholic community were put in an impossible position, and massive support swung behind the militant Provisionals. "Recruits came forward to offer their services at an ever increasing rate," wrote the Provisional IRA leader, Sean MacStiofain, about the aftermath of the curfew and the violence that accompanied the searches.

The UDA applauded the success of its ruse and privately took credit for having inspired the whole operation. Though the actions of the Protestant gunmen might well have added to the hostility the troops evidently felt against the Catholics, it is doubtful if they had much to do with the scale of the search operation. Even if the UDA was justified in its claims, it should have realized how self-defeating such actions were, as they led to increased support for the Provisionals.

Such rational political considerations, however, have rarely affected loyalist behavior. The UDA had set out to inflict further humiliation on the minority population regardless of its political effect. That was the real desire behind most of its activities.

As support for the Provisionals continued to grow, so did the Belfast organization, the backbone of the movement. By mid-1970 the city's several hundred volunteers were organized into three "battalions." The recruits came mostly from the area in which each battalion was based—in this stage of their development, the Provisionals were still very much a neighborhood force. The First Battalion covered the Andersonstown housing development along the upper fringes of the Falls area; the Second Battalion was based in the mid-Falls ghetto; and the Third Battalion was organized in the outlying Catholic enclaves of north and east Belfast, areas like the Ardoyne, the Bone, and the Short Strand, all surrounded by much larger loyalist districts. The third battalion, the most pugnacious and aggressive in the city, was responsible for most of the early Provisional violence.

The Conservatives supported the Unionist decision to go for a military solution, which suited the militaristic Provisionals perfectly. In early 1970 they had begun a small-scale bombing campaign. This was stepped up during the summer and fall. The attacks were directed against power supplies and communication installations. During one such attack the Provisionals lost their second volunteer within the space of a few months—Michael Kane blew himself up in September 1970 trying to sabotage an electricity transformer in a Belfast suburb. Like the IRA man killed in the Short Strand gun battle, he was a member of the Third Battalion.

The Provisionals acted in other ways, too. Demonstrating their power as ghetto "policemen," Provisional gunmen shot dead two local criminal racketeers in Ballymurphy in November. (Later the brother of one of the dead men would join the UDA in its campaign against Catholics and be responsible for the murders of nearly a dozen men.) As yet, however, the Provisionals did not consider themselves strong enough to take on the British army in a wide-spread guerrilla war. Since the troops had been introduced over a year before, no soldiers had been killed by IRA action. Street battles between the army and Catholic rioters continued, in spite of the Provisionals' attempts to stop them. The organization did not want to run the risk of army raids provoked by the troubles on the streets disrupting its supply of arms. For a time, contact between local guerrilla leaders and British army commanders was established in an attempt to keep peace in the ghettos. When the Unionists found out they were horrified. The right wing of the party began accusing the British and Chichester-Clarke of being "soft" on the IRA. They wanted "firm action" against the Provisionals.

The Unionist position was simplicity itself: The IRA was in the ghettos, so the army should simply go in and get them. They ignored the disaster of the July arms raids which did so much to bring support to the Provisionals. Rather like the UDA, the Unionists forgot about the political impact of oppressive measures in their overriding desire to see them imposed. On February 3rd the army mounted a search of the Clonard area in the mid-Falls and the Ardoyne in north Belfast. Severe rioting erupted. But the violence escalated when four soldiers were wounded by a Provisional gunman on the New Lodge Road, a stronghold of the militant third battalion. The riots continued for two days, and under pressure from the Unionists, the British army allowed one of its generals to go on television and name members of the Provisionals' Belfast leadership (men with whom the army had actually been talking, but of course this was not mentioned).

The following night, February 6th, a patrol of troops proceeding down the New Lodge Road was raked by sub-machine gun fire. Five soldiers were wounded, one of them seriously. As police arrived to check the wounded, a detective constable noticed that Gunner Robert Curtis appeared to be only stunned—there was no sign of blood near him. When the policeman crouched down for a closer look, however, he discovered the soldier dead, pierced under the armpit by a bullet that left almost no entrance wound. The Irish guerrillas had killed their first British soldier in Ireland in almost fifty years.

The next morning, Chichester-Clarke, pale and drawn, solemnly declared on television, "Northern Ireland is at war with the Irish Republican Army Provisionals." The Third Battalion had made its mark in the bloody history of Northern Ireland. So had the man who led the ambush, Billy Reid. Three months later he entered the realms of IRA legend, dying in a hail of British bullets as he shot it out with another patrol in the city streets. His death in the old IRA tradition was celebrated in song:

> *Tell me why, oh why,*
> *Billy Reid had to die,*
> *But he died with a gun in his hand.*
> *Tell me why, oh why*
> *Billy Reid had to die,*
> *He died to free Ireland.*

It became a popular ballad around the Belfast bars and clubs. He received another tribute in verse from one of his imprisoned cohorts which began

> *'Twas in the town of Belfast*
> *All in the month of May*
> *Three youthful Irish soldiers*
> *Set out upon their way*
> *A mission to accomplish*
> *Ireland's freedom which we need,*
> *And the leader of that gallant band*
> *Was Lieutenant Billy Reid.*

The ballad then describes, in the language of conventional sentiment, the gun battle and the death of the guerrilla:

> *But the bullet caught our Billy,*
> *His life it took away,*
> *And there on a street in Belfast*
> *An Irish martyr lay.*

The motif of martyrdom runs through the IRA tradition as strongly as the theme of victory does in the annals of loyalism. It gilds violent death with a layer of sentimentality that disguises its ugliness, its brutality. To sacrifice oneself and others for the cause of Ireland becomes a hallowed act untouched by violence's sordid reality. The rituals of IRA funerals soon became a common sight in the Belfast ghettos: the coffin draped with the republican flag (the flag of a nation that has never existed), the long cortege of men in black berets, the shots fired over the grave as the coffin goes down, making even the burial an act of defiance, and the graveside orations from the leadership exhorting more young men to rise up and continue the fight. So the ritual of sacrifice turns defeat into a kind of victory.

Other young men followed Reid into the grave with deaths less noble than his. Less noble too were the deaths they inflicted on others. In March 1971 the killing of three off-duty soldiers whose bodies were found in a ditch to the north of the city provoked a powerful feeling of indignation among Catholics as well as Protestants. Two of the soldiers were young brothers. They had been befriended by IRA men in a bar, then murdered. The Third Battalion was again responsible—this time, it was rumored, without sanction from the leadership. But sanction, as when the Provisionals claimed their first victim the year before, was more often sought *after* acts than before them.

The political protest over this event took its now expected form. The Unionists' ever-growing right wing demanded still stronger actions, asking for the immediate introduction of internment without trial—that most powerful section of the Special Powers Act. The Conservatives, on the advice of their generals, refused. The army was skeptical about the efficacy of such a move and at that time did not think the police were sufficiently informed to carry it out successfully. To placate his party, Chichester-Clarke asked for more troops. When the British only gave him half the number he requested, he resigned.

With the growing clamor from the Unionist right, the British were running out of alternatives. There were no more senior "liberal" Unionists to choose from, and the elevation of a right-winger to the premiership might lend further support to the Provisionals— so the British feared. In the end, the man who replaced Chichester-Clarke turned out to be a liberal in public and a right-winger in private or, as it suited him, vice versa. At the end of March 1971, the late Brian Faulkner became Prime Minister, the last Northern Ireland would ever have.

Terence O'Neill once said Faulkner was "the best public relations man I have ever met." Faulkner had almost beaten O'Neill in the race for the premiership in 1963, and in 1969 he was there once more, this time against Chichester-Clarke. In those days he courted the right wing of Unionism, vying with William Craig for its support. But the British recognized Faulkner as a pragmatist—he was, after all, the first member of the Northern Ireland middle class to head a government that had for fifty years been led by landed gentry like the O'Neills and Brookeboroughs. Faulkner came from impeccable mercantile stock, a family of linen mill owners. He was canny, handling political principles like a juggler handling clubs. He had endeared himself to the loyalists in 1959, when as the Minister of Home Affairs he introduced internment, a move he credited with breaking the IRA's border campaign. Faulkner made the fatal mistake of drawing an analogy between that campaign and the current violence of the Provisionals.

Internment was now a certainty; it was merely a matter of when. The British were already taking a step in preparation for the expected move. In March, the same month that Faulkner became Prime Minister, a group of British intelligence officers arrived in County Derry at an old Royal Air Force base near Ballykelly. They began setting up a secret interrogation center. The interrogation methods were also kept a closely guarded secret, so much so that the Unionists later had to disclaim any knowledge of them. They had good reason to do so, for what subsequently happened in that center brought British actions in Northern Ireland to the attention of every human rights organization in the world.

The Provisionals' campaign became more and more violent throughout the early summer of 1971. Fighting often took the form of conventional skirmishes between up to a dozen gunmen and British patrols. It was not until later that the Provisionals entered the phase of real hit-and-run guerrilla warfare. The month of July saw over ninety explosions, the most in the campaign until then. The Official IRA also took part in the fighting—the Dublin leadership had to respond to the Northern membership's pressure for "defensive" actions. Meanwhile, the Unionists waited for the miracle of internment promised by Faulkner.

Stormont was rapidly losing control of the security situation. Entire areas of the state were falling under the rule of the guerrillas, where the police and army could only venture in at great risk. The British government became increasingly committed to supporting a regime that had very little moral authority left. Stormont's final abnegation of any right to rule was reached with the use of internment, a final admission of political bankruptcy.

The consequences of Wilson's failure to take decisive political action when he committed the army two years before were becoming clear. Politics was replaced by a "military solution." Unfortunately for Faulkner and Stormont, it was a military failure. At 4:30 in the morning of August 9, 1971, internment went into operation. The army lifted over three hundred men out of a list of four hundred and fifty prepared by the Prime Minister. The detainees, often dragged unceremoniously out of their beds, were taken to holding centers and held without trial. The violence unleashed in the streets was unprecedented—over one hundred explosions rocked Belfast that month, and thirty-five people died violently (as compared to four in July). Catholics were outraged not only by the use of internment, but by the fact that it was used indiscriminately against people who were not connected with terrorism. It was a clumsy instrument, exposed as such two days later when over one hundred of those originally arrested were released. Those that were interned were eventually held in an old air force base called Long Kesh, near Belfast. They were kept in war-time Nissen huts, grouped into compounds.

Internment effectively crystalized the Catholics' opposition to the state. In protest they went on a rent and rates strike that lasted for over three years. Local government broke down as Catholic councilors refused to occupy their seats on the councils that ran the day-to-day affairs of the state. Parliamentary government dissolved—there were no opposition Catholic politicians present in Stormont. They were refusing to return until internment was ended.

Only the Catholic population suffered arrest during the operation. No Protestants were interned. But loyalist gunmen took part in the rioting and gun battles that followed the internment raids. In north Belfast two hundred homes were burned down and thousands of people evacuated as the sectarian fighting spread. Near Drew Street the effects of the years of sectarian hatred were graphically evident. A few blocks away had stood a Protestant street. In the days following August 9th, gun battles raged between local loyalists and Catholics. UDA men from the Donegal Road arrived in the street and ordered the Protestants out, their reason being that they did not want fellow Protestants living in such an exposed position.

In reality, the UDA was carrying out a scorched-earth policy—destroying streets which lay near Catholic areas to make sure the houses would never be occupied by Catholics. After they had evacuated the street, they debated whether to booby-trap some of the houses to kill any Catholic who tried to move in or simply burn them all down. They took the latter course. Within hours the street was aflame. It was a dismal sight. Homes that had been well-furnished "little palaces," as the Protestants called them, were reduced to piles of blackened rubble. Within a few days the area between Drew Street and the Donegal Road, which had contained a mixed Catholic and Protestant population, was a skeleton of itself. Only a few streets, including Drew Street, were spared, largely because they were close enough to the Falls to escape sectarian attack.

Internment was Brian Faulkner's desperate attempt to save his government and Stormont. He refused to admit that it had failed; nor at first would the British. He remained Prime Minister for another seven months, and Stormont continued to blunder through the bloody mess its policies had made inevitable. At the end of January 1972 the army, attempting to break up a civil rights and anti-internment meeting in Derry, shot and killed thirteen unarmed demonstrators. "Bloody Sunday," as it became known, was the Unionists' final outrage committed in the name of security. In March Edward Heath called Faulkner to London and told him that all security powers exercised by his government were to be surrendered to Westminster. The Unionists would be left with only a facade of power. Faulkner refused, and Heath had no alternative but to abolish Stormont and impose direct rule. Northern Ireland's fifty-year-old parliament was suspended, and a Conservative minister, William Whitelaw, was sent over by Heath to run the devastated area.

The British government at last took responsibility for the affairs of what was claimed to be part of the United Kingdom, but which had been ruled as a separate state by one party since 1921.

One of the worst consequences of that rule was already apparent—perhaps the one the British feared most and which had made them reluctant to impose direct rule in 1969—the "Protestant backlash" had begun. The UDA was now under the control of Harding Smith, the man who three years before wanted to use it as a front for an assassination gang. UDA squads were on the streets of Belfast bombing Catholic bars and shooting any Catholic unfortunate enough to come their way. The attacks had begun shortly after internment—loyalists were still not convinced that the authorities were being tough enough with the Catholic population! Their campaign escalated drastically after the suspension of Stormont and has since been a major contributor to the continuing violence. It was the final sign that the two communities Terence O'Neill had once tried to bridge were now completely polarized.

Our family had lived through sectarian unrest before, but this was the worst. Uncle Willy was the only surviving Protestant member of the family. Every Sunday evening he and his wife would visit Drew Street. It was a seemingly inseparable part of our Sunday routine. (When I was young we'd have tea and I'd listen to Willy's recounting of the D-Day landings.) After 1971 he stopped coming. In the area where he lived, part of north Belfast, it would have been dangerous for him if people found out he had Catholic relatives.

The Conservatives now faced the consequences of Stormont's misrule and their support of it. Their conduct in the internment operation brought them to the attention of human rights organizations all around the world. Revelations were being made about the torture of prisoners in the secret interrogation center set up by intelligence officers in March 1971. They were potentially very damaging, for they concerned activities involving high-ranking government ministers in serious illegalities.

In spite of being an embarrassment to British democracy, Northern Ireland government had been supported by Westminster for fifty years. By the time that support was removed, it had compromised British democracy itself.

3

The Hooded Men

Arbitrary power is the natural object of temptation to a prince.

—JONATHAN SWIFT

After being handcuffed to these men, I then had a hood put over my head, covering my head entirely and lying loose on my shoulders. It was loose on the face, though for breathing, one had to breathe up from below as it was impossible to breathe through this hood.

It is 4:45 A.M., August 11, 1971. The place is Girdwood Barracks, north Belfast, a holding center for men picked up during the internment operation begun two days before. One of the men detained there is Joe Clarke, aged nineteen, a Catholic from the Falls Road.

After being hooded I was led to the helicopter and I was thrown bodily into the helicopter. During this exercise my hands and wrists were hurt due to the others handcuffed to me not being pushed equally. (Before being led off to the helicopter, I understand that one of the hooded men, now known to be F. McGuigan, collapsed when the hood was first applied.) On being put into the 'copter the handcuffs were removed and were applied to the back of the hood to tighten it around the head. The helicopter took off and a journey which I would estimate to have taken about an hour began.

The journey took Joe Clarke into a nightmare world of sensory deprivation. Along with eleven other detainees, for almost a week Clarke was subjected to what British intelligence officers called "the five techniques." The twelve hooded men called it torture.

The helicopter then landed at a destination unknown to me and we were taken from the copter and led into a building and eventually into a room where I was made stand in a search position against a wall. My position was the same as for other men—fully stretched hands as far apart as humanly possible and feet as far from the wall as possible. Back rigid and head held up. Not allowed to relax any of the joints at all. If any relaxation of limbs—arms, elbow joints, legs, knee joints—someone came along and grabbed the limb in a rough manner and put it back into position again. After being against the wall for a few hours I was taken away and brought, I was told, to a doctor. Sometime during this period I was taken out of this room and put into a helicopter and flown away. I was always handcuffed and hooded. When the copter landed I was put into a lorry—driven short distance—five to ten minutes—beaten about the face and body—transferred to other vehicle. Holding my face—asked why—said that I did not want to be beaten again. Assured that I wouldn't be. Brought into a building—hood removed—shown detention form.

The form bore the signature of Brian Faulkner. As Minister of Home Affairs—a post he reserved for himself after he became Prime Minister—he had the authority, thanks to the Special Powers Act, to detain Joe Clarke indefinitely. In the words of the act:

Any person so arrested may, on the order of the Civil Authority, [the Minister of Home Affairs] be detained either in any of Her Majesty's prisons or elsewhere, as may be specified in the order, upon such conditions as the Civil Authority may direct, until he has been discharged by the direction of the Attorney General or is brought before a Court of Summary Jurisdiction. . . .

"Elsewhere" for Joe Clarke was a nondescript collection of wartime huts in an old air force base that had been converted into a psychological torture chamber. After being shown the detention form, he was returned to the still-secret location.

> The buildup to this collapse was frequent numbing of the hands, which—when it happened—I closed my fist only to find that my hands were beaten against the wall until I opened my fingers again and put my hands back in position. On the other occasion I tried to rest by leaning my head against the wall, but the response to this was my head was "banged" on the wall and shaken about until I resumed my position. All the time there was the constant whirring noise like a helicopter blade going around. From the sound of the noise I would say that it was played into the room where I was, 'cos on the occasions that I was taken from this room, even outside of the door of the room, the noise was noticeably vague almost to be inaudible.

The sound that Clarke and the others heard continuously was the so-called "white noise," intended to isolate them from communication and further deepen the intense anxiety created by the prolonged hooding.

> As I have said I collapsed completely after that long period of time. I was brought round and carried out of the room and brought to another room, put on a couch and examined by a doctor. I was given a drink of water and brought back out into the main room again and made resume my position as before against the wall.
>
> There then followed a series of collapsing—I could not say how many times I collapsed. Initially my hands and legs were beaten whenever this happened, and the insides of my feet were kicked until my ankles were swollen to almost twice their normal size. After a number of these collapsings I was then made sit on the floor, with my knees up to my chest, my head between my knees, and my arms folded around my knees. In this position I was swayed backwards and forwards—I presume to bring my circulation back. Whenever this was done, I was put up against the wall again in the original position. Still the noise was going steady, driving the mental resistance to its utmost. I thought that I was going mad. This noise was the only noise one heard save the groans of the other people lined up against the wall.

The British themselves later confirmed that the detainees were kept against the wall for up to sixteen hours at a stretch. The hooding, the wall-standing, and the "white noise" were three of the five techniques. Prisoners were also deprived of sleep and kept on a diet of bread and water. Clarke's statement went on:

> All the time that I was against this wall I got bread and water once and water alone on two other occasions. This was fed to me by the hood being lifted to my nose, and bread and water was fed into my mouth in this way. I should emphasize that I was fed—I did not feed myself. The cup of water was put to my mouth, and the bread was put into my mouth.
>
> I cannot possibly estimate for what duration I was against this wall and underwent the collapsing experiences and physical torture against this wall, but I would estimate that it must have been at least two full days and nights. During all the time no sleep was permitted. At the end of the periods I must say that I was extremely fatigued both physically and mentally. I was certainly verging on complete mental exhaustion, suffering delusions which were of nightmarish nature.

Having been "softened up," every so often the men were taken for interrogation. According to Clarke:

> I was taken out of this room—in to another room where my hood was removed and I found myself confronted by two plainclothes R.U.C. S.B. [Special Branch] men, one of whom was standing beside a table and the other was seated behind it. I was told by these men that I had asked to see them. I do not recollect ever having done so. I told them that I did not ask for anyone. They then began to interrogate me. These men did not introduce themselves to me, so I do not know who they were. The hood was removed during this entire interview. These men interrogated me for a couple of hours. I should say that at the start of this interview I imagined that I was talking to my brother. At the end of this interview the hood was put back on again, and I was put back into the other room and put against the wall. I asked where I was, but I was told that I could not be told.
>
> As I was against the wall this time I was given a beating: kicked about the legs, a knee was stuck in the base of my spine, and the hood was jerked back tight on my face, hurting my neck. I collapsed at the end of this beating. I was also punched in the ribs and in the stomach, as well as being nipped. I was brought round after collapsing and put up against the wall again. The nipping and punching on the arms and ribs

commenced, so I shouted "Fuck off" and punched one of my assailants.
I was then grabbed by a number of people and I was punched, kicked,
and kneed all over the body, stomach, ribs, and back of my head. The
hood was pulled tightly around my neck, nearly suffocating me. I was
then put back against the wall—for a short time against it—I collapsed.
I do not know for how long I was out. The next thing I clearly remember was sitting in this small room with the same two men as before who
again told me that I sent for them. The hood was taken off for this interview as well. This interview lasted only a very short time, a matter
of minutes. I was rehooded and taken out again into another room
where I was beaten continuously for a long number of hours. During
the beating I was asked questions concerning the I.R.A., naming various people, and they also asked me about arms dumps. During all this
time I was standing. Due to this beating—mostly about the body and
head, not face—I fell unconscious. When I awakened I was lying on a
floor, and as I was waking I was being punched. During this period of
unconsciousness, I had a dream where a friend of mine—my fiancee's
brother—bought a scrapyard. Whenever I awoke and found myself being beaten, I began to struggle—I kicked one person and punched another. I was then overcome, my hands were put behind my back, and
I was handcuffed in this position. There was an attempt to handcuff my
ankles. I was then carried down a flight of stairs into a further interrogation—by a different person than previous. The hood was taken off.
He told me that I had sent for him. I said that I did not but that I had
asked for a priest. He told me that I would get no priest there. After
a few questions I was rehooded and let outside and into another room
where I was made, hands still handcuffed behind my back, stand facing
a wall with the crown of my head leaning against the wall. As I stood
there my arms were pulled further back, causing my wrists to be cut and
torn. . . . I was left alone in this room unhooded for a few hours. This
same S.B. man came back in but was very gentle in the course of questioning me. He would have questioned me for two or three hours. He
then left me again alone in the room—this time for about six hours. He
returned when it was morning and told me that I was going back in a
few hours. I asked him where and he said to the jail.

Joe Clarke, still hooded, was flown in a helicopter back to the
place where his ordeal had begun, Girdwood Barracks in north Belfast. When he arrived he asked what day it was. When told it was
Tuesday, he replied, "It couldn't be since I was in Girdwood on
Tuesday." "That was a week ago," came the answer. It was now

August 17, 1971. The previous six days of his life had been tele-
scoped like one long bad dream.

The other eleven hooded men tell a similar story. One imagined
he had died; another tried to commit suicide; none had any idea
what was happening to them. During the six days the torture lasted,
one of the prisoners supposed that there had been a loyalist *coup*,
that Ian Paisley was in power, and that he was about to be executed
or "tortured to death."

Several of them caught glimpses of what was happening around
them. A prisoner whose hood slipped off for a second saw uniformed policemen standing near where he was spread-eagled
against the wall. Another reported catching sight of men in khaki
trousers with sleeves rolled up, looking young and fit, in the room
(which he said had sawdust on the floor) where he was kept against
the wall. They were the British intelligence officers supervising the
"procedures." Another later thought he could identify the doctor
present at the secret interrogation center as a British psychiatrist
used by the army to oversee the application of the techniques.

None of the twelve was charged with any crime, and most were
released shortly after their experience. But the controversy that
their treatment provoked would dog successive British governments
for the next six years and more. Already by the fall of 1971 there
were stories in the British and Irish press about the torture of the
detainees. The British, already embarrassed by the failure of the internment operation, were now being goaded by accusations of serious violations of human rights committed by their security forces.

In quick succession Westminster set up two parliamentary inquiries into the allegations, in hope that this would assuage public
opinion. If anything, they had the opposite effect. The first, headed
by a prominent British civil servant, Sir Edmund Compton, confirmed the general description the prisoners gave of the sensory
deprivation methods. Compton's report, published in late 1971, acknowledged that the hooding, the "white noise," the wall-standing,
the deprivation of sleep and food, were all part of what was called
the "five techniques," but it asserted that the beatings were a fab-
rication. The experience did not constitute brutal treatment or torture!

Though it was revealed that the five techniques had been used in
all of Britain's colonial wars since 1946, until the Compton report
they had never been described. The report refused to characterize
the methods as other than a form of ill treatment, but their nature

shocked many people and raised some very pertinent questions as to their legality. Could the forces of law and order inflict such treatment upon U.K. citizens? And if so, by whose or what authority? Answers were called for, prompting the establishment of the second inquiry, headed by Lord Parker. It included Lord Gardiner. Both men were highly respected legal authorities. Their brief was "to consider authorised procedures for the interrogation of persons suspected of terrorism." In the end they disagreed over their findings and the committee issued two reports—the majority report of Lord Parker and a minority report from Lord Gardiner.

Lord Parker revealed that the five techniques were an established practice in the army. They had been used in Palestine, Malaya, Kenya, and Cyprus, as well as in the British Cameroons (1960–61), Brunei (1963), British Guyana (1964), Aden (1964–67), Borneo/ Malaysia (1965–66), and the Persian Gulf (1970–71). He conceded that "some if not all of the techniques in question would constitute criminal assaults and might also give rise to civil proceedings under English law." Yet he went on to conclude that in "cases where it is considered vitally necessary to obtain information," they should be used, but only after being authorized by a minister of government who, Parker suggested, should first take legal advice.

Lord Parker justified the use of sensory deprivation by claiming that it provided the authorities with much-needed information about terrorists. The British knew little about the Provisionals. A new generation of guerrilla activists was now involved in terrorism, and the authorities were desperate to obtain some information about who they were. Parker's majority report (from which Lord Gardiner dissented) stated that as a result of the "in depth" interrogation, the following was obtained:

(1) Identification of a further 700 members of both IRA factions, and their positions in the organisations.

(2) Over 40 sheets giving details of the organisation and structure of I.R.A. units.

(3) Details of possible I.R.A. operations: arms caches, safe houses, communications and supply routes, including those across the border, and locations of wanted persons.

(4) Details of morale, operational directives, propaganda techniques, relations with other organisations and future plans.

(5) The discovery of individual responsibility for about 85 incidents recorded on police files which had previously remained unexplained.

(It is an impressive list, but only if the statistics of subsequent violence are ignored. They show that during the period after internment and until the end of 1972, violence reached the highest level ever. One hundred thirty-nine soldiers were killed in those eighteen months, compared with four before August 1971 and the use of the five techniques.)

The moral arguments justifying the use of sensory deprivation because of its effectiveness were beside the point. As Lord Gardiner was to make clear in his minority report, the five techniques could not be used, because they constituted a criminal offense. In applying them, the British army was systematically breaking the laws it was supposed to defend.

Lord Gardiner's dissent was based firmly on English common law regarding the treatment of prisoners. In his minority report he stated the legal facts quite bluntly:

> If any document or Minister had purported to authorise them, it would have been invalid because the procedures were and are illegal by domestic law and may also have been illegal by international law.

He went on with some emphasis:

> This being so, no Army Directive and no Minister could lawfully or validly have authorised the use of the procedures. Only parliament can alter the law. The procedures were and are illegal.

Should parliament act to legalize the five techniques, he wrote:

> I believe that we should both gravely damage our own reputation and deal a severe blow to the whole world movement to improve Human Rights.

Since it was clear that the five techniques were illegal, the question of their authorization took on great importance. Gardiner wrote that "our terms of reference appear to assume that the procedures were or are authorised," but concludes this was impossible *because* they were illegal. He arrived at this conclusion in spite of his acknowledgment that the British army actually taught the techniques to members of the RUC and that they constructed a special interrogation center in which to apply them—all suggesting a high level of authorization.

His claim that no minister of the British government could have approved them "specifically" because they were illegal assumes that British government ministers would not break United Kingdom laws. The only politician named in his report is Brian Faulkner, a Unionist and an Ulsterman, and therefore outside the range of this assumption. He claims that Brian Faulkner knew of and approved the procedures. Gardiner states in his conclusion:

Finally, in fairness to the Government of Northern Ireland and the Royal Ulster Constabulary, I must say that, according to the evidence before us, although the Minister of Home Affairs, Northern Ireland, purported to approve the procedures, he had no idea that they were illegal; and it was, I think, not unnatural that the Royal Ulster Constabulary should assume that the army had satisfied themselves that the procedures which they were training the police to employ were legal.

The blame for this sorry story, if blame there be, must lie with those who, many years ago, decided that in emergency conditions in colonial-type situations we should abandon our legal, well tried and highly successful wartime methods and replace them by procedures which were secret, illegal, not morally justifiable, and alien to the traditions of what I believe to be the greatest democracy in the world.

The argument in the penultimate paragraph is quite remarkable. It is surprising that a British Lord Chief Justice and former legal adviser to Her Majesty's government, should use ignorance of the law as a defense! (By analogy, John Mitchell might have argued that he did not know breaking and entering was a crime when he authorized the dirty tricks team to set to work burglarizing the Democratic Watergate headquarters.) The fact that a man of such legal eminence could employ such an obviously invalid argument indicates the extent to which Northern Ireland was clouding British thinking.

The second surprising implication of Gardiner's conclusion is that although admitted illegalities had occurred, they were no one's responsibility—apart from Brian Faulkner and those unknown persons who "many years ago" borrowed the sensory deprivation methods from the KGB. The report constitutes an admission that crimes have been committed, but there are no criminals except for

Faulkner, who is excused because of his ignorance of the law. Gardiner's hint was not the only one that suggested blame for authorizing the five techniques lay at the door of the Unionist Prime Minister. A few months before, on November 17, 1971, a spokesman for Lord Carrington, the Defense Secretary, said in the British House of Commons that the five techniques were formally authorized by Faulkner and "approved of" by the British government. Clearly the British were implying that Stormont was responsible, in spite of the fact that their own inquiries had established that the five techniques were an authorized practice in the army. In public, the Northern Ireland government did not respond to this assertion, but some years later in private, several Unionists, including Brian Faulkner, would tell a different story.

In the meantime, the British government did not behave as if it believed the Unionists were responsible. The inquiries they had set up raised more questions than they answered. The most crucial one, that of authorization, was sidestepped. But by 1973 the British were faced with the prospect of other forms of investigation that threatened to expose the vital chain of responsibility leading from the psychological torture chambers of the old R.A.F. base in Ballykelly to the highest reaches of their government.

One was the series of civil actions taken by the hooded men (and others who alleged ordinary brutality at the different holding centers after the internment sweep) against the Stormont and Westminster authorities. If these actions were dragged through the courts, the names of policemen and army officers involved in the interrogation of detainees might be revealed; this in turn might lead to the names of their superiors' being brought to account—and so on up the ladder of authority until the highest level of authorization was reached. And since this was a matter of criminal offenses, the British had to avoid it at all costs.

The other investigation was initiated by the government of the Republic of Ireland and involved the European Human Rights Commission. Potentially, this was the most embarrassing of all.

The Irish government accused the British of having violated articles of the European Human Rights Convention drawn up in 1956 to protect fundamental civil liberties. The Convention was signed by most Western European nations, including the United Kingdom and Republic of Ireland. The Commission was established to investigate alleged violations by member nations and the apparatus of a

Human Rights Court, sitting at Strasbourg, France, was set up to rule on its findings. The court had no legal power over the signatories to force them to institute criminal proceedings against the guilty if violations were proven. Its authority was purely moral, but politically very embarrassing for any nation found to be in violation of its precepts. For the United Kingdom it was especially so—the British had already been before the Commission in a case of torture alleged in Cyprus. (The five techniques were at the center of this dispute as well, though at no time during this inquiry were they described. This investigation ended in a friendly settlement.)

The Irish claimed, most seriously, that the British army and police had violated article 3 of the Convention which states, "No one shall be subjected to torture or to inhuman or degrading treatment or punishment." They also accused the British of using internment in a discriminatory way against the Catholic population, in violation of articles 14, 15, 5, and 6.

Much to the chagrin of the British, the Commission undertook to investigate the Irish allegations in October 1972. It was the beginning of the first non-British inquiry into how Northern Ireland was ruled, and it proved to be the most painstaking and thorough yet undertaken. The Conservative government immediately adopted an uncooperative stance. It was noticeably annoyed at the Commission's decision to go ahead with the inquiry and extremely concerned as to what it might reveal. They were worried principally about the identity of the men who applied the five techniques. As in the civil action suits, if they were forced to appear before the Commission to give evidence about what happened at the secret interrogation center, the intelligence officers' only defense would be to argue authorization at a higher level. To prevent this from happening, the government point-blank refused to permit anyone who was connected with the application of the five techniques to appear before the hearings. They also instructed those witnesses who did appear on their behalf not to answer any questions regarding the use of the techniques. The Irish government protested, but the Commission had no legal authority to make the Conservatives produce those concerned. It was just the beginning of the British stalling tactics.

They refused to allow their witnesses to attend the hearings held in the Human Rights Building in Strasbourg, complaining that it was not secure enough. It took the Commission three months to find a venue to suit them. They were finally held in a remote area of Norway. When the British witnesses did appear, their legal counsel insisted that they be concealed behind a screen. They refused to give their names. Instead, arguing security reasons, the British used a code system. But what became apparent as the hearings progressed was that the same witness often had more than one code number. Well into the proceedings, it became clear that their legal counsel was allowing its witnesses to read the transcript of evidence given by the previous witnesses for the Irish government. The Irish legal representatives argued that this "was a serious breach of the confidential nature of the proceedings as guaranteed by the Convention and the Rules of Procedure of the Commission." The Commission agreed, and stated that "it regretted that the respondent [British] government did not consult the Commission or its delegates before showing the verbatim record to the persons proposed as witnesses as the possible effect of such a procedure on the value of the evidence given could then have been considered in advance." In addition, the British team persisted throughout the proceedings in submitting its proofs of evidence a week late in spite of repeated requests not to do so by the Commission.

The elaborate secrecy and demand for stringent security hampered the proceedings and helped create an unfavorable impression that the Irish government was—by pursuing the issue—putting British army and Northern Ireland police personnel at risk and distracting them from their task of combatting terrorism. This was an impression the British consciously fostered. But the real reason behind the secrecy and the refusal to allow personnel involved with the techniques to attend was fear of exposing the chain of responsibility. In spite of all the steps they took to ensure that it remained concealed, they were still not completely reassured. At one point their legal team went so far as to suggest that the British government refuse to implement important political reforms for Northern Ireland until the Irish dropped their human rights case. The British and Irish governments were at the time (1973) bringing leading Catholic and Protestant politicians together in an attempt to set up a new assembly to replace the old Stormont parliament abolished the year before. The assembly would have a "power-sharing" executive that would for the first time in the history of Northern Ireland include Catholics in government at cabinet level. But irritated and worried by the continuing human rights investigation, the British contemplated using the power-sharing reform as a bargaining counter. In the end they realized that the bad publicity it might provoke would not be worth it, so the idea was dropped. But in Northern Ireland itself, cruder forms of intimidation were taking place. Several of the Irish witnesses due to attend the Commission's hearings were harassed by the army and repeatedly arrested. One was actually assassinated by loyalist gunmen.

Still, the hearings went on, the witnesses came, and one of them produced the most dramatic evidence of high-level authorization unearthed by the Commission. He was Dr. Robert Daly, the Irish government's psychiatric expert. He testified on the possible long-term psychological damage caused by sensory deprivation, arguing that, like LSD, it can render permanent injury to the mind. But that was not his most important contribution.

In all their inquiries, the British had stressed that the five techniques were taught "orally" at a joint services intelligence center. Lord Gardiner stressed this in his report: "I have thought it essential to state what the procedures referred to in the Compton reports were because they were never published or even *written down anywhere*" (my emphasis). The British authorities emphasized this as proof that the techniques were "informal"—that is, were not authorized at a high level. A document or army directive outlining the five techniques would indicate a degree of authorization the British might find uncomfortable.

During cross-examination by the British defense counsel, Daly took a slim document out of his case. The counsel was stunned to hear the psychiatrist claim that here were written army instructions about the application of the techniques—the document that was not supposed to exist.

The document came from a joint services intelligence training center in England. Daly had attended a talk there in 1969 about the uses of sensory deprivation given by an intelligence officer called Colonel Stevens. He had managed to get a copy of the document from which Stevens gave his talk. It was even more embarrassing to the British than at first sight—upon perusal it was found that it outlined *six,* not five, techniques. The nature of the sixth technique was one reason why the British had been so determined to conceal the written evidence: It described methods of physical assault on the prisoner undergoing the five techniques. Physical assault is a clearly criminal act, a flagrant breach of the law about which there can be no dispute; for a security forces document to exist which authorizes such illegal acts was a serious matter. It condoned blatant violations of the basic civil liberties of the citizens of the United Kingdom as well as those of Britain's former colonies. Dr. Daly's document was never made public. Because of the obligations of secrecy imposed upon all witnesses and their evidence, he was unable to produce the document for the press (though asked to do so by the *London Sunday Times* on several occasions in 1977). Its existence raises the important question of whether or not the parliamentary committees set up by Edward Heath in 1971 to investigate the use of the five techniques were deliberately misled. If so, then the British parliament had been misled—in effect, something of a minor constitutional crisis—as to what its servants had been doing in the name of law and order and the extent to which they had been prepared to go in condoning criminal acts.

Four years after it began its inquiry, the European Human Rights Commission produced its report—over 550 pages of argument and counterargument, of evidence in the form of statistics and statements from a host of witnesses. (It remains an authoritative source for the genesis and development of the Northern Ireland crisis.) Its decision on the use of the five techniques was stated thus:

> The Commission is of the opinion, by a unanimous vote, that the combined use of the five techniques in the cases before it constituted a practice of inhuman treatment and torture in breach of article three of the Convention.

It found that the use of the five techniques was an "administrative practice." Also by unanimous vote, it stated that

> There has been at Palace Barracks, Holywood [east Belfast] in the autumn of 1971 a practice in connection with the interrogation of prisoners by members of the Royal Ulster Constabulary which was inhuman treatment in breach of article three of the Convention.

However, the Irish government did not fare so well with its other allegations about the discriminatory use of internment. The Commission accepted British arguments that only Catholics were interned because only Catholics were then involved—in the Provisional and Official IRA—in organized terrorism. (As a matter of fact, this was not so. The authorities were not aware of, or ignored, the UDA campaign launched in late 1971.) The report then went to the court, and its decision was awaited. The British, though piqued at being found guilty of "torture," were content in that they had successfully prevented vital evidence as to the identities of those responsible for authorizing and applying the five techniques from being made public.

The court's formal judgment came eighteen months later. In January 1978 it sustained the decision of the Commission but found, to everyone's surprise, that though the British had broken article 3, the five techniques constituted inhuman treatment—not torture, as described in the report. The press seized on this and ignored the vital finding, which was that Britain, in the first internation case ever brought before the Human Rights Court, was *guilty* of violating article 3 of the Convention.

By the time the decision was arrived at, the British had also successfully blocked the other threat to the secret chain of responsibility—the civil actions taken by the hooded men against the Stormont and Westminster authorities. This was a simpler matter to deal with than the Human Rights Commission.

Some indication of government concern about the suits was seen at the very beginning of the actions. In early 1972 interrogatories were submitted by the counsel for the detainees, who were demanding compensation for injuries and suffering inflicted on them by the five techniques. One of the lawyers appearing on behalf of the British government was summoned secretly to Downing Street, the English Prime Minister's official residence in London. There, Edward Heath supervised the framing of the counsels' replies to the allegations and approved them before allowing them to be presented in the Belfast court.

All the suits were settled out of court by the British, who paid large awards in damages to each of the hooded men—the last as late as 1977. The total bill in compensation, including awards to detainees who had experienced other forms of abuse and maltreatment, came to over one million dollars. It got the British government excellent publicity—after all, they admitted wrongdoing had occurred and were paying the victims handsomely for it. But in the meantime, the wrongdoers had disappeared, as they had from the Strasbourg inquiry. Because the actions were settled out of court, no British officer or policeman was forced to take the stand and ex-

plain to a judge who gave him the authorization to so abuse and torture citizens of the United Kingdom.

From the evidence amassed by the Human Rights Commission
and from other sources, it can be inferred that the government itself
tolerated the five techniques. They were, after all, according to the
Commission's report, an administrative practice within the British
army, and the British inquiry under Lord Parker admitted as much
in 1972. A special training center existed (as it still does) to train
officers—from the navy and air force as well as the army—in the
use of the techniques. One was set up in Northern Ireland to *apply*
them. British intelligence officers outlined the methods to high-
ranking RUC men in Belfast four months before internment was introduced. All of this supposes high-level approval. The British
alleged in 1971 that high-level approval came from Brian Faulkner.
But that was not the whole story, and the Unionists knew it. The
Unionists did not, after all, institute the use of sensory deprivation
in the British army—it had been a method of interrogation employed in every colonial war the British fought since the late forties.
In private, Faulkner and another high-ranking Unionist minister
put the responsibility on a prominent Conservative politician.

Shortly before his accidental death, Brian Faulkner claimed that
it was a British government minister who first mentioned the five
techniques to him after the meeting at which the British gave the
go-ahead to internment. As told to a leading Labour MP, Faulkner's story was that the minister said to him, "If you're going to do
this internment thing you might as well see that you get some information out of it. Our chaps have some methods you might find
useful." "But are they legal?" Faulkner claimed he asked. He was
told "not to bother his pretty head about that." (This story echoes
the claim in the Gardiner report that Faulkner "had no idea" the
methods were illegal.)

Another leading Unionist in Faulkner's cabinet in 1971 also
traces the authorization to this same minister. In late August that
year, as the first rumors about the torture of detainees began circulating, there was a Stormont security meeting attended by the
head of the RUC, Faulkner, the army General Officer Commanding, and the Unionist cabinet member in question. The Unionist
can't recall who, but he heard someone refer to the five techniques.
Not knowing what they were, he leaned over to the RUC Chief and
asked him to explain them to him. The policeman whispered a de-

scription and went on to say that the RUC were more or less being forced to use them by the army. The Unionist, claiming he was disturbed by what he heard, then asked the policeman, "What's the authorization for this?"

"It has come from the very top in London," the officer replied.

"As far up as————?," naming the authority.

"Yes—it has his authority," the police chief whispered, and the matter was then dropped.

Everything since then has conspired to make sure the matter was dropped for good. Many of the policemen involved with the secret interrogation center have been promoted; one received a very high honorary award some years later and is now in command of a special antiterrorist unit (against which, not surprisingly, there have been continued allegations of brutality). And of course the authorizing minister himself has remained unaffected by the events of that August.

The broader constitutional and legal questions remain unanswered. The British constitution requires in a case such as the use of illegal methods of interrogation that there be either a prosecution or an indemnity act in parliament. During the 1919–21 Irish war of independence, for instance, such an act was passed to ensure that no British soldier would have to answer in court for any illegal action carried out during that period in Ireland. Many crimes were known to have been committed by the security forces then, and the government, wanting to avoid the embarrassment of public trials, chose instead to indemnify its servants. Constitutional requirements were thus met. But this is not the case with the events of August 1971 in Ballykelly.

Since there has been no prosecution, though crimes have been admitted, then the constitution demands an indemnity act to cover those involved in the acknowledged illegalities at the secret interrogation center in Ballykelly. No such act was ever passed, for the same reason that the government felt unable to allow the intelligence officers and policemen who took part in the application of the five techniques to appear in any court. Had an indemnity act been brought before parliament, it would have to have been made clear who exactly was being indemnified. Unlike the illegalities perpetrated during the 1919–21 period, which involved mostly ordinary soldiers of the lower ranks, those committed in Ballykelly concerned officers and government at the highest levels. It was much too sensitive an issue to be exposed for debate in parliament. The demands of the constitution, like the ordinary decencies of law and order, have been left in abeyance.

The Provisionals used the revelations about the torture to their own advantage; the less-than-candid attitude of the government made it easy for them to do so. The brutality of the state was invoked to justify morally their own, far worse brutality. In December 1973 they kidnapped a Special Branch officer, Ivan Johnston, claiming that he was at Ballykelly and had tortured detainees. The claim came before the site of the secret interrogation center was generally known. Johnston was "executed," in spite of pleas from his wife and children. One year later Inspector Peter Flanagan was drinking in a bar in Omagh, in the west of Northern Ireland. Two teen-aged Provisionals entered the bar and shot him. He tried to escape but was shot again in the men's toilet, where he died.

Flanagan was referred to in the Human Rights Commission's report as PO 4. He was a Special Branch man and the only one in the report against whom the prisoners made no allegations of brutality. In the words of the Commission, "the way in which he answered showed resentment of the situation at Palace Barracks."

The controversy ended the use of the five techniques in Northern Ireland. Heath gave an undertaking in parliament in 1972 that they were not to be used there. In 1976 the British told the Human Rights Commission, and later the court, that the five techniques were no longer being taught in the army. However, this had to be qualified by their admission that the methods were still being taught in some form. The human rights organization Amnesty International (recipient of a Nobel Peace Prize) had already confirmed this. In 1975 a government minister, replying to Amnesty, wrote:

> The main instructors [in interrogation methods] are officers of the rank of Major and above who are responsible during the practical phase of this training for close continuous control over every activity, including the application of the five techniques.

When the British gave their undertaking to Strasbourg, they argued that the methods were no longer being taught, but that officers were learning how to *resist* them. It seems the British were prepared not only to take liberties with the law, but with language as well in order to prevent this offense to the civil rights of its citizens from being dumped in the dustbin as it deserved to be.

The British cover-up set an ugly precedent. There have since been other allegations of police brutality and authoritative reports substantiating them—for example, the British Bennett Report (1979)—and from respected bodies, including Amnesty International (1978). They brought the number of official reports on security forces' abusing prisoners to five within the last decade. Yet, to date no member of the security forces has appeared in court as a result of those reports, much less any politician. The initial failure to make anyone accountable for the 1971 violations—a failure motivated by the fact that the government was directly responsible for those violations—ensured that the police and army felt free to go on ill treating and brutalizing their prisoners without fear of prosecution.

Had it concerned any other area in the United Kingdom, there would have been an outcry. But the story of the hooded men, the cover-up, the continuing problems with the police, indicate a deeper difficulty. Northern Ireland is not just another part of the United Kingdom. The fact that the Special Powers Act, operative until 1973, existed at all is sufficient proof that in Northern Ireland British standards of democracy do not apply. The act bestowed arbitrary power on government; it was an abrogation of the rule of law which made the next step—the outright violation of the law by the authorities—inevitable and easier to countenance. The Emergency Provisions Act, which replaced the Special Powers Act in 1973, is almost as Draconian, allowing for arrest without warrant and detention without charge for up to seventy-two hours.

Northern Ireland has been ruled like this since its creation, by the invoking of one form of coercion or another. It is an area where government ministers can be involved in violations of human rights more serious than anything revealed during the Watergate scandal and yet not be held accountable for their actions. It is an area where clearly the government lacks moral authority with which to persuade its citizens to obey laws it has broken itself with impunity. In the end, the British government will have to ask itself if it is worth the continual compromise and sacrifice of democratic principles to preserve the integrity of such a state.

The results of the moral failure of government were obvious: Catholic opposition to Stormont, crystallized by internment, by 1972 hardened into tacit support of the Provisionals. The guerrillas' campaign gathered a bloody momentum that, within eleven months of August 1971, carried it into the corridors of power in Westminster. In July 1972, Provisional leaders, including Sean MacStiofain,

During a riot Catholic teen-agers in a side street in republican west Belfast confront a British army armored vehicle. Such confrontation became a daily event in the Catholic ghettos in the 1970s, as the support for law and order deteriorated. FROM ARTHUR MACCAIG'S FILM *THE PATRIOT GAME*, DISTRIBUTED BY ICARUS FILMS.

were flown by British army helicopter to confer with William Whitelaw, the Secretary of State for Northern Ireland, after the abolition of Stormont. Their attempts to reach a settlement failed, but it brought the Provisionals political recognition, undermining the position of the moderate Catholic politicians then struggling to win support away from the tacticians of terror.

Oppression strengthened the Provisionals, but the Northern Ireland dialectic of violence had another, equally frightening component. The abolition of Stormont, the recognition of the republican guerrillas by the British, and their increasing violence brought into force the loyalists' ultimate sanction: assassination. To date, it has remained the most chilling aspect of the crisis.

4

"Why Us?"

A few miles to the north of Belfast city there is a cul-de-sac called Longlands Road. It is a quiet avenue of comfortable, middle-class homes, and it commands a fine view of Belfast Lough, a cold blue, rippling inlet of the Irish Sea. On a good summer's day, like that of July 8, 1976, the undulating hills of County Down, with their green patchwork of fields, can be seen clearly running along the far side of the lough. The road climbs steeply towards the splintered foothills of the Antrim Plateau, the basaltic mass which dominates County Antrim.

In 1976 the very last house at the top on the right-hand side was occupied by a young Catholic couple in their twenties. Mervyn and Rosaleen McDonald had two children: Seamus, aged two and a half, and a four-month-old baby, Margaret. It was an attractive house, secluded by a high hedge, with a little wooden gate leading into a narrow pathway that ran to their door through a small wild garden.

Catholics and Protestants were neighbors in Longlands Road in spite of the continuing violence and the fact that the area around it was frequently the scene of sectarian murder. The district is mainly Protestant, with an archipelago of small Catholic ghettos vulnerable to attack. But so far Longlands Road had been spared.

Less than a mile away stretched the large Protestant housing development known as Rathcoole, a product of the late 1950s slum clearance program, which had moved the urban working class into the suburbs. It was like Highfield Estate at the top of the Shankill or the big Catholic development of Andersonstown at the head of the Falls: bare homes of concrete block in rows, with gardens front and back, forming bleak streets swept by mountain winds in winter. Rathcoole was a stronghold of the Ulster Defence Association (UDA) which, by 1976, was the largest and most powerful of the loyalist paramilitary organizations, with a membership of thousands.

Until 1971 the UDA was a loose and disintegrating collection of loyalist vigilante groups. When Harding Smith took over—with the support of the toughest of the vigilantes, mostly from the Woodvale Defence Association—the UDA embarked upon a campaign of murder which the authorities did little to check. The abolition of Stormont, the successes of the Provisionals, and then the attempts by the British to bring Catholics into a new, reformed government structure in late 1973, gave the UDA the cause to fight a bitter war of assassination. Most of their victims were Catholics innocent of any involvement with the IRA. Throughout 1975 and 1976 the sectarian murders reached a crescendo, with republican groups killing Protestants—usually as innocent as the victims on the other side— in retaliation for the unending murders of Catholics by the UDA and other loyalist organizations.

Northern Ireland had experienced periods of sectarian murder before, but this was the worst. The local newspapers became lists of murder victims; the local radio news ended its night's broadcast with the report of the inevitable body found in the alleyway or on some bleak vacant lot or discovered in a suburban ditch. People would huddle together in their ghettos fearful of the unexpected rap on the door, the stranger in the street. But even at home they were not safe—in north Belfast a gang leader nicknamed "the Window

Cleaner" murdered Catholics as they slept in bed. The death squads struck their victims at work, on public buses, in their living rooms, in bars, and in their beds. Nowhere seemed safe. And yet, in the midst of death, life in Longlands Road went on as usual. People there still opened their doors to strangers.

Just after 6:00 P.M. on a quiet, slightly hazy summer's evening when the air seemed to ripple above the waves of the lough, a car pulled up by the McDonalds' gate. A well-dressed young man got out of the driver's seat and walked between the high hedges up the garden path. He was carrying a small case. When he reached the door he rapped it once. It was opened by Rosaleen. She looked at the stranger. "Could I interest you in a *Freeman's Encyclopedia?*" he asked politely. She said "No, thank you." He turned, walked back down the path, and got into his car. He did not go to any other house. Swinging his car round full circle, he drove back down Longlands Road, turning left towards Rathcoole Estate.

At Doonbeg Drive in the estate, he stopped his car and looked at his watch. It was just after six minutes past six. It had taken him approximately six minutes to drive to the McDonalds', make his inquiry, and return to his starting point. He reported this to a man standing nearby, a member of the north Belfast UDA and the leader of one of its most active murder gangs, the one nicknamed Window Cleaner. The gang contained six members, including a professional burglar who was responsible for murdering several Catholics as they slept. Another member was an adept bomb maker capable of planting devices in the seemingly most inaccessible places, including well-guarded republican bars.

The grounds on which they chose their victims were usually haphazard. Many of their killings were random, though some were based on information they had obtained from police contacts. Between January and October 1976, the gang killed about twenty-five Catholics in the north Belfast area.

What drew their attention to the McDonalds was the fact that, apart from being Catholic and vulnerable—generally good enough excuse for assassins to strike—they came from republican backgrounds. Rosaleen's father was a member of the political wing of the Official faction of the IRA. Mervyn, her husband, had family connections with the Catholic New Lodge Road and drank in a republican bar not far from where they lived. It was called the Wolf Tone Club, named after the eighteenth-century Protestant revolutionary, and served the small Catholic enclave in Greencastle on the shores of Belfast Lough. It was already the scene of several murders. At the beginning of 1976 a patron was gunned down by the UDA as he left the bar. Within weeks, a pregnant woman was shot in the back by the same UDA gang as she came out of the club. Though she survived, the bullet killed her unborn child.

That Mervyn McDonald drank in such a place was, as far as the UDA was concerned, enough to sentence him to death. But the UDA commander did not agonize over the motivation for the intended crime; rather, he was satisfied with the timing of the dummy run they had just made for the gang's next murder.

The next day, July 9th, was also a sunny, bright day, turning hazy towards evening. It was such good weather that a group of children were getting ready for an evening's outing, clambering excitedly into a Land Rover parked on Longlands Road a few houses away from the McDonalds. They did not notice a white Austin 1100 drive past them in the direction of the couple's home. It was 6:00 P.M.

As usual at that time the McDonalds were home having dinner, or "tea," as it is called in Belfast. Mervyn was sitting in the kitchen just off the main room, eating. Their young son was sitting on the sofa not far away. Rosaleen was holding baby Margaret, looking at the local television news and the reports of the latest violence.

The white Austin contained three men. It stopped by the house at the top of the street. The car was stolen and fitted with false number plates. Two of its occupants got out and walked through the McDonalds' gate up the garden path to the door. One of them, with long dirty fair hair, was strangely dressed for such a warm and pleasant evening—he wore a long heavy overcoat and carried something bulky underneath it. His companion walked beside him, his right hand tucked in his jacket. The driver sat in the car. There was a fourth member of the gang stationed a short distance away on a rise above Longlands Road. His position gave him a good view of the surrounding area. He was armed with a rifle and was to cover the other two gunmen while they murdered the McDonalds.

Rosaleen McDonald answered the knock at the door holding her baby daughter. She found the two men standing there. The short one wearing the overcoat said, "We're from the New Lodge. Is your husband in?" Rosaleen assumed they were friends of Mervyn's family. "Yes," she replied. "He's having his tea, but come in." They followed her into the main room.

As they entered, her husband, hearing strange voices, stopped eating and looked round from where he was sitting. He stuck his head into the main room to see who it was. As he did so, with one quick move the man in the overcoat swung his sub-machine gun round from behind his back, jammed a magazine into it, and fired a burst at Mervyn McDonald. Four rounds of 9 mm ammunition hit him, blowing off part of his head and face. He died instantly.

Rosaleen, clutching baby Margaret, started screaming. "Why us? Why us?" she screamed repeatedly. The machine gunner did not answer. Without hesitating, he wrenched the baby from her arms and dropped the little girl on the sofa beside her now hysterical brother. Rosaleen was still pleading for her life when he pushed her across the room and fired a burst into her back, hitting her four times in the spine. She fell terribly wounded in a pool of blood. It took her four hours to die.

The killer and his companion turned away from the carnage and the crying children and walked out. He swung his sub-machine gun nonchalantly by his side as he went down the little garden path between the lush hedge rows to the car. But the other gunman, who had not taken part in the killings, was ashen-faced, almost sick, and shaken by what he had seen. When he was in the car again he blurted out, "I didn't get a shot." It had been his first operation, and it was to be his last. He did not have the stomach for such work.

The driver swung the car around and they headed down the quiet avenue following the same route that the "salesman" had taken the previous evening. They passed the Land Rover, now full of children getting ready to drive off for their picnic. Nobody seemed to have heard the bursts of gunfire. In the time it takes to pack a sandwich, two people had been murdered, two children left without parents.

As the gunmen drove towards Rathcoole they noticed a police car speeding behind them. But the UDA driver was an experienced man and didn't panic easily. He simply slowed down to let the RUC car race past on its errand. A few minutes later they were safely back in Doonbeg Drive, Rathcoole. The operation, they agreed, was a success.

Back in the McDonalds' home Seamus was found by a neighbor still screaming and staring at his dying mother, while his baby sister cried on the sofa beside him. It was by then 6:15 P.M., July 9, 1976. In Northern Ireland's statistics of violent death the McDonalds were numbered 1577 and 1578. Their place on the UDA's death list is not known with any certainty. By that time the UDA had lost count.

While the McDonalds were being murdered, a few miles away in the east of the city the UDA was closing its headquarters for the evening. It is a large Victorian house situated directly opposite a funeral parlor on the Newtownards Road, one of the main thoroughfares in the heart of the loyalist territory of east Belfast. The area is dominated by the giant yellow crane of Harland and Wolfe's, the shipbuilding firm where most of the local Protestants work. It is called "the Goliath," and it towers above the maze of red brick houses.

On July 9, 1976, the streets were decorated with bunting, wooden and pasteboard arches, and flags in vivid red, white, and blue colors. The big loyalist festival of July 12th was approaching, when the parades and bands would march all over Northern Ireland celebrating the defeat of Irish Catholics nearly three hundred years before. At the corners of many streets piles of wood, old furniture, tires, and other combustible scraps stood in pyramids, ready to be burned on the night of the 12th.

There were a few UDA men still hanging around getting ready to go home. John Orchin, who handled visitors and general inquiries, sat behind his desk in the front downstairs room on the right. He chatted with Sammy Duddy, who issued the organization's press statements. The walls around them were hung with photographs of old leaders, now dead. The most famous, Tommy Herron, showed a thin-faced man in his late thirties with dirty fair hair slicked back in the style of the 1950s and wearing a black leather coat. For many years he was the vice chairman of the UDA and in control of the east Belfast area. It was a period when the UDA grew from a few hundred to, in mid-1972, an estimated fifty thousand members. The loyalist population turned to it in time of crisis when they had lost their parliament. But under Herron east Belfast became the scene of some of the worst sectarian violence the city had ever seen. His power extended to the west as well, where police suspected him of being involved in the murders of a young Catholic woman and her boyfriend in July 1972. He was a hot-headed, unstable leader, suspected by his colleagues of taking more than his cut from the UDA coffers, which perhaps explains his sudden disappearance in September 1973. His body turned up a few days later in a ditch, where it had been dumped after he had been shot in the head. The Reverend Ian Paisley graced his funeral, as did twenty thousand loyalists, including probably the UDA who had murdered him. In his graveside oration Paisley said that Herron "died in the fight for freedom and to preserve the Protestant heritage." Many who stood silently around the freshly opened earth must have smiled at the hyperbole.

Not far from Herron's photograph hung that of Ernie "The Duke" Elliott, founding member of the Woodvale Defence Association, supporter of Harding Smith in his takeover of the UDA. He was a tough guy, an assassin who reputedly read Che Guevara. This is how the UDA likes to remember "The Duke." They prefer to forget his death, which was inglorious. During a brawl in a loyalist club The Duke was cut down by a shotgun blast; his almost headless body was found the next day in a large cardboard box. His former colleagues in the Woodvale named a club after him, The Duke Inn.

As for Harding Smith himself, he was nowhere to be seen. Even today there are no photographs on the wall commemorating the UDA's one-time leader and founding member. By 1976 Smith was gone from Northern Ireland altogether. Due to an internal dispute in which Smith threatened to split the UDA, he was shot on two occasions. Both times he was badly wounded and both times narrowly escaped with his life. He took the hint and left for somewhere in England. Once in a while rumors fly around the Shankill Road, his old stomping ground, that the former head of loyalism's biggest organization is back in town. But the man who sits in the seat of the chairman of the UDA, two floors up, shows little concern about that. He is Andy Tyrie, supreme commander of the Ulster Defence Association.

Tyrie has been official chairman since May 1973. But unofficially he became leader only after the forced emigration of Harding Smith. He has remained in charge longer than any other UDA leader. His office is well-carpeted, with three telephones and a large filing cabinet. Above his desk hangs the Red Hand of Ulster, a traditional Celtic symbol that assumes a rather sinister significance as the emblem of the UDA. It is capped with a crown; the motto beneath reads "Quis Separabit"—that which separates.

Tyrie, a black-haired, bespectacled, rather portly man in his late thirties, does not give the impression of being in charge of an organization which, between 1972 and 1977, was responsible for murdering about four hundred Catholics (though figures are uncertain). Quite the contrary, there is no bigoted fanaticism, no expression of violent hatreds. Rather, the impression is of a man who thinks about the causes of the troubles, of the leader of an organization that is doing its best to get to the bottom of the muddle. Many foreign reporters have gone away from an interview with him thinking that the UDA is an organization of social workers.

For a long time the authorities seemed to be of the same opinion—or at least acted as if they were. The UDA has never been proscribed under the Special Powers Act, as has the IRA. It is still a perfectly legal organization. Its open offices testify to that. The UDA's command structure which consists of a group of about eight men from different parts of Northern Ireland who form the Inner Council, has remained intact for nearly eight years. Tyrie himself has never been arrested. More recently, the RUC has begun digging through some of its old unsolved murder files, and several UDA men have gone to jail for life. But, of all the paramilitary organizations involved in bloodshed, it has been affected least by the security forces. Yet it has killed probably more civilians than any other terrorist group in the country, including the Provisional IRA.

There is a room in the building which testifies to its violent activities. As the visitor leaves he passes it on the ground floor. It is a little shop which sells mementos and handiwork of imprisoned UDA men. There are tables made of match sticks, lampstands built out of thousands of lollipop sticks, and many paintings of the Red Hand and the Union Jack, the emotive symbols of Ulster loyalists. By 1976 the shop had about one hundred eighty UDA men in jail to keep up its supplies. Most of them are in the Maze Prison, south of Belfast. They are a small percentage of the total prison population of over two thousand, the vast bulk of them Provisionals or suspected Provisionals. And yet the UDA's percentage of the total prison population is not at all an accurate reflection of its contribution to Northern Ireland's bloody statistics.

Between 1972 and 1977 the UDA murdered approximately four hundred forty people; it wounded and seriously injured thousands more. It has been directly responsible for a massive intimidation campaign in Belfast, where about sixty thousand people have been forced to leave their homes largely because of its activities. Hardly a week goes by without its death squads striking somewhere in Northern Ireland.

There are many reasons why the UDA has evaded the police and army. Some are more legitimate than others. The British have argued since 1972 that tactically they could not sustain a second front such as might develop if they moved against the loyalists with force equal to that used on republicans. The security forces have their hands full coping with the Provisionals. The authorities also argued, as they did at Strasbourg to refute the allegation that internment was one-sided, that the UDA was not like the IRA, so massive arrests were not needed—the loyalists were not a well-organized terrorist army but more like a gang. Because information was more readily available to the police, it was not necessary, as it was with the Provisionals, to employ such Draconian measures. When the British did finally introduce internment against loyalists in February 1973, it was only after public pressure became too great to resist.

The east Belfast UDA was the direct cause. (By a coincidence, fifty years before the police were forced to use the Special Powers Act against the supporters of Northern Ireland in the same area, when they interned two east Belfast loyalists suspected of being members of a gang like the UDA.) Under Tommy Herron it conducted a vicious murder campaign that climaxed with the bombing of a bus carrying Catholic workers to their jobs. In the months before, it tortured and killed many other Catholics living or working in the neighborhood. One was found mutilated and branded with a hot iron poker. Another was so hideously tortured that the coroner said it was the worst thing he had ever seen in his life. The man, a mentally backward Catholic, had been scorched on the fingertips and toenails, branded on the back, where the shape of a cross was seared into his flesh; his eyes were gouged out, and he was beaten until almost unrecognizable. It had been an act of mercy to shoot him.

In February 1973 the security forces picked up two members of the UDA and interned them amid general loyalist outrage. At the time there were over three hundred sixty Catholics interned. A further five loyalists were picked up before the end of the month, but there were never more than seventy loyalists interned at any one time—the majority were UDA men.

Internment did not affect the UDA's killing power, but it did frighten the leadership, who were expecting it imminently to be used on a much bigger scale. In the weeks before February 1973, Tommy Herron issued a statement from the "moderate" leadership condemning the sectarian killers as "maverick elements" over whom the UDA was trying to get control. According to official

UDA statements, these were real diehards who were dissatisfied with the UDA leadership. They wanted "action," and Herron's message to the British army and the RUC was clear: Don't arrest us or the fanatics will take over. Much to everyone's surprise the ruse was quite successful. Herron was not interned, nor were the majority of those responsible for carrying out and organizing the killings.

In the following months, the UDA produced other tricks to ward off the army and police. One of their most farcical was a "kidnapping" of Tommy Herron, supposedly by young militants attempting to dethrone the still moderate leadership. (Herron was still trying to convince the authorities that he was a safer bet than some of those under him.) But their most effective smoke screen came from an idea suggested by John White, a loyalist gunman from west Belfast. He advocated that the UDA death squads should issue statements claiming responsibility, as the IRA did for its killings, under some fictitious name. "The Ulster Freedom Fighters" was advanced as a suitable cover. It was agreed on. From May 1973 the organization claimed its killings as the work of the UFF. Part of the reason why the assassins needed a cover was that they wanted to claim responsibility for their actions. Up until then the UDA did not acknowledge its murders for fear of drawing down the wrath of the British. But this meant that the killings lost some of their political impact. They were intended, after all, to spread terror among the Catholics and to demonstrate to the government that the Protestants meant business. However, many Catholics, including both wings of the IRA, believed that the assassins were undercover British soldiers or intelligence officers deliberately trying to stir up sectarian hatred. The killings were therefore not as effective politically as the UDA leaders and their gunmen wanted them to be.

After a murder, White would go to a local bar on the Shankill and call a newspaper, using the pseudonym Captain Black (Sherlock Holmes, where are you?) to make a statement on behalf of the UFF, claiming the murder. At first the UDA treated the ruse as something of a joke. But the British surprised them once again by displaying more naiveté than the loyalists ever expected. The government banned the UFF! The UDA men were amazed. One UDA man said, rather philosophically as it turned out, "How can you ban an organization that doesn't exist?"

It was not mere ingenuousness on the part of the authorities. By banning the UFF it *seemed* they were moving against the source of Protestant terrorism, while at the same time it obviated the need to confront the real problem, the UDA itself.

None of these ruses, however, would have worked if there had not been a basic ambivalence on the part of the police and army towards UDA violence. At certain levels of the RUC and army there was a belief that the leadership of the UDA was the best of a bad lot—and also could be of use. On one occasion, a UDA leader was caught by an army patrol with explosives in his car. To his surprise he was told he was free to go. The soldier said to him, "It's better the devil we know than the devil we don't." Assistant Chief Constable Bradley (for a long time a confidant of Paisley's) at one time spoke up on behalf of Charles Harding Smith. Smith was charged in a London court in 1972 with attempting to obtain illegal guns for Northern Ireland. Bradley sent a character reference to the court which stated that the accused had "been of some use" to the security forces in Belfast. Harding Smith was eventually acquitted and returned in late 1972 to resume control of the UDA (then in the midst of its first assassination campaign).

More sinister than this was the relationship that Tommy Herron had with a detective in east Belfast, with whom he met regularly in 1972 and 1973. At the meetings they exchanged information, on one occasion in the detective's house. Herron was given guns by the policeman, one of which was later used to kill a Catholic. (When Herron was found murdered, it was surmised that he had been killed by a special undercover police squad with whom he had had dealings, and who were worried in case he would reveal them. But as already mentioned it is more likely that the UDA leader was killed by east Belfast UDA men angry about his handling of the sensitive matter of money.)

Since its formation the UDA has received information about Catholics from the RUC. Usually this comes from sources in the RUC reserve, a part-time force recruited as backup to the police. In north Belfast UDA assassins—the killers of the McDonalds— were working from police files on suspected republicans. Among the names on those files were Niall O'Neill, Gerard Masterson, and Colm Mulgrew, all of whom were murdered by the gang. The first two were shot in their beds, the third at his doorstep. (The Provisionals have denied they were members, but in the case of Mulgrew they did eventually acknowledge he was a member of Sinn Fein, the political wing of the movement.)

The relationship between the forces of the state and those of the assassins is a disturbing one. But it is due directly to the nature of the state itself, where the police force is almost exclusively from the majority, who also make up the membership of the loyalist terrorist groups. They come from the same community, and they often share the same basic political goals—a safe, stable Northern Ireland freed from the menace of Catholic subversion. It is not surprising, since they overlap in these ways, that they sometimes establish a relationship that goes far beyond mere sympathy into the realms of criminal conspiracy. The politics of Northern Ireland has made that almost inevitable.

The UFF was not the only smoke screen thrown up by the UDA. It produced two others, with somewhat more benign intentions. In 1974 the Ulster Community Action Group (UCAG) came into being. It was a sort of Protestant welfare group, an attempt to get local people involved in their own neighborhoods. In the fall of that year, it went to Dublin to meet with members of the Irish government. Among the delegation was Tommy Lyttle, a long-standing UDA leader from the Shankill and an old associate of Harding Smith. It met with Irish Prime Minister Liam Cosgrave, who in spite of his fierce "law and order" image, seemed to have no qualms about talking to loyalists with paramilitary associations. UCAG's biggest *coup* of all was its successful raising of nearly twenty thousand dollars while on its Dublin trip. The money was donated by a group of Dublin businessmen and was needed to buy a minibus UCAG wanted to take handicapped people on little trips.

More recently the UDA has formed a political organization called the New Ulster Political Research Group (NUPRG). In January 1979 their delegates arrived in New York to meet with former New York City Council President Paul O'Dwyer, a long-time civil rights activist and fighter for the Irish cause. They were touring the United States to present their case for an independent Ulster as a solution to the crisis. Andy Tyrie and Tommy Lyttle had a long meeting with O'Dwyer, and all came away satisfied that they had reached some measure of understanding about the cause of Northern Ireland's current impasse.

These splinters from the UDA serve a legitimate need at one level. The New Ulster Political Research Group explored possible solutions to the political conflict. (See chapter 5.) But at another level they were undertaken for more Machiavellian reasons. They gave the UDA and its leaders favorable publicity. The paramilitaries appeared in the guise of serious men searching for a solution. It would look good should any of them ever end up in front of a judge. It continued the UDA's old tactic, begun by Tommy Herron, of convincing the authorities that its leadership is really a group of moderate men endeavoring to hold back the fanatics while desperately trying to find an answer that will bring peace to Northern Ireland.

Whatever these activities do achieve in reassuring the government or in reaching a genuine measure of understanding about basic problems, the real business of the organization is still assassination. The UDA came into being as a reaction to the Provisional IRA, the changes threatened and put into effect by the British, and the uncertainty of Northern Ireland's political future. It reflected the worst elements of loyalism under stress—anger and hatred born out of confusion, directed at the minority population against whom loyalists have for generations harbored fears and bigotry played upon by Unionist politicians. The quintessence of all these elements is seen in the UDA's assassination gangs, the so-called UFF.

In the summer of 1977, along with another Belfast reporter, I had the chance to meet with several of the UFF gunmen. The one we interviewed, whom we will call Sammy, worked in a garage when not on "active service" with his squad. He began by explaining why he turned against Catholics:

> Quite a considerable number of my friends were Catholic. I used to go to dances with them and drink with them. But when the Provo [Provisional] campaign started they would not condemn it. In a Catholic bar when they heard a bomb they would cheer and say, "there's another one away." I said, that's me finished with Catholics.

When the Provisionals' campaign got under way in 1971, he joined the UDA:

> In my area in 1971 there were about one hundred men in the UDA. About seventy of them would say that they wanted action, but when it came to it there were only three of us who actually went out.

It was the men "who actually went out" that formed the hard core of UDA assassins. The young man went on:

> We used to hit any Catholic place we could, taking an easy bar, throw a bomb into it and run. Unfortunately a lot of innocent people got

killed. I didn't like that. We try now [1977] just to kill active republicans. But it isn't always possible. If it's retaliation, you just go for the nearest and most convenient.

Sammy became something of a bomb expert, making up devices to throw into Catholic bars and, later, more sophisticated time bombs. He explained:

In the years that I have been involved in the UDA I have found there are very few men who are capable of handling a bomb. It's very rare. Somebody would be prepared to shoot people dead, but they will not handle bombs. And there aren't all that many who are prepared to cut a throat. Where a bomb's concerned, it's indiscriminate. If you leave it in a confined space it will nearly definitely kill. You should be selective but when you plant a bomb you can't always be.

Sammy insisted that the UDA were trying to be more "selective" now about whom it murdered. But he admitted:

An awful lot of people just run off and kill the first Catholic they can find. We call these "roamers" because they wander around looking for teagues [another derogatory word, like *Fenian,* for Catholics]. I feel we should be more selective, because that must be counterproductive. The Protestant population love to read about an IRA man killed, but if the press puts it across that this is another innocent Catholic killed, they say that's terrible.

Sammy was asked what effect he thought his killings might have on the Catholic population and on the political situation. He replied after a moment's consideration:

We're not trying to have any specific effect on Catholics. I suppose we're trying to tell them they can't force their views on us. If the UDA hadn't existed and we hadn't done what we did, we would find ourselves very near to a united Ireland. It's all been more of a stalling action than anything else.

When pressed for his assessment of the argument that UDA killings might be counterproductive and lead to support for the Provisionals, he replied,

It depends on the area what effect our killings have. In a middle-class Catholic area they would tend to abhor any act of violence. But in a more working-class environment anything that strikes back at the republican set-up is viewed with a lot more sympathy by Catholics. [He contends Catholics do not support the Provisionals.] If we have the capability to go into an IRA bar, it must have a very demoralizing effect on their people—that we can penetrate their security to that extent. Also if we can kill an IRA officer, it must shake them up. It also takes away from the credibility of their claim to defend Catholic areas from attack.

"I suppose it might help to recruit for the Provos when we kill Catholics," he finally admitted, but then, pausing, he added with emphasis,

But this is terror. If you want to terrorize a community you put a bomb under somebody's car or shoot somebody at their door. But there's other Catholics who might blame the IRA and say it's the IRA's fault that things like this are going on.

Sammy had other reasons for wanting to be more "selective" about his targets:

It's always better to shoot a republican and not an innocent Catholic. If it's an ordinary Catholic gets killed, the police pick the operator up and work on him and say, you're a great one aren't you; you killed an innocent man and left his family without a father. They'll put it up to him like that and make him feel bad and it's a lot more likely be will talk.

At this point he was asked how he felt about the police pursuing loyalists. He answered:

It used to be that we would retaliate quicker for the UDR and the police, because when the IRA kill one of them they're nearly always killing a Protestant. But now we've been knocked about and beaten up by the police so much that the boys don't want to go out and retaliate for them.

When asked if he had been successful in his expressed intention to be "selective," he admitted frankly he hadn't: "The unfortunate thing is that most of my victims have turned out to be innocent Catholics." (The Provisionals have only ever admitted losing one volunteer to loyalist assassins; that was John Green, a commander of the Provisionals in the north Armagh area. He was gunned down in a remote farmhouse on the border in early 1975 by members of the Ulster Volunteer Force.)

Sammy, however, was not contrite:

Personally, I'm not interested in whatever way their families take it. I know they're human beings, and their families are obviously going to grieve, but I'm after selected targets. This is a war we're in.

Forgetting his previous admission about the innocence of his victims, he went on forcefully, angrily:

I know I'll be answerable some day. It's murder, but it's in the line of duty. I am a soldier; the victims are also soldiers. The IRA is anti-Protestant most certainly. They are haters of everybody—the British, us, their own people sometimes. They will have to be stopped. The police are not my best friends. They have knocked me about when I've been inside. But every time the IRA shoot a policeman it is a direct attack on my country, our ideals and freedom. It's trying to force us into their way of thinking.

When probed about how he felt about murdering people, he was dismissive. It didn't upset him, he explained; on the contrary, "I used to get excited and sort of flushed after a job but now I can take it in my stride. It doesn't affect me now." He was asked did this lack of feeling not concern him. Sammy replied:

One man I killed—afterwards I had a feeling of joy. I could have gone out and done another one immediately. I got worried about this. I thought I was getting caught up and getting to like killing too much. I think of myself as a soldier, but in another way I still think of it as murder.

After a second's reflection he told us about one killing he regretted. He spoke almost in a whisper.

Once I killed a Protestant by mistake. One of the men in the organization came up to me afterwards and said, that was a good one you got there—he was a Prod, but he was a republican. He was just saying that to satisfy our consciences. After that I said that's me finished with operations. I was badly moved. But after a while I got over it. I try to be as careful as I can be now.

Sammy told us the UDA was careful in picking its killers. As proof he mentioned its training manual, which he offered to show us. He went out and came back five minutes later. He showed us a sheaf of papers; it was the "training manual" for assassins. Its first section began:

Once you are in a militant cell most of your authority for jobs will come from a higher level where they will also be organised. . . . Now that you are on your own you must study the art of killing. In earlier lectures you have learned the weapons you will need to use to be a good assassin. Most assassins use the heavy calibre revolver because they are very reliable and leave no empty cartridges/cases. The most popular revolvers are .38 and .45 Webley, Smith & Wesson or Magnums. There are ten places in the head where one shot will be fatal, and of course the heart is also a sure place. . . . With a booby trap or ordinary bomb or sniping it is relatively simple, the real test comes when you are face to face with your victim, you must not panic or get excited. The most important thing to remember is "not to get into conversation with your victim." The reasons for this are obvious, for example, a man in such a desperate position will try anything to escape, he would also try to talk you out of it or stall in the hope that someone will come along and rescue him; if by any chance you know the victim, don't let this influence you, it's "kill or be killed." If you take on the job you must carry it through or pay the penalty yourself.

One section described the use of the knife:

The best part of the body to attack with the knife is the throat. This is done from behind, holding the chin of your victim with your left hand, and drawing the blade across from left to right piercing the jugular vein causing death, but if your victim is bigger than you and is walking then the best way is to grab his chin with your left hand, place your foot at the back of your victim's knee-joint, then push the joint with the foot and pull back with your hand and as he goes down start the cut. The alternative method is again used from behind but this time the target is just below the rib-cage, you simply put your left arm around your victim's throat pulling him back and pushing the knife in and up, once you have done this turn the blade and pull the knife out. . . .

Once you have proven yourself as an operator just sit tight and listen, do not interfere in anything that doesn't concern you, when you are eventually chosen to take part in any big jobs, you will be briefed by your commander about the target, the easiest way in, and two or more exits, your alibi and most suitable time, then do a few dry runs to satisfy yourself on the planning. . . .

The "dry run" made me remember the "encyclopedia salesman" who'd visited the McDonalds the day before they were murdered. We copied these few quotes and returned the papers.

Sammy told us he intended to go on killing. "I just do it out of hatred—I hate Catholics," he said conclusively. As we turned to leave he remarked on there being something strange about Catholics. We asked what it was. He explained, "Protestants seem to die easy, Catholics don't. Honest, I've shot them and bombed them, and it's very hard to kill them. Sometimes I think they can eat steel." With this bizarre compliment the interview ended.

Two years after this interview took place, the UDA lost one of its most active killers, John White, the notorious Captain Black of the UFF. In 1979 he went to prison for life for the murders of Paddy Wilson, a Catholic politician, and Irene Andrews, his Protestant secretary, six years before. Paddy Wilson was stabbed over thirty times and his throat cut ear to ear. Irene Andrews also died of multiple stab wounds. White was not one of those who Sammy said "aren't prepared to cut a throat." He was suspected of being involved in nearly forty murders. The UFF was not deterred by his arrest. To date Sammy and the other assassins who make up its ranks are still active.

5

Identity Crisis

. . . this is your country, close one eye and be king.

—DEREK MAHON

A few years ago I was in a train travelling northeast from Belfast, where the track hugs the coast of County Antrim. Our destination was the little port of Larne, from which a ferry runs across the sea to Scotland, twelve miles away and visible on a clear day. Our route was through the heartland of loyalism—a jumble of factories, gardens, red brick houses, and small churches belonging to a seemingly infinite variety of Protestant sects. It is an area where industry has filled every crevice in the foothills of the Antrim Plateau, which here merge into lowlands lapped by the cold choppy waters of Belfast Lough.

It was late afternoon on a wet winter's day. A slight mist of rain was falling. Wafting over mountains or down green glens, rain lends the powerful if rather startling charm of insubstantiality so characteristic of the Irish landscape. But hanging around the big smoking stacks of the power plants and chemical works, it is dismal and depressing. Throughout these districts a sense of being ill-at-ease prevails, as if the landscape and the factories are opposed to each other, as if there is lurking still in the dimly perceived hills beyond some demon that remains to be appeased, that still unsettles the settlers with their industry on the plains and lowlands.

The British Union Jack flaps in gardens that the train runs past; or else it is the Red Hand of Ulster on flags or painted on walls alongside anti-Catholic graffiti and Protestant paramilitary slogans. The Red Hand in competition with the Union Jack is an indication that loyalties that were once synonymous are no longer perceived as such. It is a common sight in this part of Northern Ireland, which Protestants have traditionally sworn was British and would remain so. The sense of unease that was always there behind their vociferous proclamations of Britishness is now being made manifest.

The railway carriage was shabby, its walls carved full of graffiti, its seats loose and ripped, battered almost into a state of disuse. It looked as if it had been forgotten and that no one—no government body, no local authority, no well-funded transport company— would ever try to rehabilitate it, that it would just fall to pieces some day as it rolled along between the mountains and the sea.

Opposite my companion and me were three Protestant youths returning home from their apprenticeship jobs in one of the big factories nearby. They were dressed in the traditional uniform of the British working-class youth: long-cuffed jeans hung above their ankles, short boots, and short, heavy black jackets known as "donkey jackets." It was pay day, and they were exuberant, fighting among themselves, throwing cans and bottles out the window while threatening to throw each other out after them.

In the middle of the mayhem one of the youths shouted breathlessly, "No wonder they say the Irish are mad!" There was a short but sudden silence. His two companions looked at him uneasily, and he almost blushed with embarrassment. It was as if a taboo had been broken, and in front of strangers. After a second or so the biggest youth, obviously the leader of the group, shouted with bluff confidence and an aggressive voice, "Hey, what d' ya mean? We're not Irish—we're British." They laughed at each other, but rather self-consciously. It was obvious they were discomfited, unsettled, and they flung themselves with increased vigor into another round of furious and distracting activity. But they were no longer at ease with themselves or with us there as witnesses to the manifesting of a doubt which troubles Northern Ireland's Protestants, almost as their industries seem troubled by the landscape in which they find themselves.

This doubt lurks under the surface of even the most unreflective of loyalists; it reveals itself in the fact that the UDA chose the Red Hand as their emblem instead of the Union Jack; and occasionally it is expressed in their actions and statements and their ponderings. And it has become acute since 1972, when the British abolished the Northern Ireland parliament. Basically it is a problem of national identity. But it is more complex than that, involving the anxieties and fears, the feelings of being ill-at-ease, of those who centuries ago came as settlers to a land with which they were never at peace.

All colonists and settlers face the same or similar dilemmas. It is a short trip across the Irish Sea from Scotland and England, the homelands of those Presbyterian farmers who in the late seventeenth century supplanted the local Celtic tribes of Ulster. The overt racial distinctions have faded; the natives and the settlers now speak the same language. On the surface, there is nothing to distinguish them. But the surface is deceptive. In Northern Ireland history and politics still determine even the geography of Catholic and Protestant, as well as their attitudes towards themselves and each other.

Protestant geography is characterized by low hills, rolling farmlands, lowlands like those in east Antrim, and good soil. Their coastal towns are on flat plains, with wide sandy beaches in sheltered spots. Like the eastern lowlands of Antrim through which we took our train trip to Larne, these areas are heavily industrialized or else well-farmed and cultivated. Catholic geography is, in contrast, a landscape of mountain slopes, rugged terrain, small farms of stony fields; their costal towns abut wild coastlines with mountains and glens for hinterland and dangerous tides before them. The contrast is still that of settler and native: the Protestants with all the best sites, and the Catholics forced into the nooks and crannies of the inhospitable countryside. It is a contrast that persists even in the cities—compare east and west Belfast. The former, a loyalist area, is flat, gathered around the major industries at the mouth of the River Lagan. West Belfast, with its large Catholic ghetto, is an area of river valleys, mountains, and gullies where many of the streets in the modern developments terminate. While the loyalists got the best land, they left the Catholic nationalist population with the best views. But that is not what disturbs the modern citizens of the state which proclaimed its loyalty to Britain for over two generations and whose supporters are the descendants of a people who have traditionally asserted their identification with the British Empire for well over a century. Many of them now feel that their loyalty to Britain has been betrayed and abused, that it now constitutes more of a threat to them than a source of support and protection. Their confidence in Britain has been badly shaken by the events of the last decade; this has at times led some of them to question the old dogmas of Unionism, based as they are on the assumption that being part of the United Kingdom is good for Northern Ireland, as being British is preferable to being Irish. These assumptions have been challenged by Protestants before. In the late eighteenth century, Presbyterian liberals from Ulster, under the banner of the United Irishmen—a banner that, in theory at any rate, continues to be the inspiration of republicanism—fomented an insurrection against British rule. Led by Wolfe Tone, a Protestant lawyer, they believed that Ireland's hope lay in an independent republic modelled on that of the recently formed United States and French republics. The insurrection was mercilessly crushed. Since then the British have seen to it that the Protestants of northeast Ireland have remained constant in their devotion to the British crown and in their opposition to Irish nationalism.

The development of heavy industry in the northeast of Ireland throughout the late nineteenth and early twentieth centuries gave that devotion a sound economic base. The area became a bulwark against the ever-swelling tide of Irish nationalism. When it seemed that some form of Irish independence was imminent, the Protestants banded together under the banners of the Ulster Volunteer Force, a militia raised in 1912 to combat any attempt to force them into a united Ireland. They demonstrated their devotion to the British crown when the First World War broke out—the UVF was recruited *en masse* into the British army, and Ulstermen died in thousands in the fields of France. The loyalists still regard their service during World War I as their finest hour, the climax of their patriotic devotion to Britain. The Protestant working class is perhaps unique in Europe in that it is the only working class not radicalized by the experience of World War I, an experience which sparked off revolutionary movements elsewhere. But for the loyalists of northeast Ireland, it only confirmed their support for Britain and their own sense of Britishness. It hardened their suspicions of the Irish nationalists, who rose in rebellion against the British when the war was at its height in 1916. Fifty years later when members of the other UVF, the terrorist organization formed by Gusty Spence, went to jail in Long Kesh Prison, they named their prison huts after World War I battlefields. The mythology of British imperialism held them still.

The loyalists looked to Britain to reward their services. In 1921 they got that reward: their own parliament, under Westminster. At the same time they remained part of the United Kingdom. The settlement allowed Northern Ireland to return twelve members to the Westminster parliament every British general election (until the mid-sixties all twelve were generally Unionists). The entity known as Northern Ireland was born. This strengthened the loyalists' attachment to Britain, for Britain's support was required to guarantee the privileges they received as citizens of Northern Ireland. But it was also an expression of the ambivalence underlying the loyalist position in Ireland—they were British but, unlike the rest of the United Kingdom, they had their own parliament, with all the apparatus of a separate state. As citizens of this state what were they? British? Irish? Northern Irish?

The creation of Northern Ireland reinforced the remarkable social cohesion of the loyalists. Workers, farmers, businessmen, and landed aristocracy were bound together in defense of their parliament. The Unionist Party was the political aspect of a great monolith that included the Orange Order and the Protestant churches, all demanding absolute loyalty from Protestants—loyalty to their church, their party, and the Order. For workers in Belfast it meant strikes were frowned on as unpatriotic; loyalty to the state also meant loyalty to the factory owner who, like the worker, was an Orangeman, and therefore obviously must have the best interests of his fellow Orangemen at heart. There were occasions when Protestant workers broke ranks and joined the Catholics in protests, as in the hard times of the 1930s. But they were the exception. Otherwise the labor force remained docile. Nothing could compete with the power of loyalist mythology: not the labor movement, nor the trade unions, nor any social democratic tendency. As a result, most of the powerful political currents that were sweeping through the rest of Europe passed by Northern Ireland's Protestants.

In the words of Lord MacCauly, loyalism was a "caste system." The untouchables were, of course, the nationalist, Catholic population. The caste system was organized specifically to neutralize the threat from the Catholics, incorporated against their will within the borders of Northern Ireland. (The political methods of neutralizing them, such as gerrymandering constituencies, have already been referred to.)

Maintaining such a system produced a virtually racist hatred and fear among Protestants of their fellow citizens. To justify the oppression of the minority it was necessary—as it always is—to characterize the victims as deserving of their oppression. Nineteenth-century Orangist pamphlets argued the racial differences between Catholics and Protestants in terms familiar enough in the United States—whites tried to justify the exploitation of black Americans for similar reasons. These arguments still persist in Northern Ireland. They are frequently couched in the usual excremental rhetoric of racism. The UDA ballad (see page 49) celebrating the burning out of the "shit" is typical. Loyalist newssheets in the early 1970s commonly describe Catholics as "slimey excrement" to be "roasted off the streets" by flamethrowers; they are "two-legged rats," "Fenian scum" who have to be "exterminated," and so on. The underground groups that loyalism spawned to defend its beliefs—the UDA, the UVF, and other smaller gangs—have created a ritualistic brutality, accompanied by a quasi-religious mumbo-jumbo reminiscent of the Ku Klux Klan.

The racist fears are unfortunately not only expressed in words; the violence inflicted on Catholics by loyalist gangs has occasionally descended to incredible levels of brutality inexplicable outside the social context of Northern Ireland. The tortures, the terrible abuse of the victims, spring from a desire to degrade and humiliate that is typical of racist attitudes to an "inferior" group. As is common, this desire is strongest among the poorer elements of the dominant group. The unemployed loyalists, who form a high percentage of UDA and UVF membership, live in housing as bad as that of their supposed inferiors, the Catholics. The loyalists suffer deprivation they do not expect and cannot understand. The Catholic has an explanation for his oppression, the deprived loyalist does not. He cannot blame the system, since it is there for his benefit and he supports it. His anger is turned against the scapegoat that the system provides—in the present case, the Catholics. But it could just as easily be any minority group which becomes the object of the fear and guilt felt by those who benefit from the discrimination used to keep it in a position of inferiority. That is why loyalist poverty and deprivation are so much more depressing and destructive than that found among Catholics. It generates self-hate as well as a hatred of others, a feeling of hopelessness that Catholics do not share. The Catholics find the reason for their oppression in the policies of Unionist and British domination, and they turn their anger against them—legitimately enough. Traditionally, the poor Protestants have had no outlet that provided a legitimate object for their anger and frustration. But more recently, since the abolition of Stormont, there has been a tendency to blame the middle-class Unionists for the "betrayal" of Northern Ireland and the failure of its government. Coupled with occasional outbursts of resentment against the British, it is the nearest the Protestants have come to breaking with their anti-Catholic obsessions.

While the oppressed have an explanation for their own oppression, they also have a ready-made justification for the violence they use in what they believe will be successful attempts to end it. The loyalists are again, however, put in an ambivalent and confusing moral position when they resort to terror. They are to begin with breaking the laws of the government they claim to be upholding and supporting. "Sammy," the UDA assassin quoted in the previous chapter, tries to justify his killings by the usual means: It frightens Catholics into not supporting the IRA; it demoralizes the IRA by proving to their Catholic supporters that they are not succeeding in defending the ghettos. He does not admit that in fact his actions might have (and demonstrably have had) the opposite effect: "I suppose it might help to recruit for the Provos when we kill Catholics, but this is terror." He dismisses this suggestion without much thought because he cannot face up to the irrational element in his actions which have led to increased support for the very people the UDA are supposedly out to defeat. In the end he did admit "I just do it out of hatred: I hate Catholics." It is this hatred that is the most powerful motivation of loyalist terror. Generally, they do not admit it to themselves and seek to justify it by other explanations. This ambivalence and dishonesty lead to an almost schizophrenic attitude to the crimes they commit in the name of law and order.

The little handbook from which the "Battle of Bombay Street" was quoted (page 49) contains a glaring example of this attitude. The poems were all written by a UDA prisoner in Long Kesh Prison (known now as The Maze) in 1974. In his Bombay Street ballad, as we have seen, he wrote: "On the 14th of August we took a / Little trip, up along Bombay Street / And burned out all the shit. . . ." Several pages on, there is another poem entitled "Chase Them Home," in which it is alleged that the Catholics are to blame for the violence:

> Trouble started in Belfast city,
> When rebels tried, to show no pity,
> Torn and showing intimidation,
> Put the fear into our nation.
> The U.D.A. came out in thousands
> Showed no pity to the scoundrels,
> Civil Rights they marched and swore
> That the U.D.A. had caused the roar.
> Intimidation cried the Provies
> After burning their own homes
> In Bombay Street and Lower Falls

(This "poem" by the way is typical of the remarkably low level of literacy shown throughout the handbook.) The last lines, in contradiction to the "Battle of Bombay Street," claim that the Catholics burned their own homes to make the loyalists look bad. This was written by the same man who *boasted* about the fact that the loyalists had burned Bombay Street. Loyalists frequently swing between boasting about their crimes when in a defiant mood and denying that they ever did them when they are seeking sympathy.

Like "Sammy" who admitted, "I think of myself as a soldier, but in another way I still think of it as murder," the songwriter's underlying ambivalence about the actions described is symptomatic of a general confusion, in the latter case amounting to uncertainty as to what actually happened. This is a result of the social position of loyalism, a position that does not allow those who hold it to admit the reasons behind what they do. They cannot win the sympathy of the outside world by proclaiming that they kill to maintain a sectarian system; they cannot—or can only with difficulty—admit that they kill from a hatred of Catholics. Nor can they admit to themselves that they are in fact committing crimes in the name of law and order. When they do go to jail they lament, with the UDA balladeer of Long Kesh,

> *Now the loyalists in Long Kesh*
> *Have committed just one crime,*
> *To fight for God and Ulster,*
> *And stay loyal to the crown.*

It is a familiar plea. A loyalist newspaper, *The Orange Cross,* which is devoted to the concerns of Protestant paramilitary prisoners, has as its motto "Their only crime is loyalty." Indeed loyalists can with justification point out that for years the Unionist Party deliberately fostered the notion that defending Ulster meant persecuting Catholics. When the Provisionals' bombing campaign got under way, Unionists called on loyalists to attack the Republic of Ireland and even to "liquidate" (in the words of Unionist extremist William Craig) the "enemy." Many UDA men took the Unionist spokesmen at their word and ended up in jail because of it. This has been the source of a growing disenchantment with Unionist politicians, who the paramilitaries believe misled and betrayed them.

This disenchantment has spread to the British government and the policies it has pursued since 1969. It reached a peak with the ending of Northern Ireland's parliament in 1972. At that time right-wing Unionists like Craig threatened a Rhodesian-style unilateral declaration of independence. Gun battles broke out between the UDA and the British army in the Shankill and east Belfast, where a soldier was shot dead by a loyalist sniper. The loyalists were telling the British that their loyalty has its price—it would only continue if it did not conflict with the maintenance of the privileges it once guaranteed.

The British, however, never pushed policies threatening enough to Protestants to force a final showdown. They backed away from the brink on several occasions. The most serious confrontation came in 1974 with the advent of a "power-sharing" government in Northern Ireland. The British experiment was a kind of political affirmative action program giving Catholics as a constitutional right cabinet posts in an executive intended to replace the old Stormont parliamentary system. Faulkner was at the head of the executive. (Ironically enough, the man who tried to sabotage the moderate reforms of O'Neill in the late sixties had taken up the torch of liberal Unionism and was prepared to undertake far more daring initiatives.) His deputy was Gerry Fitt, the leader of the Catholic Social Democratic and Labour Party. The experiment lasted five months.

In protest against the new assembly, Andy Tyrie and the UDA, with the support of a group of Protestant trade unionists called the Ulster Workers Council (UWC), initiated a series of intimidatory actions that stopped workers from going to their jobs. Industry ground to a halt. Faulkner and Fitt pleaded with the British to move against the UDA, who had blocked the main roads with barricades, sealing off large areas. But the British did nothing and allowed the power-sharing government to collapse, giving the loyalists and the UDA their most substantial victory since the current crisis began. Yet the suspicion and disenchantment with Britain remains, becoming acute at times of political insecurity. More recently it has prompted elements in the UDA (with the support of Andy Tyrie) to pursue other solutions that have at least temporarily taken Protestants outside of the usual fossilized positions of traditional Unionist politics.

After its triumphant defeat of power-sharing in 1974, the UDA sought a more effective political role. Tyrie tried to persuade the Unionists to give the paramilitaries a voice. But the Unionists publicly would have nothing to do with him or the UDA. They rejected his suggestion that the UDA should be represented on the various policy-making bodies. Tyrie said later, "We were let down badly by the politicians, and having kept us out they hadn't even the sense to use us as a threat." The attitude of the middle-class Unionists was that the place for the ordinary loyalists was on the streets, that they had best leave politics to their social superiors. The UDA then went to meet with the Catholic Social Democratic and Labour Party (the SDLP). The meeting was cordial but ineffective. The two groups simply surprised each other at how well they got on together. 1974 also saw the UDA-sponsored trip to Dublin, where spokesmen met with Irish Prime Minister Liam Cosgrave and members of his cabinet. That trip at least produced some funds.

UDA meetings with other Catholic representatives took place and included contact with the Provisionals—but only to discuss "cooperative enterprises." The UDA spoke with Maire Drumm, a leading member of Provisional Sinn Fein. However, these friendly chats didn't deter the UDA from pursuing their paramilitary objectives. In November 1975, one year after meeting the Irish Prime Minister, UDA men planted two time bombs in Dublin airport, which the organization claimed were meant to kill him. The Prime Minister was indeed in the airport the day of the attack, but the bombs went off four hours after he had boarded his plane. Less fortunate was Maire Drumm. In late October 1976, she was assassinated in her hospital bed by a joint UDA/UVF squad.

The UDA's most consistent efforts to find a new solution came in 1978 and 1979 with the formation of the New Ulster Political Research Group (NUPRG). Its declared aim was to explore the idea of an independent Ulster, freed from political ties with the United Kingdom and at the same time separate from the Irish Republic. The group was headed by Andy Tyrie and Glenn Barr, a local loyalist politician and a comparatively articulate spokesman for the UDA. In the summer of 1978 they met with a delegation of United States congressmen visiting Northern Ireland on a fact-finding mission. The delegation, comprising Congressman Hamilton Fish (Republican–New York) and Joshua Eilberg (Democrat–Pennsylvania) went on behalf of the Committee on the Judiciary, which at the time was looking into allegations that the State Department was discriminating against certain Irish nationals in its visa policies. (Several spokesmen for Provisional Sinn Fein had attempted on several occasions to gain entry into the United States without success.) But their trip took in much more; they met with a wide variety of representatives of different organizations, including the UDA and the NUPRG. The committee published a report on the trip in late 1978.

The report contains a transcript of the discussion that took place in the Belfast Europa Hotel between the two Congressmen, Andy Tyrie, and Glenn Barr. Barr explained to the Congressmen,

> The aim and object of the New Ulster Political Research Group has been the task of formulating political policy for the UDA. The problem up to date has been that the Ulster Defence Association has always relied on the established politicians to be able to represent them politically. But we believe that over the last few years that representation hasn't been reflecting the true feelings of the grass root level people. We believe that the loyalist politicians with whom we have always identified do not truly represent our feelings.

He then went on to outline the reasons for their disillusionment with traditional Unionist politics:

> On the loyalist side, the loyalist politicians have manipulated the Protestant people, who have believed the Unionists. And we also believe that

on the Catholic side they have been used and manipulated by emotional type politicians. Because, over the years if you look at politics in Northern Ireland no one has talked about pure politics. Every election time, all you have is a flag being waved at you repeating threats to your constitutional position. The Unionists keep waving the Union Jack and saying, well, if you don't vote for us you are going to be in a United Ireland. Therefore the people go out and vote for them to safeguard their constitutional position.

Likewise on the Catholic side. Their politicians were out waving the tricolour [the flag of the Irish Republic] green, white and gold, saying, well, vote for us and we promise you a united Ireland. We are not prepared any longer to be used by these manipulating politicians. What we are saying is that we want to formulate a policy that will serve the two sections of the community in Northern Ireland, the Protestant and Catholic people.

Barr was stating an obvious truth: normal politics, along conventional class lines as it has developed in most of Western Europe, has been frustrated in Ireland because of the unsolved national question. Political parties there are organized according to their position on the national question: for or against a United Ireland or how best to achieve such a result. But Barr maintained that there were other ways of looking at the problem. He said,

We have gone through every option that has been voiced about Northern Ireland. We have considered all forms from total integration with the United Kingdom, a united Ireland, a federal Ireland. . . . We have come up with one solution. We believe the only solution that offers long-term stability to the people in Northern Ireland is an Independent Northern Ireland. Now, we have gone for a complete withdrawal of Britain out of the scene.

For loyalists to call for a British withdrawal would have been unthinkable until recently, but Barr was quick to point out that since such a call would frighten Protestants—and might precipitate a civil war—the Irish government would have to reciprocate by renouncing its claim of sovereignty over the whole of Ireland, a claim it has enshrined in its constitution. He explained that the governmental form of the new Ulster would be based on the United States constitution, providing for a presidential democracy with a bill of rights to protect the minority. Unlike the United States, however, the Speaker of the House would need a two-thirds majority to get elected which, Barr claimed, would ensure that no one group or faction could totally control the Congress, and that there would be an effective veto on the President (who would doubtless be a Protestant). "We believe," he continued, "that there has got to be a structure that will allow the Protestant and Catholic people to learn to work together." But he rejected out of hand any suggestion of institutional "power-sharing" whereby Catholics would automatically be given a certain number of cabinet posts in any government. He said to the congressmen, "We believe that power-sharing is totally wrong, the wrong way to build a new society . . . there cannot be institutionalized power-sharing in Northern Ireland because that defeats the objectives we are trying to achieve." Power-sharing, like a united Ireland, has obviously become intolerable to loyalists in a way suggesting that in spite of all the talk about working with Catholics in the framework of an independent Ulster, there are still profound suspicions and prejudices at work.

Barr further suggested that the United States might oversee the first twelve years of the new state by appointing one of its Supreme Court judges to head the Supreme Court of an independent Northern Ireland. The American jurist's task would be to make sure there was no deviation from the nonsectarian principles of the constitution. He was not put off by Congressman Eilberg's interjection that such a move would require a change in the U.S. constitution and that such changes, even when accepted, are painfully slow.

Barr explained his desire to have the United States act as overall guarantor of the new state for rather more fanciful reasons: "Suppose there was an independent Northern Ireland . . . and in about thirty years from now oil was discovered in Armagh and the British government said we should never have gotten out of there and . . . we should try to get in there again. What we want is someone from the outside that is strong enough to say, 'All right, hands off.'" (The discovery of oil in County Armagh might indeed present problems, but mainly, I think, to the picture postcard industry. Oil-drenched Irish shamrocks are a pretty horrifying thought!)

As he ended his remarks, Barr returned again to the old dilemma faced by the Northern Ireland Protestants, the one partly responsible for provoking this search for a new allegiance: "We believe that with new institutions [we'll find] a new identity for the Northern Irish people, which are the things which are lacking because they don't know whether they are Irish or British. We are in limbo.''

When Eilberg expressed some skepticism as to the survival of an independent Northern Ireland, given the violence of the last decade, Barr rejoined by pointing out what he saw as the stark alternatives:

> Well, no doubt it is going to take five, ten years for that to die down. We are not naive. But, we believe there has got to be a starting point. So, we have two options. As a paramilitary organization we can say turn the lads loose. Let them go out and shoot all the Catholics and let's have a civil war. At the end of the day we have still got to find a solution.

Tyrie began his contribution to the discussion by emphasizing one particularly galling aspect of the identity problem faced by Northern Ireland Protestants, the fact that to the British they are as Irish as the Catholics. He said,

> If, for instance, I was to take you to Bradford, or Birmingham, or London, or somewhere in England at the present time, you would be accepted as an American. But they hear my accent and they say, "Oh, he is Irish." They don't treat me as British. I am one of the black Irish.

Because Catholics were forced as a result of various forms of discrimination to emigrate much more than Protestants, they were used to this attitude and took it for granted. But it comes as something of a shock to the average loyalist to find that, after years of protesting his Britishness, he is treated by the English like just another "Paddy."

The presence of the British army in Northern Ireland has driven this home. Tyrie explained that the loyalists found themselves being mistreated just like the Catholics. Their reaction he said was confused. In prison they do not protest their mistreatment like Catholics because, in his words, "The Protestants consider they are British and if they protest too much they are backing up the republicans' demands. . . . We try to stay as much to the rules as possible." Yet he claimed the Protestants, like Catholics, see themselves as "political prisoners." He admitted the contradictions in all this. "We believe in what we are doing, you know, but unfortunately we got a bit mixed up in our aims and what we really did want and we are trying to figure out now what we are really after."

Tyrie claimed that the UDA was now beyond manipulation by Unionist politicians with their simplistic traditional slogans. "What we have done," he said, "is to look for something different and in that search we have stepped back. There has been no sectarian violence from the UDA in the last two years. We haven't been involved in any violence at all even when there was great provocation." The UDA did suspend assassinations from about mid-1977 to late 1979 for a variety of reasons, some tactical and some, as Tyrie alleges, genuine in that they did attempt to come up with some other way of dealing with the situation. He explained that he began to ask why the violence was necessary and the answer was the usual one: the loyalist groups had been misled by their politicians:

> I say, what are we fighting for and why are we killing each other and who is gaining from it? The ordinary citizen is not gaining a thing from it. It had to be that way. Well, probably not for violence for violence sake but because people said to us "Here is your enemy." They identified the enemy for us in 1921 and we have never really searched for the enemy ourselves. . . . They [the Unionist leaders] found that every Catholic was a member of the IRA which is absolutely wrong and really nonsense. . . . And what I have done and what the Council [the controlling body of the UDA] has said to the membership, is if you want to have a war with somebody then, damn, fight yours properly. If you want to fight the IRA, try to shoot them and bomb them, but don't shoot the wee man that is going to his work or the wee man just because he is a Roman Catholic or because he supports a Roman Catholic football team. [Soccer teams, like nearly everything else in Northern Ireland, take on emotive sectarian colors with Catholic teams and Protestant teams, whose supporters battle each other before, during, and after matches.]

He continued:

> We are convinced now that this has happened on both sides of the community. The Provisional IRA people I am convinced have said to their membership not to shoot people because they are Protestants. If you want to shoot anybody, shoot people you can identify as being deeply involved in the conflict. We have become educated the last couple of

years, and we know we have made progress which is very important to us. . . . We had been told in advance [by the Unionist leadership] and knew the answer—it has been a hard job to change minds. It is not complete but it is well on its way.

Tyrie echoed "Sammy" (see chapter 4) in claiming that the UDA was no longer interested in killing Catholics, but was now looking for more legitimate targets, people involved with the Provisionals or other republican groups. Familiar too were the condemnations of sectarian murder: UDA leaders since Tommy Herron have publicly spoken out against such acts while organizing them on a large scale. With organizations like the UDA there must always be a certain amount of disingenuousness in these pronouncements. But in spite of such qualifications, credit has to be given: Tyrie was making out, in a confused way, a rather more thorough-going case against Unionism than any paramilitary leader had before him.

In an attempt to get some publicity and support for their independent Ulster idea, Tyrie and Barr with other members of the NUPRG, arrived in the United States in January 1979 at the invitation of an Irish-American group based in Minnesota. New York civil rights activist and former President of the City Council Paul O'Dwyer introduced them to a group of lawyers who were constitutional experts, to advise them on the technical details involved in drawing up a constitution. In O'Dwyer's Wall Street offices they met with some Irish-American supporters of the IRA and had a long and rather metaphysical discussion about what exactly it meant to be Northern Irish—and, for that matter, what it meant to be Irish or British. Sean Walsh, a Democratic assemblyman from the Bronx, pointed to his red hair and skin color as proof of his Celtic racial characteristics, quite different from those of the Anglo-Saxon English. Then followed an intense consideration of hair color, skin color, and the makeup of the primitive Celtic tribes of Ulster. Dr. Ian Adamson, the group's historian and an expert on early Ulster, harked back to the Stone Age to find historical justification for the projected new state. He argued that the Celtic tribes of Ulster were quite different from those in the rest of the British Isles. The Irish-Americans were very pleased to hear Northern Ireland loyalists proclaim their Celtic heritage. The Northern Ireland Protestants, however, were somewhat more wary of the proponents of Celtic culture, who seemed to be advancing a concept of a Celtic master race. As he left the meeting Tyrie turned to a companion and asked rather plaintively, "Do you have to be red-haired to be Irish?" Tyrie, of course, is very black-haired.

Being sidetracked into the metaphysical realms of racial distinctions was not the way to the solutions the UDA was seeking. UDA spokesmen were groping for a way out of the cul-de-sac of Unionism, a politics that allowed no compromise because it was born out of a siege mentality and maintained by one. Yet they would not go outside the context of the six-county state to find a possible alternative. This in itself indicates that, in spite of all the criticism leveled at the Unionist Party and its politicians, the UDA still accepts the basic Unionist entity of Northern Ireland as nonnegotiable. There have indeed been changes in attitudes among the loyalists, but how significant they are is another matter. They have substituted a sheeplike willingness to follow their middle-class leaders with a sort of populist anger and frustration at the fact that those leaders misled them and are responsible for their current dilemma. This is only partly true. To be honest they would have to admit that at one time they thought it was in their interest to follow—and it was. The privileges bestowed on Protestants by supporting Unionism were many. Now that those benefits are no longer at the disposal of the Unionist hierarchy, it is not surprising that loyalists should look elsewhere.

Before they can get to the point where they can formulate the questions clearly, the loyalists must recognize the problem. Northern Ireland as a political entity has not been able to work in a democratic and liberal way. The English Liberal Prime Minister Lloyd George, ironically enough one of the chief architects of partition, put it clearly fifty years before: "If Ulster is to remain a separate community you can only by means of coercion keep them there." Coercion was used, with the results the world now knows too well. But it failed to produce even a stable, never mind a democratic society.

For an independent Ulster to function it would need the support of the Catholic population, who are dubious, to say the least, when the UDA proclaims a change of heart. The Provisional IRA has already rejected the proposal. Its goal is a united Ireland in some shape or form (though privately they have played with the idea of Ulster independence).

In 1979 it seemed Catholic skepticism was justified. During the summer the Provisionals killed Lord Mountbatten and massacred eighteen British soldiers in a single ambush on the same day. In the weeks previous to these attacks Provisional gunmen appeared on the streets of Belfast defiantly displaying their weapons. It proved too great a provocation for the UDA to resist. In the words of Glenn Barr, the organization "let the lads loose" once again. Within six weeks the same number of Catholics were murdered in Belfast—the first victims of the loyalist death squads in nearly two years. There was no further talk about new solutions to the Northern Ireland problem. The old reactive nature of loyalism was too strong to be contained by the confused soul-searching of the New Ulster Political Research Group.

It remains to be seen how long the loyalist tradition will last now that many of the political, social, and economic reasons for it have disappeared. Every year the 12th of July comes around, and the bands come out in their big bright colors. The bonfires light up the Northern skies; the rumble of the lambeg drum still rolls down the country lanes and the back streets of the Protestant ghettos. Old men, medals pinned to their chests, their orange sash a shock of vivid color slung across their coats, stiffen up for a day, try proudly to straighten old bones that might once have carried a soldier's pack in France. Young men march beside them, renewing the ancestors' claims to victory and the loyalist heritage. When the day ends the children still gather around the licking flames of the bonfires to roast potatoes, drink soda, and sing songs; their shadows leap against the gable walls of the tiny houses. But beyond the bonfires there is darkness; the future is uncertain and full of threats. As the years go by the lines of marching men grow shorter, the spirit less exuberant, the bravado nagged by doubt. Old beliefs are challenged, old loyalties questioned; the Unionist monolith has fragmented into a dozen different parties; the Orange Order seems more a folk ritual and less a political cause. Perhaps that in itself is political progress. When the day dawns over the smoldering ashes and the cleaners come to sweep them away, the loyalists must ask themselves, what in truth is there left to celebrate?

6

Martyrs

To lose beauty in terror, terror in inquisition.

—T. S. ELIOT

*I*t is a good day for a funeral. The October sunlight is clear, the air crisp with a hint of winter; a slight mountain breeze blows through the city streets ruffling the wreaths held by the girls in black, whose eyes, covered with dark glasses, are made blank and sinister. The green mountain seems closer than ever to the brick-red streets. For those who lift their heads, white specks of sheep are visible, nibbling away at the short mountain grass as they have been doing for who knows how long. Few lift their heads today, the day of Paul Marlowe's funeral. Paul Marlowe: Belfast Brigade, Provisional Irish Republican Army, blown to pieces along with two others when his own bomb went off too soon. "Killed In Action" is how the IRA describes the death.

The cortege stretches along the Falls Road. Silent crowds gather on the pavement watching the all-too-familiar scene. The puzzled faces of children, the tight-lipped men, the women shaking their heads, their arms folded, the youths determined, unmoved—it is all too familiar. The grim men and women of the Provisionals, wearing black berets, dark glasses, arms stiffly at their sides, accompany the cortege, marching with slow menace. I stand on the pavement watching it pass. A big black limousine creeps by, at its window Sean O'Neill's brother, "the Wizard," at one time the star bomb-maker of the Provisionals. He gazes without expression at the watching crowd, thinking perhaps that it could have been him up front in the coffin. In fact, there is nothing much in the coffin, little left to bury. Like the coffins of so many of their victims, that which the Provisionals now follow is filled with rocks to give the impression of a body's weight.

The young widow walks a little behind her husband's coffin. She is between two mourners and, almost crippled with grief, has to be supported. But this is a public occasion, and whatever private grief she feels is subordinated to the purpose of the IRA, which uses the death of its volunteers for a display of defiance. Family grief, the intimacies of the wife, mother, daughter, the children's final fare-well to the parent, all these must take place within the context of a special republican ritual of some significance. The dead man is first and foremost their volunteer, and whatever his private life has been, they claim him in death and claim him for Ireland. He is buried in a special republican plot containing the remains of many IRA men killed in conflicts with the British and Northern Ireland security forces. As the coffin is lowered down into the grave, three young men in black berets, wearing dark glasses, step suddenly out of the crowd, raise their arms up stiffly into the air, their fists clenching revolvers. They fire three shots and disappear as suddenly as they emerged into the crowd. That is the last act of defiance hurled against the state, proclaiming that this death is not a defeat for the guerrillas but rather another opportunity to assert their existence and their determination to continue the war.

Far away on the other side of the cemetery, which overlooks the gentle hills of County Down, British army observers watch the spectacle. They scrutinize the marchers, the faces of the mourners, through high-powered field glasses; they photograph everyone in sight from concealed positions out of which their telescopic lenses peer.

The ceremony ends with an oration from an IRA political leader.

He says the sacrifice will not be in vain; the war will go on until victory with greater resolve than before. Blood will fertilize the soil of the new Ireland. The crowds disperse quietly. The young wife goes home to an empty bed, her future blank, her past at that moment the only thing real to her. Now she must take up her role as the widow of a martyr.

Paul Marlowe, who was killed on October 6, 1976, is one of over two hundred members of the Provisional IRA to be "killed in action" since 1970. About 30 percent of the deaths have been as a result of premature explosions of the sort that killed Marlowe. The rest have been killed in ambushes, in gun battles with police and soldiers. Several have been shot by security forces in what are known as "disputed circumstances." (Witnesses claim that the police or army opened fire without provocation and the victim was unarmed; the army counters by alleging they were fired at, but the gun was not found on the dead man.) At least three have been killed by the other IRA organization, the Officials, during feuds which have broken out periodically between the groups. Loyalists have accounted for but few Provisional deaths, and these occurred in the early 1970s, when widespread sectarian rioting was more common and both sides staged shootouts with each other. When the loyalists adopted the tactic of sectarian assassination, they rarely ever got their hands on an IRA man. The only one the Provisionals acknowledge as having been assassinated by loyalists is John Green, a commander of the North Armagh battalion, who was also one of the few prisoners ever to escape from Long Kesh Prison Camp. He was murdered by UVF men in a lonely border farmhouse at the beginning of January 1975. (There is some indication that the murderers had help from elements in the security forces.)

In turn, the Provisionals have been mainly responsible for the deaths of (into 1980) over three hundred British soldiers; one hundred forty RUC men (full-time and part-time); more than one hundred members of the Ulster Defence Regiment, the locally recruited regiment of the British army; as well as for the deaths of twenty prison officers and several hundred "civilians." The last category includes the victims of sectarian attacks by the Provisionals, people "executed" for alleged informing, and—the vast majority—those unfortunate enough to be caught up in a bombing mission that went wrong. It is a grim record, particularly if it is kept in mind that the population of Northern Ireland is only one and a half million—one million less than Brooklyn's.

These statistics do not take into account the number of injuries inflicted by the Provisionals, nor the many millions of dollars of damage caused by them as the result of thousands of bombings for which they are responsible. It is an awesome, frightening record of destruction unique in postwar Western Europe. No other guerrilla army there has maintained such a campaign, against such odds, for so long, as have the Provisionals. And yet, just over a decade ago this would have seemed impossible, for then the IRA was small, discredited, disorganized, and confused. The growth of the Provisionals was rapid, the momentum of their violence relentless (and so it remains); yet it was not a simple, linear development.

The story of the Provisionals can be divided into three periods: from late 1969 to 1973, 1973 to 1977, and 1977 to date. The first period, when the Provisionals were under the command of Sean MacStiofain and, after his arrest in November 1972, several militant Belfast commanders saw the movement's greatest growth, the peak of its destructive power. The little band of ignored republican idealists became the leaders of a large and powerful guerrilla army that gained almost complete control of the Catholic ghettos of Belfast and Derry; though "guerrilla army" is perhaps not quite accurate— the Provisionals during this period were part guerrilla army, part local defense force, part neighborhood police force. Then they had the support of the majority of Belfast and Derry's working-class Catholics, and were developing rapidly in rural areas as well. Their power extended even into the prisons, where by 1972 many of their leaders were lodged. In May of that year a group of Provisionals led by ex-Belfast commanding officer Billy McKee, who had been convicted of an arms charge, won recognition as political prisoners from a beleaguered British administration. The concessions, which were granted after a hunger strike, included the right to free association within the prisons and Long Kesh internment camp, where most of the internees were held; the right to wear their own clothes; the right to extra visits and extra food parcels; and the right to refuse to do prison work. It was an implicit recognition from the Conservative government that they were dealing with a powerfully motivated political movement. Years later, political status—or Special Category, as it was called—would prove extremely embarrassing to a government bent on proving the Provisionals mere criminals.

The fatality record for 1972 testifies to their strength: 138 members of the security forces killed, including 100 soldiers; 1500 explo-

These photographs were smuggled out of The Maze (formerly Long Kesh Prison), near Belfast. They show Provisional IRA prisoners marching *(top left)*, attending a weapons class *(above)*, and training *(bottom left)*. The weapons are wooden replicas of armalites, the Provisionals' favorite sniping rifle. The prisoners were moved to Long Kesh shortly after internment began in 1971 and housed in Nissen huts where they were free to wear their own clothes, associate with members of their own organization, and more or less exercise control of the running of their compounds, in which the huts were grouped. The different paramilitary groups had different compounds, and each compound was controlled by a paramilitary officer. These privileges reinforced the perception of the paramilitary prisoners as "prisoners of war." In March 1976 a Labour government, embarrassed by this "special category" status (as it was known), removed the privileges for anyone convicted after that date. Prisoners were in the future housed in cells and had to conform to normal prison discipline. The republican prisoners resisted, and the so-called "blanket men" protests began with sentenced republicans refusing to wear prison uniforms, do prison work, or even, eventually, to clean out their own cells. As of 1980, nearly four hundred men and thirty to forty women were engaged in this protest.

sions (196 in July alone). It was a trial of strength between the Provisionals and the British army, and it seemed by midyear as if the Provisionals might have won—at least by proving that Northern Ireland was ungovernable unless they were listened to. A cease-fire was called in June. Sean MacStiofain was flown by helicopter to confer with William Whitelaw, the Secretary of State for Northern Ireland. Along with him went a group of Provisionals who were all to play significant roles in the subsequent development of the organization. They were Seamus Twomey, a hard-line Belfast commander (once a bookie's clerk, he rose to power in the city as an uncompromising terrorist); Gerry Adams, a young left-wing activist released from internment for the journey (an ex-barman, he was regarded as essential in conveying the mood of the younger guerrillas); Ivor Bell, another Belfast man, like Adams the product of a younger generation of IRA men and regarded as very left-wing in outlook; David O'Connell, the movement's political thinker. (A chain-smoking, restlessly active individual with the look of a salesman, O'Connell was the man behind the Provisionals' published political program, which had come out a few weeks before the talks: "Eire Nua"—"The New Ireland.") They were accompanied as well by a young IRA leader from Derry, Martin McGuinness. It was clearly a Belfast-dominated affair, for it was recognized that the power base of the organization rested there.

The Provisionals demanded that the British withdraw and make a public commitment to do so. Of course Whitelaw, a genial representative of the English gentry, could not possibly give such an understanding. Nor, he knew, would the British government. The cease-fire ended soon afterwards. It crumbled first in Belfast, where Twomey seemed determined that it should. But the Provisionals were not unanimously against the cease-fire. O'Connell, along with Seamus Loughran, a Belfast republican who was politically close to O'Connell, had tried to prevent it from ending. But on this occasion the militarists were strongest. The "doves" would have to wait for another day, when conditions were better, for their schemes to win acceptance. One of these conditions was the weakening of the Provisionals' campaign, particularly in Belfast.

The tactics of the Provisionals in this period reflect a degree of strength and support that they never attained again. At this stage they often engaged in set-piece gun battles with the army. One of the longest engagements of this kind occurred at the beginning of

1972 when a group of eight Provisionals lured a British army patrol into an ambush on the Northern Ireland border. They had set fire to two trucks, planting a bomb in one of them, then occupied a row of houses on the Irish side of the border where they waited for the troops to arrive on the scene. The army came but the bomb did not explode. The Provisionals nevertheless opened fire on the troops. Before long the army had raced over two hundred men into the area. The battle lasted for three hours, during which an estimated five thousand rounds of ammunition were used, but not to much effect, for both sides retired unscathed. The Provisionals were forced to abandon the attack because units of the Irish army were sent in by an already embarrassed Dublin government, which was constantly being accused by the British of not clamping down on the guerrillas from its side of the border.

The British and the Unionists made much of Dublin's difficulties in containing the activities of the terrorists, but Dublin's actions merely reflected the strength of the IRA. Dublin could not act as repressively against them as the British wanted, simply because the repressive tactics of the British in Northern Ireland angered Irish citizens to the extent that they were willing to tolerate the campaign of the Provisionals—up to a point. The Unionists and the British exploited Dublin's difficulties by insisting with gross unfairness that the violence in the North was caused entirely by Southern-based IRA activists. In the incident referred to above, for instance, the leader of the Provisionals' unit was an escaped commander of the IRA from North Belfast.

During this period the Provisionals were becoming increasingly ingenious in their skills as booby-trap bombers, a trend which was leading the organization into more classical guerrilla techniques. One incident, again on the border, near the South Armagh town of Crossmaglen, presaged the kind of attack with which the security forces have since had to deal. A patrol of paratroopers came across a fresh mound of earth on the side of one of the many narrow roads that criss-cross the border in that area. It looked obviously suspicious, so much so that the patrol was careful to move on the other side of the road. An officer described what then happened: "It was a diabolical trap," he said. "As they [a few members of the patrol] went to investigate, a mine went up on the other side of the road and killed one man and wounded five others." Reinforcements quickly arrived on the scene. But the Provisionals hadn't finished yet. When the reinforcements saw wires leading from the blast site they dispatched a scout car to follow them and, they hoped, to trace their origin to the presumed detonation point. As the armored car moved cautiously along the road, it touched off another land mine, which flung the vehicle into the air and killed both paratroopers inside it. "The attack was a typically treacherous one by the enemy," the officer commented. "It was cold-blooded and cowardly. Our boys never stood a chance." Crossmaglen and the surrounding area became a deathtrap for over seventy British soldiers in the space of a few years. Before long the army could only safely enter and leave the town by helicopter—the roads belonged to the Provisionals, who were quickly learning the subtleties of guerrilla warfare. That experience, however, was often won at a great cost of lives, including those of their own members. Many of these deaths were a direct result of what the Provisionals called their "economic war" against Northern Ireland.

From about mid-1971 "economic warfare" became one of the main characteristics of the Provisionals' campaign. This consisted of bombing attacks on shopping centers, businesses, government buildings, and power installations. It was a strategy in marked contrast to that of previous IRA campaigns. The Provisionals, always eager to claim direct descent from the old IRA that fought the British during the 1919–21 period, discount this. They argue that apart from causing a lot of economic damage to British financial interests in the North, it ties down thousands of British soldiers who must protect the vulnerable areas and who otherwise would be free to harass the Catholic ghettos and threaten the guerrillas' home bases. But it put civilians and Provisionals themselves at high risk. It demonstrated, perhaps more than anything else, the Provisionals' view of Northern Ireland as a foreign state, to be destroyed at any cost, by any means available. Shortly after the 1972 cease-fire broke down in July, twenty-seven bombs were exploded on a single day by the Provisionals in downtown Belfast, killing seven civilians and injuring one hundred fifty. The day became known as Bloody Friday and, with other similar outrages before and since, led to a sharp decline in support among Catholics.

When confronted by these horrors, the Provisionals shrug their shoulders and say it was not their responsibility—they gave warnings, and it was the fault of the authorities for not passing them on in time. However, the choice of targets—shopping centers crowded with women, a bus station, a busy street—was almost certain to lead to innocent lives being lost. Ordinary Catholics, who might have been sympathetic to the IRA, could not morally justify these tactics. When the guerrillas, who claimed status as "freedom fighters," were seen to be consistently more brutal than the state they are trying to overthrow, it inevitably resulted in a loss of moral credibility. (Guerrilla groups like the Baader-Meinhoff gang, who never possessed such credibility, are more indiscriminate in their choice of targets because they have no support base which might be threatened by their unjustifiable brutality.)

An incident in August 1972 was unfortunately typical of Provisional accidents of that period. Anne Parker and Michael Clarke were members of the Second Battalion, Belfast Brigade. She was eighteen and he twenty-four. They were sent out on a bombing mission—their target a local shop near the Falls Road. At lunchtime their car (which had been stolen earlier) pulled up outside the shop, and Anne Parker got out carrying a bag. Inside the bag was a twenty-pound bomb, apparently primed. But she did not get into the store. A woman attendant, seeing the bag, became suspicious and told the girl as she tried to open the door to "get the hell out." Anne Parker did so, returning to the waiting car, which was driven by Clarke. The bomb was still inside the bag when Parker and Clarke, in obvious panic, drove off at high speed from the curb.

Belfast streets are protected by ramps designed to slow down would-be bombers or gunmen in cars. Clarke did not see the ramp in front of him. His car speeded over it with a bump. A bystander saw what happened. He reported, "The car hit the antispeed hump in the road and disintegrated. It threw pieces of people and wreckage all over the place." Six people on the sidewalk nearby were injured by the explosion. Later a police spokesman commented grimly: "At first we thought we might have enough parts for three people, but it didn't turn out that way." The British army call such accidents "own goals," using the terminology of soccer.

Anne Parker and Michael Clarke were the twenty-fourth and twenty-fifth Provisionals to kill themselves with their own bombs within the space of two years. This might indicate that in one way the Provisionals in the first period of their development grew too rapidly, recruiting young men and women into the organization who were prepared to take risks for which they had been inadequately trained. The statistics speak for themselves. The Second

Battalion, the unit based in the mid-Falls area, lost thirty volunteers between 1970 and 1980. Twelve of those died in premature explosions, eight in 1972 alone. The Third Battalion's fatality list tells a similar story: Out of forty-one deaths in ten years, fourteen were caused by bombing mishaps.

By late 1972 this period of development was coming to a close. Support was falling away, recruitment dropping off, and in November of that year Sean MacStiofain was arrested by the Irish police and charged with membership in the IRA, an offense in the Irish Republic. He was sentenced to six months. Traditional IRA practice is that a member, upon arrest, loses whatever rank he held. Within prison the IRA has a separate battalion, and the new prisoner is expected to work his way up the ranks once again. But Mac-Stiofain angered many members when he went on an abortive hunger strike in protest at his arrest only to abandon it after some weeks. This was regarded by the Provisionals as a very bad example to the rank and file and publicly embarrassing to the movement, who expected the leadership to make the same sacrifices they demanded of the ordinary membership. Hunger strikes are a traditional IRA tactic, only undertaken as a last resort. As a matter of policy, no one is ordered to take this potentially fatal course. But once it is undertaken, they expect the hunger striker—particularly if he is a leader who has drawn immense publicity to himself, as MacStiofain always did—to persist until his demands are met or until he dies. MacStiofain's failure to do so has prevented him from regaining control over the movement he was so instrumental in founding and organizing. (Currently he is circulation manager of the Provisionals' newspaper, *An Phoblacht—The Republic.*)

With MacStiofain out of the way, the movement underwent some reorganization at the top. When he had been chief of staff that position was nearly all-powerful. Afterwards it became more subordinate to the seven-member Army Council, the guerrillas' ruling body. It also became policy to elect a Belfast man as chief of staff. This was due to the Provisionals' realization that Belfast was the key to this campaign and as such should have a ruling influence over future policy and strategy.

The first Belfast man to become chief of staff after MacStiofain was veteran republican Joe Cahill. Cahill, along with men like Billy McKee, was a 1940s IRA man. During the political crisis the IRA went through in the late 1960s (see chapter 2), he became inactive, suspicious of the growing Communist Party influence. But with the birth of the Provisionals, "the old men" of the movement once more found a role. Cahill's tenure was short-lived, however. In March 1973 he was arrested by Irish police on board a ship bringing Libyan arms to the Provisionals. He went to jail for three years on an arms smuggling charge. He was replaced by another Belfast man, Seamus Twomey, the bookie who had taken part in the cease-fire talks with the British in London.

The Belfast organization now passed into the hands of younger guerrillas whose leadership showed a more left-wing bias. The 1940s men who were so instrumental in founding the movement were in jail; the nature of the campaign began to change. The days of three-hour gun battles were over. The Provisionals could no longer parade so openly as a ghetto militia—the British had improved their security. The IRA adapted to the more stringent conditions. They became more reliant on booby-trap bombs and sniping techniques. But it was becoming obvious to many that the campaign would not be a short one, and that the kind of momentum created by the Provisionals in 1972 could not be kept going. The army's casualty rate dropped by almost half of that of the previous year. Bombings, too, fell to below the one thousand mark.

Now that MacStiofain was gone, the most public figure the movement had was David O'Connell, its political guru. O'Connell's rather dapper and smooth approach made him good television material, and he used the media to present dramatic and effective interviews and press conferences at which he outlined the Provisionals' program for "the New Ireland." With O'Connell's political domination, the movement entered its second stage of development, one which was to last for nearly four years, until late 1976. It was characterized by an attempt at rapprochement with the loyalists, which failed, and a push towards a new cease-fire with the British, which succeeded. The key to the first was the idea of the Federal Ireland contained in "Eire Nua"; the second depended on the volatile and ever more difficult tactical situation that the guerrillas had to confront.

The new Ireland envisaged by O'Connell was a federal state with parliaments in each of its four historic provinces: Ulster, Munster, Leinster, and Connaught. These would be under the aegis of the main Dublin parliament. According to O'Connell, this would ensure a certain amount of independence for the Ulster Protestants.

He hoped to convince them that in a federal Ireland they would not be swamped by Catholics and would be able to preserve their rituals and traditions without interference.

His emphasis on the concept of a federal Ireland grew throughout the early 1970s. On the publication of the "Eire Nua" document in June 1972, O'Connell stated, "We do not accept the term 'United Ireland,' because this has connotations which are damaging." He offered instead the slogan "The need to build a Greater Ulster," out of which, he claimed, the new Ireland would arise. It was in fact a form of Ulster nationalism with which he hoped to wean the loyalists away from espousing the British link. It became his theme, as did his other slogan, "Peace with justice." The latter was aimed at the British, to whom O'Connell wanted to indicate that the Provisionals were prepared to talk. His regrets over the collapse of the 1972 cease-fire had not left him, and his political ambition was to ensure that the IRA would be in a position once again to bring the government to the conference table, where important concessions might be gained.

His efforts to placate the loyalists led him to support any move made by them that he regarded as compatible with his federal concept. When the right-wing Unionist William Craig threatened the British with a unilateral declaration of independence (taking Rhodesia as his model), O'Connell came out in favor of such a move. He called for "an end to the sterile discussion of a United Ireland versus Union with Great Britain. Let us have meaningful talks about a New Ulster creating a New Ireland." Later, at a ceremony to commemorate the 1916 Easter Rebellion, O'Connell claimed, "The future of Ulster can only be determined by the people of Ulster." He welcomed any sign of Ulster nationalism, which was then growing among loyalists, who were disillusioned by the British government and wary of its intentions. In 1973 the British published proposals for a new government at Stormont. This would entail the setting up of a power-sharing executive, giving Catholics governmental power for the first time in Northern Ireland's history, as well as outlining a plan for a Council of Ireland. The Ulster Volunteer Force, the illegal loyalist terrorist group formed in the 1960s, attacked the proposals and suggested the setting up of a Council of Ulster. O'Connell welcomed the UVF statement, with its rejection of the British initiatives. For him, anything done by the Protestants that showed they were edging away from their previous pro-British politics was to be encouraged.

In 1974 he went farther than just "welcoming" statements espousing forms of Ulster nationalism. He defended the loyalist overthrow of the power-sharing government. The joint action of the UDA and its Protestant trade union support group, the Ulster Workers Council (UWC), won his praise. He said their action had "a note of authority and a ring of authenticity which was appealing. The UWC showed tremendous power and acted in a responsible way." He later went on to describe the loyalist coup—for that, in effect, is what it amounted to—as being in the "Wolfe Tone tradition," referring to the eighteenth-century liberal Presbyterian who led the 1798 rebellion against the British in Ireland. Ironically, just when O'Connell was praising the UDA/UWC action, the editor of the Provisionals' newspaper, *An Phoblacht (The Republic),* was preparing an editorial condemning them. When O'Connell found out, he was furious and forced the editor to resign.

O'Connell's policies were creating tensions within the Provisionals. Most of the Belfast leadership looked with disfavor on rapprochement with loyalism and talk of a "Greater Ulster." Since 1973 the IRA leaders in the city had been espousing more militantly socialist solutions. The older 1940s men were in jail; the brigade commander was Gerry Adams, and later Ivor Bell, both very left-wing. Though still opposed to the Communist Party's Moscow-inspired version of socialism, these men were proclaiming a democratic socialist United Ireland. However, they were not in so strong a position as before, during the 1972 cease-fire talks. The Provisionals were weaker militarily. Both Adams and Bell were eventually arrested, and there was a growing feeling of frustration within the movement. As this increased, O'Connell's "Peace with justice" policy aimed at the British began to seem more attractive—if, that is, the Provisionals could bring the government to the conference table as they had done in 1972. But how could this be accomplished if the IRA was in a tactically weaker position than before?

By spring 1974 the Belfast organization was in disarray. For a short time it was without any commanding officer. Four commanding officers had been arrested in succession by the British army. The movement was coming to rely increasingly on younger and younger recruits, some only sixteen or seventeen years of age. Most of the veteran guerrillas of 1971 and 1972 were interned, imprisoned, dead, or on the run across the Irish border. It was a good time for O'Connell's policies to win acceptance.

At this stage Belfast came under the control of Seamus Lough-ran, former electrician who had risen to prominence in the Andersonstown area as a local republican leader and a strong supporter of O'Connell's political line.

In the fall of 1974, O'Connell and Loughran made contact with a group of Northern Ireland Protestant clergymen who were impressed with O'Connell's politics. They acted as a go-between with the British government, with a view to eventually setting up a meeting between the British and the guerrillas.

In the meantime the Provisionals had developed a tactic that helped convince the British to make use of the proffered contacts with a view to ending the hostilities. As operations became more difficult in Belfast and throughout the rest of Northern Ireland, the IRA switched its attention to England itself. The strategy involved bombing in England to get the government to talk peace in Ireland. The Provisionals dispatched men who were on the run in Northern Ireland or in the Republic to carry out this campaign.

There had been bombing attacks in England before by both the Official and Provisional IRA. But the campaign that began in the fall of 1974 was more ruthless than any before it. Perhaps its ruthlessness was an indication of the leadership's desperate need to force the Westminster government to the conference table.

On October 5, 1974, two pubs frequented by off-duty British soldiers in Guildford, near London, were bombed without warning. Though the bombs were small, of ten and fifteen pounds respectively, they proved lethal, killing four people and injuring sixty-five others. Six days later three bombs went off, again without warning, at several ex-servicemen's clubs in Pall Mall and the Edgeware Road in London. On this occasion no one was killed. Shortly after this attack, the Provisionals booby-trapped the car of Conservative MP Denis Howell, but he escaped uninjured. The campaign then switched to the Midlands. Over the next few weeks there were bombings in the Conservative Club in Birmingham and at government offices in Wolverhampton. Another London pub was bombed on November 8, killing one man and injuring twenty.

As yet the Provisionals had not actually acknowledged responsibility for these attacks. But on the night of November 14 a young man called James McDaid was blown to pieces while planting a bomb in Coventry. He was from the Ardoyne in north Belfast, and in death notices in the Irish papers the Provisionals claimed him as a member of their organization "killed on active service." (His brother, Gerard McDaid, had been shot dead in December 1971 by British soldiers. He too was a Provisional.)

At about the same time David O'Connell made one of his dramatic television appearances. Interviewed on English television, he warned that the bombing campaign there would be stepped up. Shortly afterwards the worst incident of all occurred. Two Birmingham pubs were bombed, killing twenty-one people (including several Irishmen) and wounding hundreds. Not long after this the Provisionals announced that a cease-fire with the British had been reached and that, as part of the agreement, operations against British soldiers would be halted (although the right to take "defensive action" was claimed). Bombings in England also stopped. The last one went off on December 21. It was a three-pound bomb hurled from a passing car onto the veranda of Edward Heath's house in London. It broke a few windows.

Though the cease-fire got off to a false start, it was reestablished at the beginning of 1975 and persisted for six months or more. It was the climax of O'Connell's strategy. He had brought the British to the conference table through the agency of Protestant intermediaries; the bombing campaign in England proved that, though weakened in Ireland, the Provisionals could still strike with devastating effect in England's heartland. But it was just at this point, when success seemed to be achieved, that things began to go badly awry for the Provisionals, so that the second period of their development was to end in near political and military disaster.

Provisional propaganda proclaimed 1974 as "The Year of Victory." (One still occasionally sees an old "Year of Victory" poster, tattered and faded, on gable walls in Catholic areas of Belfast.) What the "Victory" consisted of was that, in return for halting attacks on British soldiers and stopping the English bombings, the British agreed to phase out internment and empty the prisons of all those held without trial. They also allowed Sinn Fein, now recognized as a legal political party in Northern Ireland, to open and run so-called "truce monitoring centres" staffed by Provisionals to oversee the cease-fire. They also allowed wanted members of the IRA's leadership to return to Northern Ireland and issued instructions to the security forces that these leaders "were not to be arrested unless actually suspected of or just seen committing a crime." Over and above this, the Provisionals later claimed that British Foreign Office officials involved in the negotiations with IRA representatives had given a written agreement to make a public declaration of the British government's intention to withdraw from Northern Ireland.

The ending of internment was an important booster for the Provisionals both politically and militarily. Internment without trial was the single biggest grievance the Catholics had. The Provisionals hoped by ending it to be able to turn this success into political dividends and at the same time reorganize and restaff their much-diminished units in Belfast. The "truce monitoring centres" would be used as Sinn Fein party political offices and establish the Provisionals as a political force that would eventually overtake and push out the moderate Catholic politicians of the Social Democratic Labour Party. The president of Sinn Fein, Rory O'Brady, described the centers as "the very legs on which the truce stands." Those legs were soon to prove extremely wobbly. The Provisionals, faced with a situation in which they might develop politically, showed little or no understanding of how to take advantage of it.

To begin with, O'Connell, the chief architect of the cease-fire, was arrested by the Irish police in the spring of 1975 and convicted of membership in the IRA. He was to spend most of the cease-fire period in a Southern jail. There was no one of any political stature in the movement who could take his place. O'Brady, the president of Sinn Fein, showed none of O'Connell's flare for publicity, nor did he exhibit any political leadership at all. He performed badly in public and was an uninspired speaker. With O'Connell gone, the Provisionals began to drift rudderless.

Twomey, the militant Belfast chief of staff, had agreed to the cease-fire for mostly tactical reasons. But he remained as always very much a background figure concerned with the military and tactical matters; he showed little or no political leadership. The cease-fire was putting strains on the Provisionals, caused partly by the fact that the organization was an amalgam of different political tendencies. The pro-O'Connell tendency was politically "moderate," seeking to establish the Provisionals as a political force in Northern Ireland. The other tendency was more militant, left-wing, and throughout the cease-fire period, increasingly anxious and wary of the way the movement was going. There was talk of splinters and factions; left-wing activists in Belfast did resign.

They were alarmed at what was happening in the city. The Provisionals, no longer under pressure from the British, began to develop economic interests in the west Belfast area, where they were soon running drinking clubs, taxi services, garages, cooperative shops and stores (these were the brain children of Seamus Loughran), and housing allocation in the large, overcrowded housing estates. The latter were under the control of a man the English papers dubbed "the Godfather." He soon acquired a rather unsavory reputation for putting his friends into houses that were needed by more deserving families.

What was happening to the Provisionals might be judged from an incident in the fall of 1975 that involved "the Godfather."

My mother and father had been seeking a larger, three-bedroom house for about fifteen years to accommodate their family. There were two of my sisters, one with her husband, and a boy still at home. They shared a two-bedroom house. Although my married sister was far gone in pregnancy, they were unable to find a place of their own. The Housing Authority, aware of the housing chaos in west Belfast, told my mother that if a house became available in her street, then the only way to acquire it was to squat. Because of her long-standing efforts, the Authority assured her that they would legalize her occupation of the house. When one house did become empty my parents, their children, and son-in-law did so, only to be informed that the house had already been allocated—by the local Provisional IRA leader. He arrived with six teen-agers and told them to get out. When asked for an explanation he informed them that the Provisionals had their own housing list and that the house was already allocated to somebody else whose name was on this list. The list, of course, was not a public one, and it was never produced. My mother and father at first refused to go. Attempts were made through the night to contact the Provisional leadership in order to register protest and ask for their case to be treated fairly. They stayed put through the night. Next morning they visited one of the much-vaunted truce monitoring or "incident" centers, where they were told an "enquiry" would be held. After waiting for over an hour, it became apparent that no such "enquiry" was to take place. Returning home they were again confronted by the Provisional leader and his gang, who became more threatening. They then decided to move back to their old, quite tiny house. There was no other recourse—to contact the police was unthinkable and would have been considered treasonous. In such situations ordinary people are powerless. (Two years later the Provisional leader involved in the eviction was shot dead near the drinking club he ran. He died in what are known in Northern Ireland as "disputed circumstances." The Provisionals alleged he was felled by an army sniper as he left the club late one night. The army denies this and claims it was an internal killing. All that is definitely known is that it occurred during a period when the IRA was undergoing a reorganization that some say involved the purging of "gangster" elements. Since his killing, his name has not appeared on the yearly "Roll of Honour" published every Easter to acknowledge IRA or Sinn Fein members killed by the security forces. This would tend to substantiate the army's claim that his death was the result of an internecine struggle.)

This kind of behavior was hardly a good advertisement for the new Ireland of the Provisional IRA. There were other rumors of growing corruption and gangsterism throughout 1975, until it seemed that the guerrillas were turning into a local mafia.

Unfortunately, though the aggressive campaign against the army was suspended, the violence did not cease. In fact, in some ways it grew worse. The UDA and UVF, angry at what they thought was another British compromise with republicans, stepped up their sectarian assassination campaign. But this time murders of Catholics were revenged on Protestants by the Provisionals and other breakaway republican groups. Soon a vicious "tit-for-tat" pattern emerged, in which more civilian lives were lost than at any other time during the present emergency.

A foretaste of what was to come emerged in late 1974. An outbreak of sectarian violence from the UDA in north Belfast was met by a ruthless series of retaliations, in which for the first time more Protestants were killed than Catholics. The republicans retaliated throughout 1975 and 1976. Of course, as with the English bombing campaign, the Provisional IRA did not publicly acknowledge its involvement for some time. After all, theoretically, Irish republicanism is nonsectarian, having been founded by people like the eighteenth-century Presbyterian Wolfe Tone. But in April 1975 the Army Council did issue a statement that hinted at least at Provisional responsibility for sectarian killings. It said, "The action of IRA units will be related to the level of violence and hostile activity by crown and sectarian forces," the latter being obviously the Protestant paramilitary groups.

The first clear indication of how deeply the IRA was involved in

The funeral of Belfast Provisional spokeswoman Maire Drumm, who was assassinated by a squad of UDA/UVF gunmen in her hospital bed in north Belfast on October 28, 1976. Her husband Jimmy, on right, shoulders the coffin while a Provisional IRA guard of honor fires a volley over it as part of the ritual of republican funerals. Jimmy Drumm, like his murdered wife, was a long-time Belfast republican and was one of the old IRA who joined the Provisionals after the split in late 1969.

sectarian retaliation came on June 4, 1975. A man called Francis
Jordan was shot dead by British soldiers as he attempted to plant
a bomb at a Protestant bar in Bessbrook, County Armagh. A few
days later a notice appeared in an IRA newspaper claiming Jordan
as a "Captain" in the Provisionals and stating that he had been
"killed on active service." It was the first public acknowledgment
that Provisional IRA men were engaged in sectarian attacks. Six
months later an IRA gunman, James McGrillen, was shot dead by
soldiers on the fringe of a loyalist area near the Catholic development of Ballymurphy just after he had opened fire on a group of
Protestant teen-agers. McGrillen was given full honors as an IRA
hero, even though it was difficult to make claims that he was killed
while engaged in any legitimate "freedom" struggle.

The Provisionals' sectarian activities reached their horrifying
peak in early 1976. The Protestant UVF, now as fully active as the
more violent UDA, killed five Catholics one night in the remote
area of South Armagh, traditionally an IRA stronghold. The next
day a squad of Provisionals stopped a van carrying Protestant
workers to their jobs, lined them up alongside the narrow roadway,
and mowed them down at point blank range with automatic weapons. They murdered ten men within as many seconds. Afterwards
republicans tried to justify the killings by saying that it stopped further sectarian attacks on Catholics in the area. But this cessation of
paramilitary violence had perhaps more to do with the fact that the
British flooded the South Armagh district with soldiers, including
units of the elite Special Air Service (SAS), undercover troops who
engaged in sometimes controversial actions.

The massacre of the workmen shocked and horrified the Catholic
population as much as it stunned the Protestants. So long the victims of sectarian violence themselves, Catholics believed that their
cause was a legitimate one, even though they might not support the
methods chosen by the Provisional IRA to press it. But atrocities
such as the murder of the ten Protestant workmen undermined the
moral position of the minority by exposing those who claimed to be
fighting on their behalf as prepared to use methods as vicious and
indiscriminate as those used by the loyalist sectarian assassins.

The erosion of the Provisionals' moral base for their campaign
continued throughout the cease-fire period. In late 1975 it proceeded even more rapidly—there was a violent outbreak of feuding between the Official IRA and the Provisionals. Eleven people were

murdered in as many days by both factions, including a seven-year-old girl. Eileen Kelly was shot in the back by Provisional gunmen who burst into her home and tried to shoot her father, who escaped. The Officials proved as ruthless and callous. Among their victims was Owen McVeigh, a man with no connection with the Provisional IRA. Official IRA gunmen shot him in the head as he lay, already wounded, in front of his young daughter. One of the killers was heard to shout as he raced from the house, "We went to the wrong house!"

Rory O'Brady was dispatched north to explain what was going on to an angry Catholic population, sick to death of murder and weary of republican rhetoric. He apologized for the murder of Eileen Kelly but could do no more than justify the Provisionals' violence against the Officials by accusing the latter of being Communists and gangsters. It was a truly pathetic performance and only further discredited O'Brady and his politics. At the end of 1975 the British government could with justification claim that what the security forces had to deal with was no longer an armed, politically motivated insurrection but sheer gangsterism.

Support for the IRA reached an all-time low in the ghettos. There was yet a further blow to morale; it concerned the failure of the guerrillas to get back on a war footing. Contact with British officials was broken off by the beginning of 1976. The movement began gearing itself up for resumption of the hostilities only to find that many of its operations, particularly those staged by the Andersonstown units in west Belfast, were constantly preempted by the British army. Dozens of volunteers were picked up en route to bombing missions. It soon became obvious that the successes of the security forces had something to do with informers. A lot of intelligence was being garnered by the authorities. It was eventually established that a high-ranking Belfast Provisional was the source. He was subsequently "executed" outside Belfast, and the killing was made to look like a suicide.

Beset by informers, compromised by corruption, its energies spent in sectarian attacks and internecine feuds, the Provisional movement looked as if it might disintegrate. But it survived. Part of the reason was the nature of the Northern Ireland situation itself and the continuing failure of the British government to find a political solution. As long as the British were there, an armed republican guerrilla group would be able to justify its existence. There was also a successful reform effort mounted in 1977, which helped extricate the Provisionals from the confusion of the mid-seventies. The third stage of development of the Provisional IRA involved the transformation of the movement from a loosely knit paramilitary group into a more secretive, cellular guerrilla force capable of striking once again with deadly effect against the British security forces.

The reorganization began around the time Gerry Adams, the young Belfast left-wing activist jailed in 1973, and Ivor Bell, another leftist commander, were released from prison. It will be recalled that it was their removal from the scene that had allowed O'Connell to gain the upper hand. On their return they successfully counteracted his influence, and the Provisionals once more adopted a militant left-wing nationalism such as they had espoused briefly in 1973 and 1974. But more than this, they began the actual reshaping of the structure of the group.

The original organization of the IRA was on a neighborhood basis—the brigades, battalions, and companies recruited volunteers from the areas that the units covered. This helped fulfill the Provisionals' self-proclaimed role as a Catholic defense force, but it also meant that it became increasingly easy for the security forces to identify and isolate the source of any given operation. As the years passed, British intelligence built up a good picture of the IRA men in the different areas, so that if, say, the First Battalion based in Andersonstown claimed responsibility for a shooting, the army would have a list of activists in that area whom they would pick up and question. It made for bad security for the IRA.

On the other hand with the cell system (which the Official IRA had adopted in the early seventies), activists were brought in from different neighborhoods, organized according to expertise, and then disbanded when the operation was carried out until needed again. By 1978 the Provisionals were capable of mounting intense, if short-lived, offensives. In one month of that year they set off more explosions than in any similar time period since the crisis began.

Ironically, the most interesting view of the Provisional IRA as it moved into another decade came from a secret report drawn up by the man who later became the general commanding officer of the British forces in Northern Ireland, Brigadier Glover. Dated January 4, 1979, and entitled "Northern Ireland: Future Terrorist Trends," it gives a comprehensive analysis of the structure, manpower, resources, and the political options of the Provisionals. The document fell into guerrilla hands as it was en route from one army official to another. They immediately published extracts in their own newspapers, and complete copies of the document soon found their way into the hands of a few reporters.

The British army analysis begins by admitting:

> The Provisional leadership is deeply committed to a long campaign of attrition. The Provisional IRA (PIRA) has the dedication and the sinews of war to raise violence intermittently to at least the level of early 1978, certainly for the forseeable future. Even if "Peace" is restored, the motivation for politically inspired violence will remain. Arms will be readily available and there will be many who are able and willing to use them. Any peace will be superficial and brittle. A new campaign may erupt in the years ahead.

This, of course, contradicts the security forces' public statements, which always emphasize how weak the Provisionals are and how soon they will be beaten. It is not a comforting thought for any British government that its army will be embroiled in such a bloody and frustrating confrontation without any end in sight. Yet it is an assessment that carries the authority of the upper ranks of the army itself. The report goes on to say:

> In 1977 PIRA adopted the classic terrorist cellular organisation in response to their difficulties. . . . The Provisionals cannot attract the large numbers of active terrorists they had in 1972/73. But they no longer need them. PIRA's organisation is now such that a small number of activists can maintain a disproportionate level of violence. There is a substantial pool of young Fianna [junior IRA] aspirants, nurtured in a climate of violence, eagerly seeking promotion to full gun-carrying terrorist status and there is a steady release from the prisons of embittered and dedicated terrorists. Thus though PIRA may be hard hit by security force attrition from time to time, they will probably continue to have the manpower they need to sustain violence during the next five years.

It appears from the document that the army has a much higher opinion of the terrorists than ever admitted by British officials. Under the subheading "Rank and File Terrorist" we read:

> Our evidence of the calibre of rank and file terrorists does not support the view that they are merely mindless hooligans drawn from the un-

employed and unemployable. PIRA now trains and uses its members with some care. The Active Service Units (ASU's) are for the most part manned by terrorists tempered by up to ten years of operational experience.

The report describes accurately the social nature of the movement:

Leadership. PIRA is essentially a working class organisation based in the ghetto areas of the cities and in the poorer rural areas. Thus if members of the middle classes and graduates become more deeply involved they have to forfeit their life style. Many are also deterred by the Provisionals' muddled political thinking. Nevertheless there is a strata of intelligent, astute and experienced terrorists who provide the backbone of the organisation. Although there are only a few of these high grade terrorists there is always the possibility that a new charismatic leader may emerge who would transform PIRA yet again.

As for the immediate future, the report concludes with some foreboding:

Trend in Calibre. The mature terrorists, including for instance the leading bomb makers, are usually sufficiently cunning to avoid arrest. They are continually learning from mistakes and developing their expertise. We can therefore expect to see increased professionalism and the greater exploitation of modern technology for terrorist purposes.

The document also acknowledged that though the Provisionals did not have the kind of support they enjoyed during MacStiofain's tenure as chief of staff, there was enough tacit support to keep them going. And, the report correctly asserts, "The fear of a possible return to Protestant repression will underpin this kind of support for the Provisionals for many years to come. Loyalist action could quickly awaken it to a much more volatile level."

The document shows that the British have grasped clearly the social nature of the Provisionals, as well as understanding that the key to success or failure in this campaign is in Belfast: "A further influencing factor is that the PIRA leadership appreciate that their campaign will be won or lost in Belfast. Although operations elsewhere are important, and in the border area easier to achieve, success in Belfast is critical." This is well put: the difference between the current IRA campaign and that of 1956–62 or the earlier outbreaks of republican violence is the control the Provisionals have gained in the slums and ghettos of the state's capital. A failure to achieve this in the 1956–62 offensive rendered it peripheral and finally futile. This would happen again if the British managed to make operations in the city impossible and if the terrorists lost all support among the Catholics there. However spectacular the Provisionals' attacks might prove in the remoter areas of Northern Ireland, they would reduce the movement to another "border war," which the British would find easier to contain and which would be politically less embarrassing.

The report outlines estimates by British intelligence of the structure of the guerrilla organization. They are fairly accurate by all accounts. The estimate is that as of 1979 the Provisionals had about five hundred full-time activists, armed and well trained, in Northern Ireland. (This again contrasts sharply with the public estimates of IRA strength, which the British have always given in much lower numbers than this.)

The active service units are under the control of the Northern Command, which is currently led by a Belfast Provisional. His units are supplied by the general headquarters (GHQ) based in Dublin. GHQ is responsible for provisioning the guerrillas with money, arms, and explosives. It is mainly controlled by 1940s republicans too old for active service in the North. The overall commanding body of the Provisionals is the Provisional Army Council (PAC). Its seven-member body is also based in Dublin. The head of the council is the chief of staff, who until recently was Seamus Twomey. (He was arrested in 1978 by the Irish police and jailed.) The Army Council determines general policy and strategy. It has a direct link with the Provisionals' political wing, Sinn Fein—perhaps the weakest element of the whole organization. It has never been allowed to develop politically simply because it is completely subordinated to the military organization. Provisional Sinn Fein has always been something of a doormat for the IRA, and its weaknesses became glaringly obvious during the 1975 cease-fire period, when it failed utterly to make any political progress in the North in spite of the concessions won by the guerrillas. Currently, its president is Rory O'Brady. Its two current vice-presidents are Gerry Adams and David O'Connell, who give the party political balance and represent a conciliation of the main political trends within the whole Provisional movement.

The document gives a detailed breakdown, based on British intelligence estimates, of the arms supplies and the finances of the Provisionals. It calculates that "armed robbery within Ireland is almost certainly the greatest source of income for PIRA." The amount it provides is close to $1 million a year. This compares with an estimated total overseas contribution from organizations supporting the IRA of $250,000. Of that, the British claim, about $100,000 or more comes from the Irish Northern Aid (NORAID) in the United States, the biggest pro-IRA lobby in America. (They add though that "actual remittances" might be much greater than those registered on the books of NORAID.) The report claims that

> the largest item of expenditure is probably pay for the terrorists and for those who work full or part time for Provisional Sinn Fein (PSF). A report of June 1978 indicates that normal terrorist pay is now 20 pounds [about $44] per man (as supplement to the dole) [welfare]. We estimate that some 250 people would draw this and perhaps 60 would get 40 pounds [$88] per week.

This comes to about $840,000 per year. To this has to be added the expenditure on the families of imprisoned IRA members, each of which receives a weekly sum of about $45. This accounts for $400,000 or so per year. The totals—including money for travelling and other expenses—add up to an overall yearly expense for the Provisional IRA of 780,000 pounds, or about 1.8 million dollars. When this is subtracted from their estimated yearly income of almost 950,000 pounds, approximately 2.2 million dollars, it leaves them with 170,000 pounds, or about $400,000 to spend on arms.

As for weapons, the British estimate that the Provisionals are continually able to increase their number of hand guns, sub-machine guns, and rifles of different kinds to offset what the security forces are able to recover in raids and arrests. After giving the figures for the different kinds of small guns used by the IRA, there is a note which adds, "Estimate (1) is based on known receipts by PIRA and forensic knowledge of weapons used by PIRA but not recovered. Their actual holdings are probably some five times greater." This would mean that as of March 1978 they possessed approximately four thousand small arms weapons—or eight guns for every activist in Northern Ireland. The Provisionals' main weapon is still, according to the British, the armalite, a light, highly porta-ble, easily concealed combat rifle effective at ranges up to one hun-dred fifty meters. Since the early seventies the Provisionals have been receiving quantities of these guns mainly from the United States. They are used in street ambushes, sniping attacks, and even assassinations. Among the other more recently acquired weapons are M60s. These American-made heavy general-purpose machine guns are capable of shooting down a helicopter. The Provisionals are believed to have about five of them. They regard them as some-thing of a prestige weapon, one which made its destructive debut in the border area of South Armagh and in Belfast. In the South Armagh village of Crossmaglen in late 1979 the Provisionals killed three soldiers in one burst from an M60 they had placed in a hi-jacked van. Use of the M60 in Belfast gives some idea of the kind of tactics the guerrillas have evolved to cope with a hit-and-run war in an ever more heavily patrolled city. In early 1980 the Provision-als took over a house at the junction of the Falls Road and the Whiterock Road, which runs by the Ballymurphy housing develop-ment, an IRA stronghold. They held a couple and their four young children hostage for two hours while waiting for a patrol from the Duke of Wellington's Regiment stationed on the Whiterock Road to come into view. As it was moving along the Whiterock Road, the Provisionals opened fire on it with the M60, killing Private Errol Pryce, a twenty-one-year-old bachelor from Sheffield in the north of England. The patrol returned fire, and in the exchange several civilians were wounded. The terrorists escaped in spite of being within yards of a large army base and in an area that was saturated with troops. The aftermath of the killing was typical of such inci-dents, with local people claiming that the army "went on the ram-page," threatening and abusing everyone in sight, and the army strenuously denying it.

All such attacks do not end so happily for the guerrillas. Belfast is now a city saturated not only with uniformed patrols but with un-dercover British soldiers in plain clothes who only distinguish them-selves by putting on an orange armband when there is trouble. (Orange, the color of all loyalist insignia, is not the most tactful one to choose under the circumstances.) The British introduced plain-clothes patrols early on in the campaign. But in recent years they have come to rely on this disguised surveillance much more, as an incident that occurred in May 1980 reveals.

A plainclothes army patrol was driving along the Antrim Road in north Belfast, the scene of several M60 machine gun attacks, many sniping incidents, and multiple sectarian murders. It is always a potential trouble spot. The patrol became suspicious of activity around one corner house and decided to get out of the car to investigate. As they did so, the long barrel of an M60 was poked out from an upstairs window of the house in question. It opened fire on them, killing one of the soldiers, who fell dead within a few feet of a four-year-old girl. A shopkeeper who was nearby described what happened:

> I heard a burst of gunfire—there must have been 80 or 100 shots. I went out of the shop and there was a man lying dead on the ground. Four men wearing orange armbands jumped out of a Ford car and some of them collected guns from the boot [trunk]. A second car arrived on the scene containing four more men who were also wearing orange armbands. These soldiers went to the back of the house as uniformed police and soldiers arrived at the scene. It was chaotic. There seemed to be bullets flying everywhere and these boys in the orange armbands seemed to be all over the place. They were firing at the house and the women and children on the street didn't know where to run for safety. A few minutes later they took out one man whose head was bleeding rather badly. They marched him to a Ford Cortina and drove off.

The police recovered a small arsenal from the house, including the M60, the third one lost by the Provisionals to the security forces. It could be seen by passersby, who had to duck for cover, protruding from the upstairs window of the bullet-peppered house. Four men were arrested at the scene, and later the Provisionals claimed responsibility for the death of the soldier.

Setbacks such as this will not deter the Provisional IRA. As the British army document noted, they are committed to a long and bitter guerrilla war, which they hope will achieve their socialist republic. The Provisionals' continued capacity to strike with devastating effect was shown in late August 1979. On the 27th of that month, Lord Mountbatten, the Earl of Burma and first cousin to Queen Elizabeth II, was sailing his boat, *The Shadow,* in Donegal Bay, not far from his summer home of thirty years, Classiebawn Castle. On the boat with him were Paul Maxwell, a fifteen-year-old local boy who had been hired to crew *The Shadow;* Lady Patricia Bradbourne, Mountbatten's daughter; and her husband, Lord John

Bradbourne. Along with them were their twin fourteen-year-old sons, Nicholas and Timothy, and their grandmother, Dowager Lady Bradbourne. As *The Shadow* paused to haul in a lobster pot there was a terrific explosion on or near the boat. Andrew McClenaghan, sailing nearby at the time, said, "The boat just disintegrated. From where we were sitting fishing, it looked as if someone had just thrown a huge box of matches into the air."

The Earl of Burma, Dowager Lady Bradbourne, Paul Maxwell, and Nicholas Bradbourne were killed. The Provisional IRA had delivered a blow right to the heart of the English monarchy itself.

Before that day had ended, however, there were more, equally horrifying deaths. On the other side of Ireland, near the quiet little village of Warrenpoint at the head of Carlingford Lough, the guerrillas had set up another booby-trap ambush, one which would prove to be the most bloody so far in their history. Seven hours after the Mountbatten killings, a convoy of British paratroopers was rolling down the quiet country road under the shadow of the beautiful domes of the Mourne Mountains. The border with the Irish Republic was a short distance across the lough. Reporter John Hamill, writing in the *Rolling Stone,* described what then took place:

The Land Rover passed in front of a parked hay lorry, followed by one of the trucks. Suddenly, the earth shudders violently. The truck is lifted and bounced, landing on its side with a screech like some great gored metal animal. The second truck turns over in the middle of the road. Both are ablaze. Pieces of paratroopers are scattered on the road, blasted into the trees, caught in the hedges. The smell of gasoline, burned flesh and explosives assaults the first passing motorists. . . . One soldier stumbles in a circle, on fire, then sits down and dies. "Help me . . . help me . . . help me" begs a soldier, running to a motorist. . . . Radios squawk and Major Peter Fursman, 35, rallies his men and leads them at a run to an abandoned lodge 200 yards down the road, leaving behind a litter of weapons, splintered friends and burning vehicles. Fursman draws his troops into a dazed semicircle behind the granite gatepost and shouts into a field radio for a "quick reaction group."

Within minutes the whirr of three helicopters—troop carriers—are heard. White smoke from the cooling vehicles is blown away as Fursman directs Lieutenant Colonel David Blair's lead chopper, loaded with a relief column of the Queen's Own Highlanders, onto the road.

Another button is squeezed as Blair and his radioman step from the chopper. The gatepost roars and a monsoon of granite slivers rips through the paratrooopers. Fursman disintegrates. Blair is killed two steps into his relief mission as nine more paratroopers are splashed into fleshy chunks across the road. The screaming and the fire begin again.

Eighteen British soldiers died in the double ambush. An English tourist, the son of a Buckingham Palace coachman, was shot dead by soldiers who opened fire on him as he stood on the other side of the lough transfixed by the bloody spectacle.

The soldiers' deaths were to some extent overshadowed by the widespread rage and denunciations at the killings in Donegal Bay. Mountbatten was universally loved by the English and close to the royal family not only as a blood relation but as a respected adviser. The Irish were disgusted by his death, but as always in Ireland when the Provisionals carry out a sensational attack, there is ambivalence about condemning it utterly.

The Provisionals regarded the 27th of August 1979 as one of their "best" efforts, stunning proof to the world that after a decade of guerrilla war, imprisonment, internment—after every legal means the government has been able to use to contain and beat them—they could still mount such operations. In Belfast a Provisional spokesman gave an insight into their attitude towards the Mountbatten killing. He received a phone call from a New Zealand newspaper and was asked, "Why did you kill that harmless old man?" The Provisional answered, "Why are you calling me from New Zealand?"

By 1980, the left-wing Belfast leadership had the upper hand in the movement. The Provisionals have now decisively rejected any rapprochement with those seeking some sort of Ulster nationalist solution, which lately the UDA has been advocating (see Chapter 5). O'Connell, now politically active again as a vice-president of Provisional Sinn Fein, has had to modify his talk of a "Greater Ulster"—which in some ways resembles the UDA's concept—and bow to the program of his more militant colleagues.

In an interview in the Dublin magazine *Magill* given in the summer of 1978, a high-ranking Provisional from Belfast said, "The IRA is absolutely opposed to any suggestion of any negotiated independence for the six counties. It is not the solution to the Irish problem because it does not break the back of British imperialism in Ireland. It would maintain loyalist supremacy and would be a complete block to a socialist republic."

The spokesman admitted that the ten years and more of bloodshed had achieved "virtually nothing," yet justified the continuation of the Provisionals' violence in a typically republican mode. He said, "We can't give up now and admit that the men and women we sent to their graves died for nothing. The struggle must continue until victory is achieved, and we are determined to do that." He added, "There will be many more funerals."

Patrick Pearse, one of the leaders of the 1916 rebellion in Dublin, subsequently executed by a British firing squad, is often quoted by the Provisionals. He once said, referring to another generation of Irish martyrs in the struggle against the British, "While Ireland holds these graves, Ireland unfree will never be at peace." It has become the IRA's most emotive slogan—an overt appeal to the dead to justify the continued sacrifice of the living. The Irish are known for their open acceptance of death and their deep attachment to the dead. When spring comes they flock to the cemeteries to tend the graves of their relatives. It is more popular than going to the parks. They weed out the remnants of winter, clean off the rust from the graves' railings and repaint them, usually a bright silver. On a Sunday afternoon the whole family goes along with sandwiches wrapped in paper and bottles of soda and picnic beside their dead. The cult of the martyr is a corruption of this acceptance of death, an otherwise healthy thing. It is a cult which has made people a slave to sacrifice. The movement espousing it has in its turn helped create a society in which the living are consoled by the dead, and death becomes the motivation for more deaths.

7

Police Story

*N*o one would have thought there was a war going on. Inside the plush lounge of the suburban Belfast hotel young couples, well dressed and relaxed, drank by the long marbled bar. One wall was covered with gilt-edged mirrors, and the carpets sank softly underfoot. The glass-topped tables were clean; there was a large fireplace at one end of the lounge and an impressive stairway leading to a ballroom. It was early evening; only one man sat by a table. He was dark-haired with a thin mustache and wore a neat tweed jacket. He looked up impulsively at me as I walked into the lounge; it took him only a split second to realize who I was.

Detective Sergeant Miller was sitting with his large black folder on the glass-topped table before him. It was shut. He was sipping a whiskey. I asked him what it was and hailed another round of the same. He looked occasionally at the young suburbanites by the bar as they drank, talked, and flirted. They seemed to him an unwelcome distraction. He smiled a little as he overheard a young man's story about his problems at a checkpoint—that's why he was late, he explained to his date. Detective Sergeant Miller looked away, his gaze returning as it always did to the black shut folder in front of him. He seemed to be thinking that if only they could see what was in this, it would put them off their drink.

Ten years ago Miller could probably have popped into his local pub on the Catholic New Lodge Road near his old police station for a drink without anyone paying attention to him. He was on speaking terms with most of the barmen. In fact, he saw to it that his favorite barman was immediately released after he had been picked up during the initial internment swoop on the morning of August 9, 1971. "I was disgusted and amazed," Miller told me while complaining about the failure of intelligence he claims led to the disastrous mistakes made during that operation. "I was also embarrassed. I walked into the interrogation room in Girdwood Barracks and found my bloody friend sitting at the other side of the table staring at me. I said, 'What are you doing here?' He said, 'How the f— do I know?' "

Now, as a member of the Royal Ulster Constabulary, there were few places he could go in Belfast where he would feel safe. There were definitely none on the New Lodge Road—or in any other Catholic area—and increasingly few in loyalist districts as well. The Provisional IRA, which since 1970 has killed over one hundred of his colleagues, would regard him as a prime target. Apart from being a policeman, Miller had since 1975 been in charge of the intelligence unit of the special antiterrorist squad, the innocuously named Regional Crime Squad. The squad was set up, partly at his suggestion, specifically to break the power of the Northern Ireland paramilitary gangs. Its success in doing so has been matched only by the allegations of brutality made by prisoners it has brought in for questioning, allegations which have haunted its progress for the last five years and prompted two full-scale inquiries into its methods.

When I brought the drinks to the table, he was resting his elbows on the folder. "So, we were talking about McGurk's," he said softly, resuming a conversation we'd had earlier on the telephone. In December 1971 a rundown Catholic bar near the New Lodge Road was demolished by a bomb that killed fifteen men, women, and children—the highest number so far killed in any single explosion in Northern Ireland. At the time I spoke with him I was researching a book on Protestant terrorist violence, looking into the incident, which was then unsolved. Miller, whom I had already met once, agreed to fill me in on the details of the bombing and the progress of the investigation, in which he was playing a major role.

He lifted the folder. "Here, look at that," he said, handing it across the table to me. "That's what we have." I opened the black folder. It contained a series of colored photographs of the victims of the bombing, as well as other sections with photographs of people killed in different incidents. I turned page after page, victim after victim: old men and women, a young couple, a young boy, a mother and her daughter who had just stopped into McGurk's to see the woman's husband after returning home from evening mass. Their talk about the coming Christmas was ended by a fifty-pound gel-ignite bomb left at the side entrance of the bar by a man in a long overcoat.

Miller watched me as I turned the pages, my eyes running quickly over the frightening, queer look of the last agonies of death, the rigid gestures on contours over which I was too afraid to pause for very long. I didn't really want to look. A murderer has a dreadful intimacy with his victim, an intimacy that is strangely shared by policeman, and reporter, who are often made privy to the last moments of the victim's life. It is an intimacy I never wanted and found distasteful. The last moments of anyone's life should only be shared by those closest to that person. That is one reason why murder is such a gross violation, because it intrudes so violently on the infrangible. I passed the folder back to Miller.

Because he was no longer capable of being shocked himself, he wanted to see my shock, perhaps to reassure him that people were still capable of such response. He watched me for a moment, then opened the folder, glancing at page after page of murder scenes: a soldier with his head split in two by a high-velocity bullet; a Catholic woman whose body was cratered with ugly red holes, the victim of a UDA assassination, sprawled over a chair in a taxi waiting room.

He paused, looked up at the soothing surroundings as if it were another world, and sat back in his seat. He took another sip of whiskey and said, "I believe it was the UVF."

"That did McGurk's?"

The remains of McGurk's Pub on North Queen Street, north Belfast, after a gelignite bomb leveled it on the evening of December 4, 1971, killing fifteen Catholics. During the attempted rescue operations Provisional IRA gunmen killed a British major not far from the devastated bar. Six years later, after much dispute as to who was responsible, a Protestant paramilitary member was sentenced to life in prison for causing the explosion.

"Aye."

"But at the time—1971—the UVF wasn't active," I added after a moment's thought.

"Well, son, you might be right—they didn't call themselves that—but we think whoever did it is now operating in the UVF. At the time, though, the only really active loyalist gang called itself the Woodvale Defence Association."

He seemed weary of labels. I sounded pedantic. However, I needed to get the matter of which organization was responsible cleared up for my research. I persisted. "The Woodvale Defence Association was the founding faction of the UDA," I said. "It was one of the first of the vigilante groups to take to violence and assassination." He nodded in agreement. But his eyes looked past me towards the door to the lounge where they rested, scrutinizing a newcomer to the bar. "There was a lot of confusion about McGurk's after the explosion," I said. "The Provisionals were blamed; British undercover squads as well . . ."

He smiled at me rather indulgently and replied with soft but emphatic speech. "That's politics, son. I deal with the end result, the dead body."

Like most policemen, his experience of "politics" is as far from the abstract theory behind the act of violence as it is possible to get. For him there seemed to be only the overwhelming reality of the end result. Again he paused and looked around him at the bar, as if comparing it in his mind to the dingy little room of McGurk's. He explained to me what happened that night. What he told me was this:

Everything was normal for a Saturday night, and the thirty people who were drinking that December 4th were chatting about the coming holidays, the daily violence, their lives that had to be conducted in the midst of death. Most were in their mid-forties or older. Upstairs in the apartment above the bar, where the owners lived, a young boy, Jimmy Cromis, was playing with one of the owner's children. Nobody noticed any strangers in the bar. Shortly before 8:45, Mrs. McGurk came in with her young daughter to talk to her husband, who was serving behind the bar. They were returning home from evening mass at the local church down the road a little. They were standing near the side entrance. At 8:45 P.M. a Mr. James Reid was talking to Mr. McGurk when another one of his customers, sixty-two-year-old Malachy McLaughlin, shouted to him, "Someone has put a stink bomb in here!" Those were the last words that many of the drinkers were ever to hear.

What the customer had smelled was the burning fuse of a large bomb packed into a parcel and left at the bar's side entrance. Seconds later there was a blinding flash and McGurk's pub collapsed in a cloud of crumbling masonry. By the end of the night fifteen bodies had been dug from the ruins. Ireland was stunned.

"McGurk's was just a wee local for the old ones and their wives. We think the bombers were aiming at another bar, one run by the IRA farther down the road. They couldn't make it in time and left the bomb at the first pub they came to. That was McGurk's. Most of the victims died of burns and suffocation. When the pub collapsed the gas mains exploded. Only two or three were mutilated by the bomb blast. See?" I saw and looked away. "That wee fella Cromis who died upstairs was completely unmarked. The doctors said he died of shock. The wee girl McGurk and her mother were killed, but the da survived. That's the way it goes."

He went on to explain why the controversy had arisen as to who was responsible. In a frantic effort to get at the victims the police brought in a heavy bulldozer and shifted most of the rubble to a site across the street. But in doing so they destroyed vital evidence as to where exactly the bomb had been placed. Because of this forensics experts were not able to establish accurately whether the bomb had gone off inside the pub or outside, which in turn fueled the widespread speculation as to who had planted the bomb. The Unionists immediately stated that it was a Provisional IRA bomb that went off prematurely when being made up inside the bar. The Provisionals retaliated by claiming it was the work of British army undercover squads. The controversy continued for six years.

"I was in the New Lodge station at the time. I helped dig the bodies out," Miller resumed. "PIRA killed the military O.C. [officer in command] who was directing traffic and rescue operations at the time. That didn't help—you'd have thought they'd have held off. After all, it was their people trapped in there. Afterwards I went to the morgue with the bodies to wait for the relatives to come and identify them. I sat there all night. It was a damp, cold winter's night, if I remember rightly."

"How did you pass the time?" I asked him.

"I ate fish and chips mostly," he answered matter-of-factly.

After about an hour Miller got up to leave. I walked him to the car park outside the hotel, which was sealed off by a ring of security gates. He walked slowly across to his car, looking from side to side. When he reached his car he looked under it, inspecting the back and front very carefully. Many policemen have been killed by booby-trapped cars. He took a different route home every night to the quiet north Belfast suburb where he lived. Even there though, living with anonymity, he was not safe. A colleague's home in a nearby area had been bombed by the Provisionals on two occasions. The second time a woman visitor whose husband, another policeman, had been murdered recently by the IRA, was injured in the explosion.

Miller's folder was under his arm. He told me he took it everywhere he went. It was almost as if he felt the need to shock people with the stark realities of violent death in Northern Ireland. "People get too smug," he said to me as he climbed into his automobile and looked over at the hotel we had just left. He pondered something for a moment and then added in weary tones, "But what can you do?" It was a rhetorical question. He told me to call him to let him know how my research was going and drove off towards the hotel gate.

When I spoke to Miller for the last time, in 1977, he had suspects. He was working all out on another bombing when by accident the McGurk's killings came up. Someone talked, a name was mentioned. By late 1977 a man was arrested and charged with the mass murder. One year later he was convicted and sent to prison for the rest of his life.

Detective Sergeant Miller was not an ordinary RUC man. He was English, for one, and he was a strictly "professional" cop, a kind the RUC needs more of. As a body it has been plagued since its formation in 1922 with problems that stem directly from its relationship to the state of Northern Ireland. It was largely because of these problems that the current crisis there was precipitated in the first place. It was the inability of the police to deal with the rising violence in 1969 without adding to it that forced the British government to send in its troops. Subsequent inquiries set up by the Unionists themselves—under pressure from Westminster, of course—concluded that the RUC had behaved irresponsibly during the tense and disruptive days of 1969. Recommendations in the fall of that year led to the disarming of the police and the disbandment of its auxiliary wing, the B-Specials. An English officer was put in charge of the force, and its uniform was even changed, from a deep blue to a bottle green.

The attempt to "civilianize" the RUC failed for reasons that had more to do with the nature of Northern Ireland than with the caliber of the men who served in it. The RUC was never intended to be a normal police force on the lines, say, of the English constabulary. It was first and foremost the front-line defense force of the Northern Ireland government. Unlike police forces throughout the rest of the United Kingdom, the RUC was heavily armed. It was mainly recruited from one section of the community, the Protestant-loyalist section. Catholics never made up more than 10 percent of its total membership. Catholics never accepted it as their police force. Even during the halcyon days of Terence O'Neill in the mid-sixties, there was a residual hostility and resentment for the police, whom the Catholics saw as a kind of occupying army in their ghettos. When the collapse came in 1969, the RUC was expelled from the Catholic areas and has since been able to reenter them only with great danger and difficulty. The events of those days of civil riots and disruptions merely crystallized a state of affairs that had always existed in Northern Ireland, where the police were seen as the instrument of a government not acceptable to a large minority of the people.

The 1969 debacle was the first of several bad blows to the morale of the RUC. Expelled from whole areas, disarmed, criticized by government inquiries, the police were in no position to resume the role of "peace keepers." Their reputation sank still further during the early years of the 1970s.

When the Conservative Party came to power in 1970 and the confrontation between the Catholic population and the security forces moved into the guerrilla war stage, the police were pushed farther into the background; the army's role became increasingly important. What major responsibilities they were given, that of assisting in the compiling of lists of men to be interned without trial on August 9, 1971, led to greater discredit. The political section of the RUC, the Special Branch, proved that its sources and its information were out of date and inadequate. The resulting arrest operation was dogged by this—the wrong men were arrested, the wrong houses were raided, and the hard-core leadership of the Provisional IRA easily evaded the net that was so clumsily thrown around the Catholic ghettos. What followed brought the RUC under the unwelcome scrutiny of the inquiry set up by the European Court for Human Rights at Strasbourg. Allegations of torture and ill-treatment of people arrested during the internment swoop and afterwards were the first of many to dog the efforts of the RUC and embarrass its political masters in Stormont and Westminster. The gap between the police and the Catholic community grew ever wider and made the RUC's job increasingly difficult as information about the Provisionals became harder to get. The very use of internment made normal police work redundant and undermined the very foundations of investigation.

Morale continued to slump in 1972, with the emergence of the loyalist assassination squads, which the police seemed completely unable to contain. By the end of the year the RUC's detection rate dropped to 21 percent—down 10 percent from the previous year. During the same period indictable crimes rose by 16.4 percent. This meant that though nearly two hundred people were murdered (including members of the security forces) between August and December 1972, only thirteen people were charged with murder.

The successes of the loyalist gangs alienated Catholics even more. It was believed that the assassins and the police were in collusion, or that the police simply did not want to act against fellow Protestants. The Conservative government was pressing ahead with its policy of military confrontation with the Provisionals and gave little thought to the difficulties of rehabilitating the RUC in the eyes of the minority. But this was the ultimate security problem, one which the activity and presence of the army only postponed.

The RUC has always been at the center of the British government's security dilemma; the force's fortunes are a direct reflection of Westminster's overall political approach. With the Conservatives, who handled the Northern Ireland crisis as a colonial problem, the emphasis was on the army. The Conservative Party tended toward the recognition that they were confronted by a guerrilla war that could only be dealt with effectively by the military. As a result, the RUC became more and more redundant. However, with the coming back to power of a new Labour administration in 1974, there was a decided change of direction in British policy, one which put greater responsibility on the police force.

Being a party supposedly based on Socialist principles, the Labour Party could hardly admit that the war in Northern Ireland was colonial in nature. The key concepts, therefore, in the Labour government's approach to the problem were "Ulsterization" and "criminalization." While out of office, Labour Party leader Harold Wilson developed an overall scheme for putting these ideas into operation. In 1971 he announced his "15-Point Plan" for a British withdrawal. One important aspect of this plan was the ending of internment. It stressed that "all against whom criminal charges were preferred would be subject to normal criminal procedures." Wilson had previously described internment as a "recruiting sergeant for the IRA" and recognized the debilitating effect it had on police work, because it avoided the need to build up cases to enable the police to bring all those charged to court.

With Labour back in power the gradual phase-out of internment began in late 1974. It was part of the cease-fire deal the Provisionals worked out with the British, but even after that understanding came to an end, in mid-1975 or thereabouts, the Labour administration continued its policy of releasing all those being held without trial. Labour's attitude toward internment was based not only on pragmatic objections as to its effects on police work, but on the guiding principle that the Northern Ireland crisis could only be handled successfully if the paramilitaries' claims to be fighting a "political" war were undermined—that was the meaning of "criminalization." This, Labour believed, would negate their support in the ghettos and allow the RUC to take on the job of defeating the terrorists. On the other hand, internment, by its very nature, was an obvious admission that the crisis was not an ordinary one caused by simple criminals, so it had to be removed before the emphasis on police work, the courts, and due process of law could be restored. A commission had already been set up under the previous Conservative government to look into the problems of processing cases of people charged with terrorist offenses.

The commission, chaired by Lord Diplock, published a report in December 1972. Among its recommendations was that if the use of internment and detention was to be avoided, then the only practical legal alternative would be trial by judge alone. Juries were too vulnerable to intimidation. The Diplock report dealt with the important subject of the admissibility of confessions by the accused as evidence of guilt. Under English common law, any statement made under coercion or threat of any kind is deemed inadmissible. The Diplock recommendations were not so stringent. They widened the admissibility of confessions as evidence to include any statements not made as a result of "inhuman or degrading treatment," in other words, any statement which was obtained without violating article 3 of the European Human Rights Convention, of which the United Kingdom was a signatory.

The major recommendations were incorporated the following year in the Emergency Provisions Act. The sections of the act relating to admissibility of statements as evidence give the police a much freer hand in the methods used to obtain them, and the non-jury courts more leeway in accepting them as proof of guilt. This became crucial for the reemergence of the RUC as an effective force. The British recognized that if the police were to contain the violence without the aid of internment, then it was of vital importance to allow them considerable leeway in getting convictions. Criminalization would only work if the police could show that it was able to succeed without resorting to such extralegal means as internment or detention without trial.

Another step towards the criminalization of the paramilitary organizations came with the ending of "Special Category Status," or political status, which the Conservative Secretary of State for Northern Ireland, William Whitelaw, had conceded to imprisoned members of the various paramilitary groups in the summer of 1972. (See chapter 6.)

Along with internment, political status, with its attendant concessions, was an open recognition that the violence of the Provisionals and other paramilitary groups was politically motivated, not "criminal" in the ordinary sense of the word. It was an admission that the Labour government was not prepared to make, publicly at any rate, and so political status was abolished shortly after internment's ending. Any person convicted of a terrorist offense after March 1976 was to be treated like an ordinary criminal. The Provisionals have tried to counter this move by refusing to wear prison clothes, do prison work, or—currently—clean out their cells (leading to most degrading conditions in which they live surrounded by their own excrement). They have also launched a campaign of assassination against prison officers. To date twenty have been murdered. After a hunger strike at the end of 1980, the British eventually made some concessions to the prisoners' demands.

Criminalization was the first move in the direction of "Ulsterization," which simply meant giving the Northern Ireland police the primary role in dealing with the violence. It was hoped that this would gradually lead to a reduction of British army commitments and even to eventual withdrawal. However, when Labour began this program, the RUC was still suspected—even hated—by the minority and still operating outside the ghettos, where the guerrillas held sway. Reforms were necessary. Labour had already implemented sweeping changes within the police in 1969. From 1974 onwards it continued those reforms, though in a less drastic and dramatic way.

After 1974 the policemen who tended to get promotion were those with neutral political backgrounds, that is, who did not come from the old Unionist–Orange Order club with which the police had too long been associated. The intention was to develop a professional, not overtly sectarian force that could operate against loyalist as well as republican terrorists and thus, in the long term, reassure the Catholics. The last two chief constables of the RUC, Kenneth Newman and Jack Hermon, have impeccably neutral political lineage. Hermon, who took over in late 1979, in fact was at one time something of a figure in the Lower Falls area, where he was stationed for some years. He gained a reputation there for being tough but professional, not by any means the archetypal loyalist intent on making things difficult for the minority. Even the local IRA leaders begrudgingly admitted that he was fair.

Other changes were instituted with Labour in power. One of the most significant involved Detective Sergeant Miller and the setting up of the Regional Crimes Squad. Previously the police had mainly relied on the work of the Special Branch to gather intelligence about subversives. But this intelligence was too often not coordinated with other branches of the force like the Criminal Investigation Department, whose responsibility it was to prepare the actual cases to be brought against suspected terrorists and to conduct interrogations. Miller had long advocated greater coordination between the different units within the RUC in order to rationalize its structure and make it more efficient. In July 1975, after a spate of particularly vicious sectarian murders by the Ulster Volunteer Force, the Labour Secretary of State for Northern Ireland, Merlyn Rees, ordered the establishment of such a coordinating body. It was at first known as the "A" Squad, and it was to pool the efforts of the Special Branch, the Criminal Investigation Department, and British army intelligence. Beginning with a small nucleus in 1975, it quickly developed into a force of over one hundred men that not only coordinated the work of different police branches, but also improved liaison between the different divisions based throughout Northern Ireland. Four Regional Crime Squad subdivisions were established: the Headquarters Crime Squad, the Belfast Regional Crime Squad, the Regional Crime Squad North, and the Regional Crime Squad South. Miller was put in charge of the "A" Squad's intelligence unit, based in RUC headquarters in south Belfast. In the unit, which is the brain of the Regional Crime Squad, are Special Branch officers, CID detectives, and British intelligence officers. All information gathered from these various branches of the security forces is pooled and now computerized to be made available to the squad.

The Regional Crime Squad's list of successes is impressive. Initially it scored more effectively against the various loyalist terrorist groups than against the Provisionals. Shortly after it was set up it cracked one of the most dangerous Protestant gangs in Northern Ireland. A UVF gang based in North Armagh had been largely responsible for a series of sectarian outrages between 1974 and 1975. These included a string of murders of local Catholics that had earned the area in which they occurred the name of "Murder Triangle." Between 1972 and 1975, thirty-four killings occurred here for which the UVF was mainly responsible. In August 1975 UVF terrorists stopped a van containing members of a popular Irish dance band, the Miami Showband, and lined them up along the side of the road while a gang member planted a bomb in the back of the vehicle. As he was doing so, it exploded, killing him and another UVF man. The remaining members of the gang machine-gunned the musicians, killing three of them. Within weeks the Regional Crime Squad (then still known as the "A" Squad) rounded up suspects. Successful charges were brought against two local Protestants, both former members of the security forces. Since then the UVF has been relatively inactive in the area it once terrorized.

Later that year the Regional Crime Squad delivered another severe blow to the UVF when it rounded up twenty-six members of that organization and charged them with a long list of crimes, including four murders. Subsequent convictions neutralized the UVF in one of their strongest areas, southeast Antrim, from where most of those arrested had come.

Already, however, there were signs of coming difficulties. Allegations of brutality were made when the Squad was investigating the Miami Showband killings—loyalists held for questioning claimed they were beaten and abused and spoke of the RUC in a way normally associated with nationalist protests. To ensure such assertions would not affect their prosecution of the southeast Antrim UVF men, the Squad members were scrupulously careful to record every interview they held with the suspects and to photograph them before and after each session of questioning.

Such precautions did not stop the allegations, at least from the Catholic nationalist community. In early 1977 the Regional Crime Squad conducted a large arrest operation in south Fermanagh near the border with the Irish Republic, where the Provisional IRA had recently carried out a series of bombings and shootings. Twelve suspects were taken to Castlereagh Holding Center in east Belfast for questioning. Shortly afterwards one of the men, a school teacher, gave an interview on BBC television. His allegations of mistreatment proved so serious as to provoke strong demands for an inquiry into police practices in the holding center. Castlereagh soon became the center of a growing controversy. The holding center is a large complex of huts surrounded by high barbed wire fences and strongly guarded by British soldiers. Inside are the interrogation rooms of the Criminal Investigation Department. Suspects are questioned by two officers at a time; although these are generally CID men, Special Branch officers are often present. The CID officers can be those attached to the local police division, or they can be from one of the four divisions of the Regional Crime Squad. As the resources of these units became greater, their part in interrogations became more and more important.

The twelve suspects from south Fermanagh alleged beatings, threats, and other forms of intimidation, which, they said, were used to try and force them to sign confessions of guilt. Their allegations were echoed by many others who had been questioned in Castlereagh. In the fall of 1977 a group of thirty lawyers involved in handling cases brought before the courts issued a statement which warned: ". . . ill-treatment of suspects by police officers, with the object of obtaining confessions, is now common practice, and . . . this most often, but not always, takes place at Castlereagh RUC station and other police stations throughout Northern Ireland."

As well as the flood of allegations about maltreatment, there were other factors causing concern in legal circles in Northern Ireland. One was the statistics relating to convictions. These showed that in 1976 out of twelve hundred or so cases brought before the courts, nine hundred convictions resulted. Eighty percent of these convictions were handed down on the basis of confessions. This compared with a figure of between 50 and 60 percent throughout the rest of the United Kingdom. The overall rate of conviction before the Diplock (nonjury) courts reached 94 percent of all cases with which they dealt by the fall of 1977!

Many lawyers found this a distressingly high figure and argued that the obvious dependence on confessions for convictions was undermining the whole legal system. Disquiet spread to the Police Authority, a body appointed to act as overseer of the force. Its legal adviser resigned, claiming that the abuse of prisoners was not being checked by RUC authorities and that allegations of brutality "stood unrefuted and without identifiable culprits."

In late 1977 the highly respected world human rights body Amnesty International sent a mission to Northern Ireland to investigate the allegations. It consisted of a Dutch lawyer, a Danish doctor, and a member of Amnesty International's international secretariat. They spent eight days interviewing individuals and organizations in Belfast and elsewhere. Most of those they spoke with were complainants, but the mission also met with high-ranking police officers, politicians, doctors, and lawyers. They spent several hours visiting Castlereagh Holding Center itself. They investigated allegations made by seventy-eight people who claimed to have been beaten and abused. The mission documented cases of women who alleged that their interrogators threatened them with rape, of men who claimed to have been beaten on the genitals, and prisoners forced to stand for prolonged periods against the wall (reminiscent of the "in-depth" methods of interrogation used in 1971—see chapter 3), choked, deprived of sleep, and threatened with assassination. Two people to whom the mission spoke alleged they had been hooded, and others complained that RUC officers told them they would be dropped in loyalist areas after their interrogation if they did not cooperate with the police.

Amnesty International's report was published in June 1978. Its conclusions were:

1. On the basis of the information available to it, Amnesty International believes that maltreatment of suspected terrorists by the RUC has taken place with sufficient frequency to warrant the establishment of a public inquiry to investigate it.

2. The evidence presented to the mission does not suggest that uniformed members of the RUC are involved in the alleged maltreatment.
3. The evidence presented to the mission suggests that legal provisions, which have eroded the rights of suspects held in connection with terrorist offences, have helped create the circumstances in which maltreatment of suspects has taken place.
4. The evidence presented to the mission suggests that the machinery for investigating complaints against the police of assault during interview is not adequate.

The report recommended that a public inquiry be set up with powers of reviewing the rules relating to interrogation and detention, the admissibility of statements, and the machinery for investigating complaints against the police. It also advocated that, pending the establishment of such an inquiry, steps should be taken immediately to protect suspects being interrogated by the RUC against possible maltreatment.

The report did note, however, that there were few complaints ever made against the uniformed branch of the RUC. Most allegations concerned the detective units. Ironically, of the one hundred and more deaths suffered by the police at the hands of the terrorists, the vast majority of them have been uniformed constables.

At the time the Amnesty report was being prepared for publication, the British government, under Labour Prime Minister James Callaghan, announced the setting up of its own inquiry—the third such set up by the British to investigate alleged violations of human rights since 1971. It was headed by Judge H. G. Bennett. The scope of the inquiry included police interrogation methods and the procedures for handling complaints against the RUC. However, the Bennett Committee did not undertake to look into the vital question of the use of section 81 of the Emergency Powers legislation relating to the admissibility of signed confessions as evidence. This was outside the terms under which the government established the committee. But the general conclusions published in the committee report of March 1979 substantiated the findings of Amnesty International. The report stated firmly, "Our own examination of medical evidence reveals cases in which injuries, whatever their precise cause, were not self-inflicted and were sustained in police custody." It recommended, among other things, the installation of closed circuit television cameras in all interview rooms used for interrogation. These, the report says, should be used by supervisory uniformed staff, with other monitors for senior uniformed police officers. It also stressed that the tendency to refuse admission of lawyers to see their clients while they were being held—a common complaint made by prisoners—had to be stopped immediately and that prisoners had to be given "an unconditional right of access to a solicitor [lawyer] after 48 hours," which is the period of time allowed under the Emergency Provisions Act before legal representation can be asked for.

The same month the report was published there was a disquieting indication of how strongly reforms within the RUC were needed. In March 1979 Dr. Robert Irwin, a doctor attached to Castlereagh Holding Center, resigned. He announced that he had treated dozens of injuries suffered by prisoners that could not possibly be self-inflicted, as the RUC claimed when accused of maltreatment. He pointed out that in one case a prisoner suffered a fractured eardrum, an injury which could not possibly have been self-inflicted because there is simply not enough leverage in the human arm to enable someone to so damage himself.

The fact that Dr. Irwin was a Protestant made his statement extremely damaging to the police, who could not very well accuse him of being a pro-IRA propagandist. More embarrassment followed when another doctor attached to an RUC station in Armagh, Dr. Denis Elliott, also resigned. He said his professional oath made it impossible for him to continue his duties there. Elliott's announcement was given added effect, since he was not only a Protestant, but a former local councilor for the loyalist Official Unionist Party.

The attention given to the RUC's interrogation methods resulted in a dropping of convictions in 1979. For the time being anyway, there seemed to have been a halt to the more unacceptable methods used by the police to get confessions. But the problem remains. It is a consequence, not so much of the caliber of individual policemen—the RUC, as a police force, contains a proportion of thoroughly professional officers determined to act against all terrorists regardless of their political orientation—but of the political role in which the force finds itself.

"Ulsterization" has meant that the RUC is under extreme pressure to get the convictions needed to prove that it can handle the security situation without resorting to unpopular methods like internment and detention. The British, determined to shift more and more responsibility for security matters back to the police, have been anxious to show that their policy of making the RUC the primary antiterrorist force is working. Government officials have been prepared to turn a blind eye to the extralegal methods of interrogation used in holding centers and police stations like Castlereagh. Many judges have also been prepared to do so. One went so far as to state that certain lawyers in Northern Ireland were paying too much attention to allegations of police brutality and thus distracting the force from its objective of defeating the Provisional IRA. This has been a familiar argument, used by loyalist and British politicians as well as police officers. Their arguments are that there exists a conspiracy to discredit the RUC by IRA sympathizers. But the misconduct of certain police officers is too well documented to ignore or dismiss in this way. RUC misconduct is exploited by the Provisionals in an attempt to garner whatever moral authority they can for their acts of violence. In the end though, the responsibility for the RUC's bad publicity rests with the British government and its insensitivity to the particular circumstances which make the role of the Northern Ireland police so open to criticism in the first place. The fact remains that the almost all-Protestant RUC is not ready to assume the kind of duties expected of it by the government. Pretending that the police have to deal with mere criminals is utter folly, as well as dangerous for the policemen. It is a futile and deliberately misleading attempt to ignore the political dimension of the Northern Ireland problem. Refusing to recognize the motivation of the Provisional IRA will not make it any less of a threat. That will only postpone the day when the political problems underlying the crisis can be dealt with honestly and bravely.

In the meantime ever more disturbing facts about the RUC emerge that only underline the peculiar political makeup and involvement of Northern Ireland's police and show that internal reforms will be limited in effect as long as the overall political aspects of the situation remain as they are. In previous chapters it was pointed out that there is evidence of links between the security forces and the terrorist gangs of the Ulster Defence Association and the Ulster Volunteer Force. Information in the form of confidential files has been passed from the RUC Reserve to the UDA about suspected IRA men and sympathizers. At least three men have been murdered as a result. (See chapter 4.) In 1972, an RUC detective formed a relationship with former UDA leader Tommy Herron and had actually at one stage given weapons to the loyalist assassination squads. More recently there have been unsettling revelations about the connections between some policemen and the loyalist gangs.

In the spring of 1980 a group of RUC men were brought to trial in Belfast after an investigation into a series of incidents that included murder, the kidnapping of a priest, the bombing of a Catholic bar, and hijacking. Two policemen, Sergeant John Weir and Constable William McCaughey, were charged and convicted of murdering a Catholic shopkeeper in June 1977 in revenge for an attack by the Provisional IRA. The shooting was carried out in collaboration with local UVF men. The sergeant and constable were also convicted of kidnapping a sixty-one-year-old Catholic priest, Father Hugh Murphy, whom they threatened to murder if the body of an RUC man was not returned by the Provisionals, who had fatally wounded him during an ambush. McCaughey was also charged and convicted of bombing a Catholic bar with two other policemen in 1978.

One of the remarkable things about this case was the sentences handed down by Chief Justice Robert Lowry. While McCaughey and Weir were given life sentences, the other policemen involved in the bar bombing were let off with suspended sentences. McCaughey's father, who aided his son in concealing the priest on his farm, was also released with a suspended sentence. In his summing up Lowry stated that the action of McCaughey in murdering the Catholic was "understandable" but "inexcusable." He described it as "really an act of retribution, or revenge because of other murders that had been committed." The victim was a totally innocent man, a father of eight children with no connection to the IRA or the republican movement. Why it was "understandable" to murder such a man under any circumstances was not at all made clear by Justice Lowry.

An attempt was made to represent the fact that the officers were brought to trial as a triumph for RUC impartiality. However, the trial was brought about not so much because of painstaking police work but rather thanks to McCaughey's wife. Apparently he beat her regularly; she became fed up with his repeated abuse and went to the police with the inside story of his connection with the UVF. The case was therefore thrust upon them. Mrs. McCaughey has since divorced her husband.

Such cases have not apparently discouraged the policy of "Ulsterization." The RUC are now seen commonly in areas of Belfast where they could not go before; they man roadblocks and checkpoints and undertake patrols in the hostile ghettos of Andersonstown, the Falls Road, and Ballymurphy, where they provide more and more targets for the IRA. Since 1977 the British army in Northern Ireland has been effectively under the control of the RUC. In only two areas can the army mount special operations without first being requested to do so by the local division commander of the police. These areas are the border section of Armagh around the Provisional stronghold of Crossmaglen, and west Belfast. Elsewhere, the army's role has become increasingly subordinate to that of the police. It is part of the slow process of British disengagement, with a long-term goal of returning security to the police and the locally recruited regiment of the army, the Ulster Defence Regiment.

Ulsterization, however, remains a superficial approach to serious problems. The RUC does not go into the ghettos as a police force, but as a paramilitary body, as it has done since the creation of Northern Ireland. It is greeted as such by the majority of the Catholics. It is a hopeless and fatal solution that tries to deal with security problems without tackling the political issues underlying them. As long as the British government pursues this course, the lives of many policemen will be needlessly lost in a futile attempt to find a military solution to a political problem.

Of course, Detective Sergeant Miller would not agree. With every conviction of a terrorist the police might feel closer to their goal of "normalizing" Northern Ireland. But for every Provisional who goes to jail, another takes his or her place. Putting people in jail will not hold a state together, even if it should achieve some sort of temporary peace. The ugly reality is that there will always be conditions for another outbreak of terror, another round of ambush, murder, and repression. And the long funerals of policeman and terrorist will, unfortunately, wind their slow and solemn way through the lanes and narrow streets of their respective home districts for many years to come.

8

Letters from
a Belfast Ghetto

. . . and men strike and bear the stroke
Of war as ever, audacious or resigned,
And God still sits aloft in the array
That we have wrought him, stone-deaf and stone-blind.
                                    —EDWARD THOMAS

*A*t least once a month for the last ten years or more that I have
lived away from home, a family letter with its familiar bulge arrives
in my mailbox. On the profiled head of Her Majesty Queen Elizabeth the Second which adorns the British stamp is the black and
broken ring of the Belfast postmark. The bulge is caused by the collection of cuttings from local papers that my mother usually en-
closes in the envelope. They tumble onto the table with their grim
reports and headlines of death and destruction. It is a war correspondence. And so too are my mother's letters. But they are a war
correspondence of a more valuable kind. For she is one of the people on whose behalf the war is supposedly being fought.

She is a handsome, brown-haired woman in her mid-fifties. She
has five children. Her husband worked for most of his life as a truck

driver and until a few years ago was never out of work. Then his firm closed down, and he became one of the thousands of Northern Ireland men who have been joining the ranks of the unemployed with a rapidity not seen since the 1930s. Like other women faced with the worsening economic state, she took on a series of badly paid jobs to supplement the unemployment and retirement money my father was receiving, a small amount indeed by American standards. The last five years of economic uncertainty have provided a gloomy background lit only by the gunfire and explosions of the sectarian and political violence.

She lives in west Belfast, one of the largest working-class Catholic districts in Northern Ireland. It has in some areas an unemployment rate of 40 percent and over among males. She found a job in a canteen in a local electrical parts factory brought into the area in the early 1970s to try and alleviate the unemployment problem. It offered three hundred jobs; over three thousand men applied for them. Though she often worked seven days a week serving and cleaning in the canteen, she never brought home more than the equivalent of forty dollars a week. In February 1978 she wrote to me, "I have become one of the unemployed. We were all laid off work three weeks ago after 140 men in the factory lost their jobs." The company was losing money and had to cut its work force and abandon its previous plans to give jobs to over one thousand Catholics from the district.

My mother remembered the hard days of the thirties, when she was a child in the Markets area near downtown Belfast. Her father worked in a big bakery, but he was frequently laid off work. The poor sections of the Markets contained some of the worst housing in the United Kingdom and during the 1930s was plunged into seemingly perpetual poverty. People resorted to the money lender and the pawnshop to help them out. My mother recalled:

My life was not very colourful; it was just poverty and hunger all the way. I remember the time I got a free pair of shoes—and you had to be barefooted before you got anything free in them days. I got wearing them for a couple of days and then your ma needed them for the pawnshop. You took them to the pawnshop and got the lend of three shillings and sixpence and that kept the family fed for another three or four days. But you had to stay home from school or the teacher would want to know where your shoes were, and God knows you were humiliated enough without having to stand up in front of the class and tell them your ma pawned them.

And then we had the so-called moneylenders. There was so many of them. I'll give you a few of their names. First there was Emma Ervine. She was the one my brother and I feared most. She lived in Bond Street, the next street to ours. She lived up the stairs; it was only a two bed-roomed house but there was also a family living downstairs. I remember having to climb those old creaky stairs, usually on a Saturday, for the lend of ten shillings. She must have known the different footsteps, for she used to give a yell before you got to the door. "What the hell do you want, wee Rodgers? I hope it's not money! Did your ma pay the interest on the last ten bob I lent her?" "I have it here for you, Mrs. Ervine," I'd whisper.

Well, you got your ten bob and you were glad to get down them stairs. The next one was called Bessy Malone; then there was Maggie Hasty and Sarah McKenna. Most of these women were second-hand-clothes dealers, and they made a few pounds and started the money lending business. My older sister Mary got a job in the summer picking potatoes. She had to leave the house at half past six in the morning to walk the mile and a half to where the lorry was waiting to drive them to the potato fields. Usually it was an hour's long drive out to the country. They worked ten hours a day for six days a week and the pay was eighteen shillings. It was slavery but you were glad to get it.

Moneylending in the poor areas is a thing of the past. When the Provisional and Official IRA took over the running of the Catholic ghettos in the early 1970s, one of the first things they did was force those parasites who were still thriving on the hardship of the poor to pack up and leave. It is one of the few socially beneficial actions to their credit.

With two sisters and two brothers, my mother grew up in a tiny two-bedroom nineteenth-century house in Raphael Street, directly behind the gasworks. The great gray-ribbed, cylindrical gas tank still dominates the Markets. On winter evenings the thick sulfurous fumes from the gas works would fog up the streets, seeping into every crack and crevice of every room with its all-pervasive smell, hanging in the damp air like a heavy noxious curtain. There were, however, certain advantages to living so near the gasworks. Huge piles of coal were stacked near the back of my aunt Mary's house where she lived in later years just around the corner from Raphael Street. Whenever she wanted a shovelful of coal, all she had to do was open the door to her backyard, stick out the shovel, and help herself.

Depression and poverty took its toll, and the only recourse for relief was often drink. Every street had at least one corner bar where the men would congregate in the evening, nursing pints of black porter. Women were not accepted into the world of the pub; there was a side entrance where they would go carrying cans to be filled with porter. If they were too old to make the short journey, then they would send one of the neighborhood children. Drinking by women was frowned on. The only ones who could really get away with it were spinsters and widows—but then they were already morally suspect.

Wife beating was common, and accepted. My mother wrote to me once, recalling an incident which occurred in the next-door neighbor's house. She mentioned it because it was not unusual. The husband came home drunk and started to abuse his wife.

> I heard her screaming and went to the backyard to listen. Then I heard the back door open and heard her running into her backyard. I climbed up on our wall to take a peep at what was going on. The poor woman was trying to get into the entry when he came running out after her with a fork and dragged her by the hair on to the ground. Then he stabbed her several times with the fork. I jumped off the wall and went into the house to tell me da. But he wouldn't do anything. All he would say was that it was "between man and wife." Yet, I remember him very well . . . crossing the street to stop a man who was kicking his oul dog.

James Connolly, the Irish socialist revolutionary who was executed by the British in 1916, remarked that in Belfast women were "the slaves of the slaves." Men, crippled and frustrated by grueling work or the lack of it, would go home to take it out on those over whom they had any power. It was a vicious circle of violence and self-hatred.

When my mother was still a young girl, her father left home, never to return. The events leading up to his departure were something of a mystery until much later, when her older sister Mary explained why the marriage had collapsed. My mother wrote:

> It all started as far as I can remember when my ma just stopped talking to my da. She ignored him completely. When he came home at night from work she would sit in a corner and not even give him a glance.

We all thought it would last for only a few days; but it went on and on and on, year in, year out. She grew sadder and sadder. She stopped going out. And she would just sit by the fireplace with an oul shawl wrapped around her shoulders staring at the flames. One day my da didn't come home. They never saw each other again. He came back from London where he'd gone for her funeral—but that was all. He never said anything about why they fell out. Neither did she.

It was Mary told me why, years later. My ma had a wee baby boy who died of pneumonia. She saved up thirty shillings, all she had; she wanted to spend it on a headstone and a plot of land for his grave. She gave it to my da to go and buy the headstone and make arrangements for his son's funeral. But he spent it on drink and the child was buried in the paupers' grave—a big unmarked pit in Milltown Cemetery. It broke her heart to think of her son in a paupers' grave and she never forgave my da for that, never until the day she died. His name never again passed her lips.

Her mother died when I was about four. I remember the funeral well because it was the only one I ever attended that had horse-drawn coaches. By then my mother's sisters and brothers were long married, with families, and had generally prospered enough to own small stores. My aunt Mary had a "sweetie shop," which is still doing business; my uncle Tommy owns a Bookies Betting Shop and runs a taxi service with his wife. So the funeral of their mother was a memorable affair. It was a splendid sight to see: the black, plumed horses pulling the coach with the coffin over the cobble-stoned streets of the Markets. Behind the cortege rose the gas works, ever present, a stark contrast to the procession, as were the narrow, cramped little streets through which it passed. Funerals, like marriages, are an excuse for the Belfast working classes to splash out. Death and marriage are two of the high points in their lives, which they mark with as much celebration as they can possibly afford. The rest of their life is made up of a usually dull routine—of scraping together enough money to get through the week, of work or the search for work.

My mother looks back on her upbringing believing that things can never again be that bad—the abject poverty and humiliating dependence on local charity have been removed to a large extent by the welfare state. The Markets is still by European or American standards a very poor area, but the old nineteenth-century slums have mostly been replaced with modern dwellings that have inside toilets and bathrooms. Families are still large, as they are in all the Catholic districts, and work scarce. But the people now have the welfare check to depend on instead of the fickle charity of individuals or the church.

Inevitably a lot of the letters I receive from home are mainly concerned with passing on the names of those recently killed or the incidents of violence which mark everyday life. They also give some idea as to the difficulties ordinary people have doing simple things usually taken for granted elsewhere, like shopping. A letter dated December 19, 1978, from my mother begins:

> Well, Jack, as you will see from these few clippings that the war here is hotting up again. The prison officers are being blown up and shot every day. I have just heard the news today that another soldier has been shot dead, a policeman blown up and God knows what tomorrow will bring.
>
> I was in the town last week trying to do a bit of shopping. I went into Littlewoods first. I was only in a few minutes when the bomb alert went and I had to leave my shopping down and run like the devil. I then went round to the C&A store. Another bomb alert went off. The same thing—run like hell; and that happened four times in different stores. I just gave up and made my way up Castle Street to a taxi stand, glad to get out of that mad town.

Fortunately, on this occasion no one was injured—the buildings were cleared in time. It was part of the Provisional IRA's "economic" war against Northern Ireland. That war is, according to Provisional propaganda, being fought to protect women like my mother and other working-class Catholics from British imperialism. However, the organization, in taking upon itself such responsibility, never seems to consult the experience of those whom it affects most directly: the poor, harried women trying to get a little Christmas shopping done in peace. It is just another instance of the very wide gap existing between the aims and aspirations of the Provisional IRA and its actual methods. An economic war that affects working-class people so directly and only is indirectly effective against British interests, if at all, is hardly striking a blow against imperialism.

It has proven costly in terms of human life. At the beginning of 1978, during one of the worst bombing campaigns Northern Ireland has yet sustained, a series of firebombs went off in a suburban hotel near Belfast. Twelve people died. The bombs were planted by the

Provisionals, who later claimed that their warnings to clear the building had been heeded too late. They apologized for the loss of life. My mother wrote to me about the deaths.

> I suppose you've heard about the La Mon House hotel? Them poor people were just out for a night's entertainment and look how they died. People here are disgusted by it. Even the Provisional supporters said it was awful. It has turned an awful lot of people against them, Jack. Is any cause worth such loss of life? They said they were sorry! But they shouldn't be planting bombs where people are eating and drinking having a wee night out. What kind of war is that, will you tell me?

However, though genuine, such indignation does not affect the tactics of the terrorists for very long. They are not answerable to anybody. After a lull in the bombing campaign, which lasted long enough for the people to forget the last "accident," the Provisionals were back in action bombing stores, shops, and other areas where civilians gathered. One of the most foolhardy attacks of all was made on the Belfast-to-Dublin express train, the *Enterprise.* In a letter from my mother dated November 2, 1978, she wrote:

> I suppose you have heard about the poor old Enterprise getting bombed. The woman that was killed on it came from Leeson Street. She had been living in Dublin a few years and was coming up to visit her aged parents who still live in Leeson Street.

The terrorists seemed to have planted the bomb in or near the bathroom in the restaurant car of the train. Mrs. Joan McKernan was having a cup of tea when it went off, killing her. In the letter mentioning the murder, my mother included a little clipping from a local newspaper. It was a death notice from an Irish organization of which Joan McKernan had been a member. The fact that she became yet another innocent victim of the IRA's so-called economic war against British imperialism underscores just how foolhardy and callous its tactics are. Apart from everything else, the *Enterprise* is one of the few cross-border links in Ireland, one used mostly by working-class Catholics (the people on whose behalf the Provisionals claim they are fighting their campaign). Why an organization which wants a united Ireland should attempt to break this link is a mystery to most people.

The same letter contained more cuttings with lists of death notices and *In Memoriam* notices. They provide a sad but interesting cross-section of the means by which people get killed in the city. There was a column for Joan McKernan, killed by the Provisionals' bomb:

> Joan, loving wife of Gerry and dear sister of Eileen, Eternal rest grant unto her, O Lord. Not our will, O Lord, but Thine be done. . . . O Holy Child of Jesus, lead her to the throne of your heavenly Father. . . .

The next column was devoted to Jim Fogarty, a supporter of the Official IRA whom the Provisionals murdered on November 3, 1975. This was the third anniversary of his death. The notices were decidedly more militant, containing the curious mixture of Irish Catholic belief and political jargon typical of the republican tradition:

> Jim—murdered 3rd November, 1975, by cowardly gunmen of the fascist Provos. They took away your life, Jim, but they'll never take the memory we have of you. We'll make them all regret. Always remembered and sadly missed by his loving brother Paddy, sister-in-law Betty and baby Karen. . . .

Beneath this, another one began,

> In loving memory of James, murdered by a coward's bullet. St. Anthony pray for him. . . .

In these and other *In Memoriam* notices, it is quite common to find the language of left-wing politics beside references to the saints and Mary, "Queen of Ireland."

The next column across from Fogarty's was devoted to the McCrory brothers, both of whom were murdered on separate occasions by loyalist gunmen:

> In loving memory of my two brothers, Cornelius (Neil), murdered November 3, 1976, and Patrick Pearse (Pearsy), murdered March 13, 1972—R.I.P. St. Patrick pray for them. Gone are the brothers I loved so dear, silent the voices I loved to hear. . . .

Beneath this we read:

> In proud and loving memory of my dear friend Cornelius who was murdered by loyalist thugs on November 3, 1976, aged 17—R.I.P. To those who think of him today a little prayer to Jesus say.

In yet another notice for Cornelius, it states he was "murdered for his faith"—the usual phrase for Catholics who are the victim of sectarian assassination.

Grief is a great leveler. The conventional sentimentality of these little death notices is nonetheless poignant for being that. Though sentimental, they are curiously restrained, excepting of course the outbursts of political rhetoric. But the grief of the ordinary people is generally apolitical, and they all express it in the same terms. The Northern Irish are not effusive (except when drunk) even when confronted by the saddest or most painful experiences. I can read through my mother's letters and rarely find an expression of any length of her feelings about the tragedies by which she is surrounded. Instead, she mentions and lists them with a relentless objectivity. From a letter of November 1977:

> Well, Jack, have you settled down in your new home, or do you miss old Belfast anymore? Not much change here. The war is still going on and not getting any better. Two weeks ago they [the Provisionals] burned the Greenan Lodge Hotel down; this week a few shops in the town and numerous other places. And to make matters worse the firemen are out on strike. The shootings and kneecappings go on.
>
> Do you remember Sammy Hyland? Well, the British army went to his house a few weeks ago and asked would he go with them to look at a suspicious car. When they got him outside they nearly murdered him. He was in hospital for two weeks with 24 stitches in his head and a lot more injuries.
>
> There was a young fellow named Sammy Murphy shot dead last week in Bernagh Drive. He joined the British army three years ago and came home to see his mother who lived in Andersonstown. They were out shopping together and were coming up the street when a taxi drew up beside them and two of the boys jumped out and started shooting. That was on a Friday. He was leaving the army the following Monday. He was buried last week.

She concludes with a joke:

> I heard a joke the other day, that they were kneecapping the dogs in Ardoyne because they were carrying their tails to the army.
>
> Eileen has just called me to the window to see the snow. It is coming down very heavy and the air is full of thunder and lightning.

A few months later, in early 1978, the story is the same:

> The troubles here are not getting any better. In the last couple of days the IRA have shot and killed one member of the Ulster Defence Regiment. And this morning they booby-trapped another UDR man's car as he was taking his child to school. It blew up killing him and his ten year old daughter and the wee baby that was in the back is critically ill. There was another shooting at the corner of Andersonstown Park. A plainclothes policeman was passing in his car and they riddled the car. He is in hospital seriously wounded. Another policeman was shot down in York Road, and a woman who was passing at the time was shot dead in the cross fire. I could go on as each day brings a new tragedy. There seems no end to it. . . .

"Each day brings a new tragedy." My mother's letters do not distinguish one from another by political criteria; in that I think they are a fairly accurate barometer of the feelings of the majority of the people of Northern Ireland in their response to the killings. This does not mean, however, that political aspirations have lapsed. I suppose my mother is like the majority of Andersonstown Catholics in that she would like a united Ireland and wants to see the British army leave as soon as practically possible. She is in tacit sympathy with the aims of the Provisional IRA, insofar as she understands them, but she can at the same time find their methods reprehensible.

It is really the bedrock of basic agreement with the aims of the IRA on which that organization's whole campaign can rest and base itself for the indefinite future. At times the bedrock is stronger than at others. In the early years of the troubles, support for the Provisionals was evident in many of the letters I received from home, through the detailing of little incidents of the kind that never made their way into the newspapers. I have one from mid-1973 in which my mother wrote:

> The Provisionals are still very strong, Jack. Many people defend them and say that they are not as bad as the papers and politicians make out. Last Sunday the priest in St. Paul's got a shock when he was attacking them for killing some young soldier in a booby-trap. Some man stood up and shouted him down saying he was doing the work of the British. Then he stopped and walked out and shouted that he wasn't coming back. Your da was very angry and said that no one had the right to talk like that in chapel and that the Church was better off without the likes of him. I don't agree with shouting at priests now, but I think they are not being fair by preaching like that. A lot of people afterwards told me that the man was right and that if there wasn't the IRA in 1970 many chapels would have been burnt to the ground by loyalist gangs.

Such a challenge in a church would have been unthinkable before. But the authority of the Church, like the authority of the state, has weakened since 1969. Among young teen-agers that weakening is quite dramatic. Partly it is due to the general feeling of rebellion; more specifically, it has been caused by real resentment felt when the hierarchy has seemed one-sided in condemnation of the violence.

A few years later I witnessed another incident that revealed discontent among the Church's flock. I was quite surprised one day in late 1976 when walking through the lower Falls area near the towering spires of St. Peter's Cathedral, which dominate the streets around them, to see a drunk man standing outside the cathedral hurling violent abuse at priests and bishops. Though he was swearing at the top of his lungs, no one intervened to chase him away. A few people looked at him curiously for a moment, shook their heads, and walked on. Obviously, there is a general feeling of dissatisfaction and disappointment in the air, which many tacitly acknowledge. I don't know what this man's particular grievance was, but he was proclaiming something about the Church "betraying the people."

My mother's letters reveal that other forms of authority are under pressure. One that suffered badly was the school system. When I was a child attending first the local Christian Brothers and then the secondary school, discipline was hard and stringently enforced. The little rhyme sung by Falls Road children earlier in the century was still appropriate:

> *Our wee school's a nice wee school*
> *Made of bricks and plaster,*
> *The only thing that we don't like*
> *Is our wee baldy Master.*
> *He goes to the pub on Saturday night,*
> *He goes to Mass on Sunday,*
> *To pray to God to give him strength*
> *To slaughter us on Monday.*

Punishment was generally cruel and often arbitrary. Pupils were beaten with a variety of instruments, some of which would not have been out of place in a medieval torture chamber. From my own experience, I recall that most usually beatings were administered with a heavy, short, but very thick leather strap; it often had studs along the edges, and one or two teachers lined the insides of their straps with three-penny bits—a sturdy little hexagonal coin, long out of use now. Others improvised with long thin wires, canes, and hurling sticks.

However, by mid-1973 the teachers in the ghetto schools were completely outgunned, as another letter from my mother testifies:

Anyway, Thomas came home early today and told me that his school was taken over by the Official IRA. They were all in class at about eleven when they saw a group of young fellas coming up the driveway. They were hooded and carrying guns. They went into each classroom and told the teachers to be quiet. Then they pushed the teachers into the storeroom and locked the door. The Officials had heard about the punishments being given in the school and thought they were too much. After the teachers were all locked up they read a statement in each class. Thomas didn't pay much attention to this, he said it had something to do with history. He said everybody thought it was a laugh. They left the teachers in the storeroom and gave the keys to the boys. They said they could let them out whenever they liked. Some of the boys did not want to let them out at all and said they should throw away the keys. But they were afraid they might suffocate then they'd all go to jail for murder, so they opened the doors. You never know what is going to happen next in this place, do you?

This occurred during a time when attendance had fallen off drastically. In 1972 and 1973 riots were everyday events in west Belfast. When one broke out, the children in the local secondary schools—entirely working-class—would simply get up, leave the classrooms, and flock to the scene of the stonings. There was little the school authorities could do to prevent this flood-tide of rebellion. Many of their pupils were already using high-velocity rifles when out of school, having been inducted into the Provisionals' youth movement, "Na Fianna Eireanna," at a still earlier age. (In 1972 alone, thirteen young boys belonging to the youth movement of the Provisionals were killed.)

A Belfast teacher who was a friend of mine mentioned another incident that indicates the kind of problems the authorities face. One afternoon after school he was driving down the Falls Road on his way home. At an intersection not far from the school he stopped at a traffic light. Two boys wearing masks walked over to the car, pulled a gun, and told him to get out. "This is a hijacking. The Provies need your car," the one with the gun said. But when the teacher turned to face his coercer the boy's mouth fell. He lowered his gun and said with obvious embarrassment, "I'm sorry, sir, I didn't recognize you." The gunman backed away from his teacher and waved him on. The teacher told me he knew who it was from his voice—a thirteen-year-old in one of the lower classes he taught. Next day at school the teacher was greeted with a big grin from the blushing pupil. "What could I do?" he asked me despairingly. "I wouldn't tell the police—I couldn't even if I wanted to. I'd be dead if I did, you know that. You can't take a boy up to the front of the class and cane him for attempted hijacking, can you? I suppose I could have taken him aside and told him a few homilies about violence, but he knows more about violence than I do. I go home to a quiet flat in a tree-lined middle-class area where they never see a saracen or a soldier. He goes back to Ballymurphy where he's liable to arrest at any time, where the streets are full of soldiers pointing high-velocity rifles at you everywhere you go, where your door's liable to be kicked in the middle of the night. It's really hopeless."

At the beginning of 1979 I received a letter from my brother-in-law, who described what happened to his brother, a known local gangster wanted by the IRA (in its role as a kind of ghetto police force) for various robberies. The IRA were unsuccessful for several years in catching up with him. He wrote:

> You remember, Ronnie, my brother, he was having a bit of trouble before you went away. Well, the police caught him and he was put away for a year and a half but just as he got out and was beginning to start fresh he was picked up at the Lake Glen where he was at a dance with his girl friend. Only this time he was not so lucky—it was not the police but the Provies who got him. After a long struggle he managed to cause the driver of the car that was taking him away to crash. But his fight was in vain for outside the car instead of making off before the police arrived, the four other occupants of the car beat him up badly before one of them produced his gun and shot Ronnie in both legs. Because of the bad beating he was given before he was shot the police are treating it as attempted murder. Lucky for Ronnie both bullets passed through his legs and he was out of hospital after only nine days stay. We are just hoping that he settles down and does not try to get revenge. I think all of his friends have been shot at one time or another. His friend who lives next door to my ma was shot dead by the Brits after driving through an army barrier. That's two that have been killed that way.

Random hijacking of cars in west Belfast is very common—teenagers without any organizational affiliation do it for joy rides. Unfortunately, the army pursues a policy of shoot first and ask questions later in such cases, with the result that many young lives are lost quite needlessly. In the case mentioned in the letter above, when Ronnie's friend from next door was shot dead, the army had been told that the hijackers were armed. After opening fire on the stolen car and killing one of the youths, the soldiers found a toy gun lying on the back seat.

Ronnie was sixteen when he first became a renegade, after graduating from the Official IRA. All his friends, who formed a sort of gang that robbed post offices and pubs, were his age or younger. They were all apolitical. They had never known politics as such—only violence. Of course, it was "political violence"; I suppose they reasoned that if you can use violence for political aims, then why not use it to get what you want in other spheres as well—money, drink, clothes, or whatever. The morality of politically inspired murder was obviously too subtle for them, or perhaps they were somewhat more sophisticated and had reached a kind of cynicism. But from the experience of Belfast, it is probably true to say that

A riot on the Upper Falls Road, near Andersonstown, Belfast, in August 1979, shortly after the ceremonies marking the eighth anniversary of the introduction of internment. The British army's armored personnel carriers are retreating to the police station which they use as a barracks. Its high wire fence can be seen in the background.

once you have taken the step of morally justifying murder for the achievement of limited political goals and you proceed on a campaign of death and destruction, you run a grave risk of undermining basic moral constraints that normally hold a community together. It would be unfair to blame the Provisional IRA for being solely responsible for this—the forces of the British government hardly set a worthy example of respect for law and order. In any case, respect for laws only comes when the laws are seen to be just. Even so, the ruthlessness and often callous disregard for human life shown in many of the Provisionals' tactics has had a traumatic and destructive effect on the very moral fabric of the community. In 1979 crime was so rife that there was little even the Provisionals could do to stop it. Entire areas like the Divis Flats, once a republican stronghold, became "hole-in-the-wall" style hideouts and sanctuaries for gangs of youthful bandits. There was a widespread black market in stolen goods throughout west Belfast. The RUC, according to the locals, did not interfere; it was accused of allowing the criminals to do what they liked in order to build up support for bringing the police back into the Catholic areas again.

Since the Provisionals adopted their more secretive "cell structure," they have been less effective as a ghetto police force. When they do emerge to render "punishment" for alleged "crimes against the people," they are faced with the prospect of being caught between the criminals and the police. One day in the early summer of 1980, for instance, a Provisional IRA punishment squad consisting of two men kneecapped several youths on the Whiterock Road in Ballymurphy. Seconds after the punishment was administered, an RUC Land Rover drove up the road and opened fire on the Provisional IRA men. One escaped, but the other, Teddy O'Neill, aged twenty-three, was shot dead. (A witness added the disgusting detail that O'Neill was only wounded at first and then was shot again by a policeman who stood over him. This allegation has been made in several other incidents since 1978, and republicans claim that the police have a policy of immediate and summary execution of any Provisional whom they apprehend in suitable circumstances.)

The brutalizing violence affects children in many ways. When my youngest sister Eileen was thirteen, my mother wrote to me with concern:

Poor wee Eileen has bad nightmares lately. She can't sleep and is always getting up in the middle of the night to switch on the lights. She says she's scared of the dark now. She tells me she dreams about soldiers. It's been like this ever since she saw that wee Scots soldier shot dead at the top of our street. She was playing in the fields when it happened. She came running in and told me that the women were saying the rosary over his body, lying on the street. I'm taking her to the doctor tomorrow to see if he can give her something to help her sleep at night.

This letter testifies that when death strikes even the usually hated or disliked, they are treated poignantly and with respect. The rosary is said over the dying soldier, whom the women would no doubt have been cursing if he were alive—grief is the leveler. The letters show a resigned acceptance of violence that almost appears to be a kind of indifference at times. The references to the daily murders become perfunctory, to be mentioned in passing. When the sectarian killings reached a peak in 1975, my father wrote:

Things are much the same in Belfast. The sectarian killings have started again and you have to watch where you go. . . . There is nothing much happening in Andersonstown. . . .

A month later he wrote to tell me my eldest sister, Katherine, was getting married soon. At the end of his letter he added, "Well, everything is quiet at home except for the assassinations which we are getting used to again."

What is considered quiet by Belfast standards might be put in perspective when it is remembered that between February and July 1975, the times these last two letters were written, eighty people were murdered—not including soldiers and policemen—in sectarian attacks. The majority of the killings were in Belfast; my sister's wedding day was marred by nine sectarian murders within the period of a few hours.

The sectarian killings put the greatest strain on the ordinary people and create the worst horror throughout the community. Katherine occasionally wrote to me about the murders, echoing something of the thrill of fear that went through the streets as the dawn broke over another battered corpse:

I have enclosed some pieces of recent news you might be interested in. Things here at the moment seem to be slipping back to the old routine of sectarian murders. The UVF said in a statement that the murders would start up again. And following that two bodies have been found. The first found was a replica of a previous murder. The victim, a Catholic, had his head crushed by a sledge hammer and large stones. It was really horrible. The fellow was set up at his workplace. The latest body was just found this morning, shot through the neck at Black's Road. But he is not dead. . . . I wonder will there be any more murdered by the time you read this. I hope not as this kind of thing really scares me. . . .

The sectarian murders made it very difficult for people to cross borders of the different ghettos. This was particularly difficult for many Belfast families like my father's, who had Protestant and Catholic relatives. My uncle Willy, my father's oldest brother, the only remaining Protestant in our family, was one of my favorite uncles. It was his chair covers from Canada with the pictures of the Mounted Police with their peaked caps and red uniforms at which I used to marvel when younger. Though, being a Catholic, I always preferred the U.S. Cavalry. He visited us regularly, once a week. Then, after 1969, his visits became infrequent. The outbreak of sectarian murders in 1972 ended them completely. For almost four years my father did not see him. Then in 1976 my mother wrote of a chance meeting they had in the city center:

By the way, Jack, you know who your da bumped into last week? Your Uncle Willy. He hasn't seen him in donkeys years. He met him near Royal Avenue. He has had to move from his old home because of the troubles and now lives in a quieter area. But he won't come to Andersonstown. You know he's just as frightened of his own side as he is of the IRA—you know what the UDA would do to him if they found out his brother was a Catholic? But he promised as soon as the troubles were over he'd be up to see. We might never see him again the way these troubles are going. It's awful the way your own family can't feel safe coming to see you. Your da was always very fond of Willy. . . . He was asking for you. . . .

That was in the summer of 1976. Four years later the killings continue, and my father has seen his brother only once since. When their sister Agnes died in February 1977 they met at the funeral. It was a misty, wet day, sodden with a bleak drizzle. The street was full of black glistening wet umbrellas. The two brothers met in the little parlor just before the coffin was carried out into the damp gray winter's day. I witnessed the scene. My father smiled and said, "How've you been keepin', Willy?" Willy, a big-boned, white-haired man with gentle eyes, nodded and replied, "Auck, you know how it is at my age. I'm not getting any younger. But you can't complain. . . . These oul troubles are a nuisance." "Aye, Willy," my father replied, "both sides are to blame. Just rascals if you ask me, rascals!" Willy nodded quietly in agreement, then shook hands with Agnes' son Gerry, out on parole from the Maze Prison (Long Kesh), where he is serving eighteen years for Provisional IRA activities. But that did not matter.

The brothers parted without ado after the funeral, true to characteristic Belfast form: One's feelings are not expressed directly. Effusiveness is equated with falseness, even weakness, in Belfast. I found their restraint full of poignancy. It was almost as if it were a testimony to the depth of their feelings for each other. Against the hard background of their lives perhaps it is inevitable. As with most Belfast men and women, self-expression is an indulgence that they almost despise—except if drunk, of course. Then, like the slaves of ancient Rome during the feast of Saturnalia, excess of every kind is excused.

The sectarian dangers which helped keep them apart persist to date. They tend to make even the most innocuous act a dangerous business—taking a short-cut through one area to get somewhere else, for instance, can become a frightening experience. When my father fell seriously ill in March 1980, my mother was forced to take a long circuitous route to the hospital, which lay in south Belfast near the loyalist ghetto of Sandy Row. She first decided to take a more convenient, shorter route to the hospital through Sandy Row itself. It was also cheaper, it meant one less bus fare, a fare she simply could not afford. She wrote:

Jack, there is something I must tell you. I travel to the City Hospital seven nights a week and last Tuesday night I thought I would take a short cut over the Boyne Bridge and down through Sandy Row and on to the Lisburn Road. I got over the bridge and had just got into Sandy Row when I saw three women standing chatting. I saw these heads turn and watch me come along and as I started to pass them they shouted into my face, "We'll fix you, you fenian bastard—you do this all the time"—meaning that fenians take the liberty of going through Sandy Row. I had a good half mile to walk to get to the end of it and I was scared and glad to see the end of it. When I told Katherine the next day she said, "Ma, if I had been with you I would have collapsed."

And so it goes on, affecting human contact at every level. For nearly a decade now there have been only two developments that seemed to offer a way out of the morass. The first was the more serious—the attempt to establish a power-sharing government that would allow Catholics a real voice in the political future of Northern Ireland. That government took office in January 1974 and resigned less than five months later, due to loyalist resistance and widespread industrial protests coordinated by the UDA. Ever since there has been virtually no further political progress; instead there has been a political vacuum. It was because of that vacuum that the second development occurred in August 1976. That was the birth of the Peace Movement.

The story of the Northern Ireland Peace Movement is now well known. It began when three children of the Maguire family from Andersonstown were killed by a runaway IRA car whose driver the British army had shot dead. The incident horrified people all over Ireland. Innocent lives had been lost on countless occasions before, but the deaths of the Maguire children came when the people's morale was reaching an all-time low, battered almost senseless by violence that seemed increasingly pointless. In reaction, enormous crowds of Catholic women took to the streets of Andersonstown to protest and demand an end to the Provisionals' campaign. They gathered at street corners and in parks and sang songs of peace. They prayed. Soon they were accompanied by hosts of Protestant women, who held hands with the Catholics, sang, and prayed with them. Three leaders of the movement emerged, Betty Williams, Mairead Corrigan (the dead children's aunt), and Ciaran McKeown. The first two were ordinary Andersonstown women, the third a journalist. Soon they were appearing every night on local television. Within days their expansive goals and unrestrained optimism were highlighted in the world media. Everybody, it seemed, including the media, wanted desperately to believe that this was the way out of the bloody mess. The movement's leaders became celebrities as their marching and praying spilled over the border into the Irish Republic and then to England. In November 1977 Betty Williams and Mairead Corrigan were awarded the Nobel Peace Prize. The movement had reached its peak.

However, as the letters from my mother during the period when the Peace Movement was growing suggest, the impression it made on the outside world was quite different from that made on the working-class people in Belfast. Many of the latter did not share the optimism or enthusiasm for the movement as conveyed by the media. About one month after Mairead Corrigan, Betty Williams, and Ciaran McKeown became household names, I received this letter from home:

> How have you been keeping these last weeks? Andytown has been getting lots of publicity recently. We are all waiting to see what will happen next now the Peace Women have taken to the streets. No, Jack, I haven't joined in. In my eyes they are well intentioned but I don't think they can last. In some areas they are strong enough, but mostly in the better off places. In areas like the lower Falls and Leeson St. they don't want them. Eileen told me the other day that in her school the children of Peace Women get beaten up by the other children. I think they are in danger of getting carried away with themselves. Everytime you turn on the T.V. they are being interviewed. Now they're talking about bringing peace to the whole world! Never mind just Northern Ireland. Maybe they think that by standing and praying and singing "When Irish Eyes are Smiling" peace will fall out of the clouds. If prayers would work we would have had peace years ago. I don't think it will change this place.

Within months of taking to the streets the Peace Movement was already running into difficulties. Many Catholics began to see the condemnations of violence as being one-sidedly directed against the Provisionals. However, when the Peace leaders did attempt to redress the balance by criticizing British army brutality, they were accused of being soft on the Provisional IRA and lost many of their Protestant supporters. The simple and uncontroversial demand for peace around which everyone could unite simply covered a multitude of real differences. But as soon as people began to think about what was actually meant by peace, those differences emerged. When they did, they were to be the usual differences that had made Northern Ireland into the crisis-ridden state it is, and these differences finally ended the Peace Movement.

After the period of praying and marching came to an end and the movement tried to organize itself along practical lines, these problems rapidly destroyed it. It seemed that without the atmosphere of quasireligious emotion, without the great gatherings, it was swiftly fading into the background while the violence went on as ever. When Betty Williams and Mairead Corrigan received the Nobel Peace Prize in 1977, my mother wrote to me about them:

> Jack, you want to know my opinion about the Peace People now. I don't have much interest in them. You very rarely hear about them in Belfast. I think the movement is dying slowly. . . . I did hear that Betty Williams has left Andersonstown and went to live in the Malone Road.

The Malone Road is a wealthy, middle-class district of south Belfast, greatly resented by the ordinary people, both Catholic and Protestant, because of its apparent immunity from the problems and violence always afflicting their lives. The story that Betty Williams has moved into such a rich area has been a rumor circulating in the ghettos since the beginning of the Peace Movement. It is symptomatic of a suspicion that the whole movement was somewhat bogus and not really able to identify with the needs and sufferings of the average Catholic or Protestant. For them, going to live on the Malone Road is like moving to the Bahamas. (In fact, the Peace Movement has opened its headquarters on the Lisburn Road, not far from the Malone Road, which might perhaps account for the last round of rumors.)

There has been no movement or political development since the Peace Movement which has offered even the flimsiest basis for hope—none certainly that has attracted any prolonged attention. In 1980 the Conservative government under Margaret Thatcher did launch a new initiative containing various proposed alternatives for some form of devolved government for Northern Ireland. My mother never even referred to them in passing in her letters. I doubt if she would know or care to know what they were. Her lack of interest was typical; it was representative of the general weariness, the apathy which greets another British proposal. That weariness is understandable. It is produced partly by the feeling that the British government of whatever political persuasion is not really concerned about Northern Ireland enough to give it serious thought, and that the proposals—couched as always in the woolly, dead language of British civil servants—are motivated mainly by a need to save face. The government can at least say, "Well, we tried, didn't we?"

In the meantime the war goes on, numbing those it does not kill, brutalizing those who are involved in it on both sides. Feelings that have to cope with violent death on a daily basis soon become exhausted—how much grief and horror can a person deal with while still going on about his or her everyday life? The fact that everyday life can still go on in some form makes the frequent violent disruptions, often ending in death and injury, even more difficult to deal with—you are constantly being lulled into believing as you walk down the aisle of the supermarket, sit drinking your beer in a bar, or watching football on television, that life is normal. Then the fabric is shattered, and the crying wife or daughter, the hysterical onlookers who witnessed another act of violence in their parlor, on their street, remind you that Northern Ireland is far from normal.

In order to survive, people must withdraw from the tragedy, suppress the grief. As I have pointed out before, repression of feeling has always been a cultural characteristic of Belfast working-class people. Real feelings are not expressed easily; self-expresssion is deemed merely squandering one's feelings. It is as if experience has taught them that there are very few occasions in their lives that are worth "an expense of spirit." They are, instead, tight-lipped and rather grim. But suppressed grief corrodes the spirit like an acid. No one ever really forgets.

What is there to hope for? All that can be said with certainty is that the list of atrocities, political blunderings, downright bullying, military and paramilitary brutality that have made life so awful have not changed the basic good nature of the people. Belfast people are still on the whole nice to children, stray dogs, and strangers. My aunt Martha will still insist with great force that the Northern Ireland people are kinder than those in the Irish Republic because of the way the southerners mistreat their donkeys. My mother, who is no great lover of dogs, will doubtless let Cindy, the local stray, into the house this winter to lounge for a few hours before the fireplace. During the years which have seen Northern Ireland become an ever more militaristic society, these abiding characteristics are something to be thankful for, and grow ever more poignant.

9

To Analyze
the Obvious

*Whether the British ruling class are wicked
or merely stupid is one of the most difficult
questions of our time, and at certain
moments a very important question.*

—GEORGE ORWELL

In 1969 there were six hundred prisoners held in Northern Ireland's Victorian jails. By 1979 the figure had risen to 2,600—the vast majority there for offenses connected with "the troubles." Of those, some four hundred are living in cells filled with their own excrement, wearing only a blanket for covering, and kept under lock and key for twenty-four hours a day. These prisoners—almost all of them Provisionals—are protesting over the removal of political, or "Special Category" status; they are refusing to be designated criminals and to wear prison uniforms. They claim their actions were motivated by political aims. The British had until March 1976 accepted that, but with the beginning of the "criminalization" plan, Special Category was abolished, and the prisoners reacted by refusing to cooperate with the prison authorities. This eventually led to lock-ups, overflowing latrine pots, and cell walls smeared with excrement. Here human beings crouched in dim light as in some ghastly dream, wrapped in filthy blankets. The prisoners wanted the world to recognize that they are not ordinary criminals. The following facts would certainly back up their view of themselves, as would any knowledgeable account of the last decade of Northern Ireland's troubled history:

In August 1979, to mark the tenth anniversary of the British troops' presence on the streets of Northern Ireland, the London magazine *Time Out* published the statistics of violence for that decade:

> 1,932   dead
> 20,421   injured
> 26,516   shootings
> 6,309   explosions
> 3,018   bombs neutralized
> 8,076   armed robberies
> 2,736   malicious fires
> £276,000,000 in damage compensation
> £46,000,000 in injury compensation

By August 1980 the figure for the number killed stood at 2,052.

Currently there are some 12,000 British soldiers on the streets to back up the 7,000 policemen, 4,500 police reservists, and almost 8,000 members of the Ulster Defence Regiment. This commitment is thought to cost one-third of the estimated £1.5 billion subvention required from the British government for Northern Ireland each year.

Behind this military and police strength is a battery of legislation unique in Western Europe. The Northern Ireland Emergency Provisions Act (1973) which superseded the Special Powers Act, allows the authorities to arrest without warrant and hold a suspect for up to seventy-two hours; Amnesty International found that though illegal, it was "standard practise" for the police to deny access to a solicitor (attorney) during this period; it allows a house or building to be searched without warrant and the authorities to take possession of any item or property therein. Then there is the Prevention of Terrorism Act (1974). This allows the authorities to hold a suspect for up to seven days without charge: under this act a citizen can be deported from one part of the United Kingdom to another without being told why and permanently excluded. (Chile and Indonesia are apparently the only other nations where the law allows indefinite deportation.) While the Emergency Provisions Act applies only to Northern Ireland, the Prevention of Terrorism Act operates throughout the United Kingdom. Thus, from a beginning in 1968 when civil rights marchers were demanding reforms in Northern Ireland, the "troubles" have led to a weakening of basic civil liberties throughout the United Kingdom. British democracy has been poisoned by repressive legislation that in many ways resembles the kind of laws the civil rights movement set out to change in Northern Ireland.

What is the result of all this—the violence, the massive security commitment, the repressive legislation? Does it bring a solution to the problem any nearer than it was ten years ago? The result is merely to establish a kind of equilibrium where the terrorists' actions are more or less balanced by government measures. Perhaps this is what former Home Secretary in the Heath government Reginald Maudling meant when he spoke of "an acceptable level of violence." The guerrillas can't break through to a victory over the security forces; the security forces can't eradicate the guerrillas. This deadlock offers no hope of a solution in the near future.

Of course, there can't be a solution unless the situation is discussed. But in the five years between 1974 and 1979 Northern Ireland was discussed only once at the annual Labour Party conference, and then it was begrudgingly allowed a one-hour debate on a Friday afternoon. Currently the Conservative government of Margaret Thatcher has shown only a half-hearted attempt to produce a political initiative—a set of proposals published in the summer of 1980 offering various alternative forms of devolved government for discussion. It provoked little or no enthusiasm and was not really taken seriously. The magnitude of the problem dwarfs the tinkering efforts suggested in the proposals.

There is no immediate prospect of a new Northern Ireland regime. Under the present circumstances it would be impossible to create a government that would have the support of local Catholics if it did not include power-sharing and recognize in any settlement the long-term aspiration of the Irish people towards unity. On the other hand, it is hard to see a regime including such provisions being able to function without incurring the opposition of right-wing loyalist forces, both political and paramilitary. As with the military-guerrilla confrontation, these two opposing political tendencies cancel each other out and produce the inertia of continued direct rule from London.

There is the ever-present difficulty of getting an honest admission as to what the "problem" is. Official British attitudes blandly suppose that it is a matter of "law and order." Since the inauguration of the twofold "criminalization" and "Ulsterization" program by Labour in the mid-seventies, both of the main British political parties have refused to acknowledge that there is a fundamental political issue at stake. They have chosen instead to concentrate on a propaganda exercise meant to show that the terrorism is criminal and that, if only the "godfathers of terror" can be removed, then the Northern Ireland problem will cease to exist.

Official attitudes and genuine beliefs are different matters. The British army's own assessment of the situation, referred to in chapter 6, intended only for the eyes of the military, is far different from official pronouncements. It at least recognizes the fact that the violence is primarily political, and because of that there seems to the army to be no immediate hope of an end to the guerrillas' campaign.

The opinions of the ordinary people of England and Ireland are also out of step with that of the British government. Repeated opinion polls have shown that the vast majority of both Irish and English citizens want a British withdrawal from Northern Ireland. One taken in 1978 showed that 53 percent of Britons polled called for a withdrawal, compared to 30 percent who were against it. The following year, a poll conducted by the Economic and Social Research Institute showed 56 percent in favor of such a course and 33 percent against. Only 25 percent wanted Great Britain to maintain the constitutional link with Northern Ireland. Britain's largest-selling newspaper, *The Daily Mirror,* has reflected the general sentiment favoring withdrawal. On August 14, 1978, its front-page headline declared, "Ulster: Bring Home The Troops." It repeated this call on August 14, 1980. In 1979 a poll conducted in the Republic of Ireland showed that 70.8 percent were in favor of a British withdrawal; 67.9 percent wanted a united Ireland; 21 percent supported the IRA, while 41 percent claimed they sympathized with its aims.

Yet, in spite of the fact that the overwhelming majority of both British and Irish citizens seek a British withdrawal from Northern Ireland and that a clear majority in Ireland support a united Ireland, the British government continues to adhere to the wishes and political demands of the Unionists, who make up some 2 percent of the total population of the United Kingdom. The British government has accorded this tiny minority a wildly disproportionate say over the future of both Ireland and the United Kingdom. It might well be asked why.

There always has been within the British ruling circles a conservative bloc which has maintained that it is of vital military and strategic importance for Great Britain to retain some grip on Ireland. In the early 1970s the right-wing ginger group within the Conservative Party, the "Monday Club," published a pamphlet entitled "Ireland: England's Cuba." The far right analysis sees the troubles in Northern Ireland as the beginning of a subversive takeover in Ireland, one which would bring a left-wing junta to power and admit Soviet influence to England's doorstep. Many who might not go that far still see it as being of crucial significance that Northern Ireland remain within the United Kingdom in order to retain an area which is important to Britain's North Atlantic defense. Former Conservative Prime Minister Edward Heath has said as much in parliament. The fear is that if Northern Ireland became part of a united republic then it would join the nonaligned countries (as did the Republic of Ireland) and British bases in Northern Ireland would be lost to the NATO pact.

These strategic considerations might be enough to persuade the military authorities, as well as perhaps the British Foreign Office, to hang on indefinitely to Northern Ireland. However, it is doubtful if they would be powerful enough in themselves to determine overall British policy towards Ireland. In any case, if in any future settlement the prospect for a united Ireland was visualized, such things as British bases and NATO commitments would be negotiable. There is another factor at work, and I believe that it is based on a genuine fear.

The "Protestant backlash" has unfortunately been used as a rallying call so often in recent Irish history—always when the Unionists feel the need to pressure the British into bending to their political requirements—as to be regarded now with disdain by many in the Catholic community and outside it. There never, after all, has been a backlash on the scale so often hinted at, only the threat of one. Yet it has remained the principal reason the British advance for staying in Ireland. They fear the turmoil that would follow a withdrawal would consume the six northeastern counties in a holocaust and even spill over into England itself, where there are millions of Irish immigrants.

There is also the delicate question of the loyalties of the indigenous security forces, the Ulster Defence Regiment and the Royal Ulster Constabulary. The Ulster Defence Regiment is the largest regiment in the British army; its members have had, since 1971, a history of loyalist paramilitary connections. Between 1970, when it was formed as a replacement to the B-Specials, and 1975, over eighty serving or former members of the regiment were convicted of serious terrorist offenses, including many murders of Catholics. UDR guns have a habit of finding their way into loyalist hands. The UDR is the only regiment in the British army continually to have been engaged in Northern Ireland, so it has an impressive knowledge of the countryside as well as extensive contacts with loyalist paramilitary groups. In 1975 a Unionist politician, perturbed at the rumors then current about a possible British withdrawal (this was during the last Provisional IRA–British truce), made an inflammatory speech in which he said, "We may well have to become the 'Queen's Rebels' in order to remain subjects of any kind." His appeal was generally thought to be directed at the UDR, which, it is assumed, would be the backbone of any loyalist resistance to a move towards unity with the Irish Republic.

Faced with such a force and uncertain about the loyalties of the Northern Ireland police, the British government might be reluctant to push ahead with disengagement if it thought that would lead to a UDR-backed right-wing coup. Currently, the policy of "Ulsterization" has led the government to rely more heavily on the UDR as its front-line troops, even pushing them into Catholic ghettos in Belfast where previously it was thought too provocative to send them. Along with the RUC, the regiment would be the main military force available to whatever regime, if any, the government tries to establish in Northern Ireland.

"Ulsterization" is merely a compromised form of withdrawal, one which hands over front-line security to the virtually all-Protestant forces of the RUC and UDR but still retains the backing of the British army. As such it is only certain to continue antagonizing the Catholics without reassuring the Protestants and offer no prospect of a peaceful solution. For too long British policy towards Ireland has floundered from one such unseemly compromise to another. If one looks for dates when some decisive action should have been taken and was not, one must take in the whole of the nineteenth and twentieth centuries. But the greatest and most disastrous compromise of all was the creation of Northern Ireland itself to placate the Unionists and their allies in the Conservative Party. It is to this that one must return to find the root of Northern Ireland's difficulties and the continual failure of subsequent British policies to achieve a just and peaceful solution to the crisis.

Partition defied the mass of the Irish people's desire for unity. It denied them their rights as a majority and created within the boundaries of the six northeastern counties a state where those who sought unity became a minority. The Unionists, who constituted a minority, were allowed to carve for themselves an area in which they could hold out against the tide of nationalism with a comfortable majority. Thus a minority of Irish people were accorded the power to divide the Irish nation.

Any future attempted solution has to deal with this fact: Partition created an artificial political situation that excluded a section of the population inside "Northern Ireland" from power and prevented the majority of the Irish population from progressing towards the goal of a unified, independent Irish republic. Such efforts as power-sharing to reform the Northern Ireland state are in effect forcing further artificial structures upon a state that is in itself artificial and designed in the first place to preclude the goals that power-sharing intends to achieve.

The British historian A. J. P. Taylor has called India and Pakistan "non-historical states" created by the British through partitioning. The same is true of Northern Ireland. It too is a non-historical state, in the sense that it does not conform to national needs nor cover an area that can be said to be the basis for a nation. It does not even constitute the traditional area of Ulster, one of the historical provinces of Ireland. Northern Ireland was carved out of Ulster, jettisoning three of the nine Ulster counties because they contained a majority of nationalists who, it was feared, would undermine the Unionist position.

Though now there is much talk of "Ulster nationalism," the Unionists at the time of the creation of Northern Ireland had no such ideas. They were expressing a desire for union with Great Britain, not any national aspiration. Of course, there is no such thing as a people's unilateral right to union with another country; yet the British have granted the Unionists that right and have given them a veto over the dissolution of the union with Great Britain. They have done this in defiance of the historically justified aspirations of the Irish people for the creation of a state that would conform to their cultural, ethnic, and economic sense of nationhood and that legitimately recognizes the whole of Ireland as an indivisible unit. The British have continually frustrated those aspirations. Not only that, but since 1921 they have armed, financed, and politically supported a group within Ireland that is determined to resist those aspirations with violence. The UDR and the RUC, as well as the illegally armed paramilitary units of loyalism, are now entrenched behind the Northern Ireland border and, should the Westminster parliament ever decide on a policy of withdrawal and support for a united Ireland, might well confront the British with an intractable military problem. That the British created the problem themselves would be of little consolation under the circumstances.

Yet in spite of this gloomy possibility, the only course for the Westminster government to undertake that will lead to a long-term solution is withdrawal. Unionists have always threatened a coup d'etat. Possibly their feeling would change if they were made to realize that, regardless of their threats, withdrawal was inevitable. Loyalist violence, like Unionist rhetoric, is aimed at convincing the British to stay, the implication being that if they go, worse will follow. But if the Westminster parliament were to say, "We're going anyway," the raison d'etre for such violence might be removed. This, a more optimistic prognosis, would depend on the Protestants' good sense and ability to recognize the futility of further sectarian terrorism. It also depends, obviously, on decisive British action.

This would mean the necessity of establishing an all-Ireland conference attended by Northern loyalists and Catholics as well as Dublin government representatives. Loyalists would have to be reassured that they would not become, as the Northern Catholics did, a repressed minority within the state. Minorities suffer repression when they are perceived as a threat, as the Catholics were within Northern Ireland. The Protestants, however, could not pose a similar threat to a united Ireland. Once the British left, the loyalists would have little to fight for—they could not hope by terrorism to bring the British back. Whatever sense of Ulster nationalism there is among Protestants is not strong enough to lend emotional support or political backing for a loyalist campaign aimed at establishing a Protestant state independent from Ireland. Such a state, in any case, would be too small to be economically viable. When these factors are taken into account, it seems unlikely that the circumstances would exist for prolonged violence from a recalcitrant loyalist population once the trauma of British withdrawal had passed.

Looked at optimistically, an Irish constitution with built-in guarantees of civil and religious freedom for the Northern Protestants might be the balm for the wounds suffered over the last few decades. As it stands, the Irish constitution contains several articles that maintain a special place for the Catholic Church and its teachings. Some liberals suggest that these are the source of loyalist fears of a united Ireland. Such things as the ban on divorce and legal restrictions on contraception, it is argued, have driven the loyalists into a fury of hatred against the Irish. This absurdly assumes that loyalism is a liberal force. If anything the conservative Paisleyite would actually share many of the moral assumptions of the conservative Catholic. However, as a matter of principle, anything smacking of preference for one religion over another would have to be written out of the constitution of a new Ireland.

Such a reunited nation would face considerable problems, not the least of which are economic. Parts of Northern Ireland, those with nationalist Catholic populations, suffer unemployment rates of up to 49.2 percent among adult males. Its industries are failing rapidly. Attempts to bring in outside investment are very costly and only partly successful. Irish economist Anthony Coughlan has argued that many of Ireland's economic woes were aggravated by partition. In *Estranged Relations: A Brief Guide to Anglo-Irish History* he wrote:

> Partition deprived the new Irish state of one-third of its potential population and half the country's taxable capacity, thus significantly diminishing the home market.
>
> The result was that both North and South leaned separately, as it were, on Britain instead of supporting one another. The South for decades was heavily dependent on the British market for her agricultural exports—which were especially important for Britain during the Second World War—while Northern Ireland's industries have remained heavily dependent on subsidies from the British government.

Couglan believes that the ending of partition would be economically beneficial to both North and South, as well as improving relations with Great Britain itself.

A government of reconstruction would be faced with the remnants of the Northern crisis, not only economic woes, but the results of many years of bloodshed and violence. The Provisional IRA would have to be dealt with, not to mention the various loyalist paramilitaries. As with the loyalists, it is difficult to conceive of a nationalist guerrilla army gathering any support for a continued campaign once the British have departed and the guerrillas' expressed main goal has been achieved. There might indeed be opposition within the IRA to handing over power to an all-Ireland government's own security forces. But it would not be sufficient—nor would this issue be able to win enough support among the war-weary Catholics—to permit another round of violence to get underway.

All this is necessarily futuristic. It is a tragedy for Ireland that its sense of nationhood is still not realized and must still be talked of in terms of some future time. But until that time comes, Ireland, North and South, will experience the deforming effects of frustrated nationhood. Cruelty and violence will prevail over trust and cooperation. Democracy will continue to be twisted out of shape until it resembles a form of totalitarian state rather than one with the social aspirations traditionally associated with the Irish and British peoples. And the attendant sacrifice, already too long, and the suffering, already too great, will continue to waste the youth and weary the old. It is to be hoped that the achievement of such a goal will come before its fruits will be too bitter to be enjoyed.

Glossary

APPRENTICE BOYS. A loyalist body with strong links to the Orange Order. Its members march once a year in Derry to celebrate the Protestants who in 1688 shut the gates of the city against the Catholic pretender to the English throne, James II. A confrontation between the Apprentice Boys and local Catholics led to a serious outbreak of violence in Derry on August 12, 1969, which in turn set off a series of riots throughout Northern Ireland, forcing the British government to introduce the army.

B-SPECIALS. Set up in 1920 before partition as part of a Protestant militia recruited to reinforce the police in northeast Ireland, the B-Specials remained as an auxiliary force for the Royal Ulster Constabulary when it was created two years later to defend the newly established state. They soon gained a reputation among Catholics for bigotry and violence. In August 1969 the B-Specials played a controversial role in the civil disruptions, which led to the force's abolition by the British Labour government, which replaced it with the Ulster Defence Regiment, under the control of the British army.

CENTRAL CITIZENS DEFENCE COMMITTEE. Established in the aftermath of the August 1969 riots to coordinate Catholic defense groups throughout the Belfast ghettos, it soon became a vehicle for the Irish Republican Army until more conservative Catholic elements gained control. In some areas, however, the local defense committees were absorbed by the Provisional IRA as it grew in strength.

COMMUNIST PARTY OF IRELAND. A Moscow-oriented "Stalinist" party with little popular support but exercising power within the trade unions. Its growing influence over the Dublin leadership of the Irish Republican Army in the mid-sixties led to dissatisfaction among the IRA's more traditional members. The Communist Party of Ireland advocated the abandonment of the armed struggle against partition and the pursuit of peaceful political goals. The dissension this caused in the IRA created a split in late 1969, out of which came the Official IRA and the Provisional IRA.

DEMOCRATIC UNIONIST PARTY. Founded by the extreme loyalist leader the Reverend Ian Paisley in 1971, it is a vehicle for right-wing Unionist policies, though with a populist, working-class base. It is closely associated with the fundamentalist Free Presbyterian Church set up by Paisley in 1951, and several of its leading members are, like Paisley, ministers of that church. The Democratic Unionist Party (DUP) has been growing steadily in influence since 1971, winning support away from the other Unionist parties.

FIANNA FAIL. The largest political party in the Republic of Ireland, founded by Eamonn DeValera in 1926 after he split from Sinn Fein. Fianna Fail, adopting a pronationalist approach and vowing to end partition peacefully, went on to become the party of government of the Irish Republic for most of the state's sixty-year history. It was in power in the late 1960s and early 1970s when the present Northern Ireland crisis erupted. Many observers see it as being more sensitive to the national question than any of the other main parties in the Irish Republic.

FINE GAEL. Founded in 1933 as a right-wing, pro-Fascist party, it grew into the second largest of the Irish political groupings (after Fianna Fail), with a more conservative line. It formed a government in coalition with the Irish Labour Party in 1973 and under the leadership of Liam Cosgrave was responsible for a crackdown on the Provisionals and their supporters. But many found the "law and order" image of the government unacceptable in view of its mainly anti-IRA bias, with little or no criticism being levelled by Cosgrave or his ministers at British and loyalist atrocities in the North and South. The coalition government suffered a crushing electoral defeat at the hands of Fianna Fail in the summer of 1977.

IRISH LABOUR PARTY. A trade union–based, mildly reformist grouping in the Irish Republic with only marginal support among the Irish working class (who traditionally support Fianna Fail). It has acted more as a platform for political independents rather than as a genuine labor party on the European Social Democratic model.

IRISH REPUBLICAN ARMY. The nationalist guerrilla organization which fought the British during the 1919–21 war of independence. The outcome of that struggle was the acceptance of the treaty offered by British Prime Minister Lloyd George, which acquiesced in the partition of Ireland into the Free State (later the Republic of Ireland) and Northern Ireland in 1921. The IRA split into pro- and anti-treaty factions and a civil war resulted in which the pro-treaty faction triumphed. The IRA then went underground and fought a series of increasingly futile campaigns against both the Dublin and Northern Ireland regimes. There was a leftward tendency in the 1930s which led to a split in the organization. In the 1940s, 1950s, and early 1960s, the IRA conducted sporadic and unsuccessful campaigns against the Unionist government in Northern Ireland, but it won little support from local Catholics there, and by the mid-1960s was regarded as something of an anachronism. During this period another Communist Party-dominated leftward tendency developed among IRA leaders in Dublin like Cathal Goulding, who were disillusioned by the failure of previous campaigns. At the same time the crisis in Northern Ireland reached violent proportions, galvanizing the Northern-based IRA into action and eventually splitting the movement into those who favored a violent attack on partition and those who continued to pursue the line of compromise with emphasis on political and social action. The former became the *Provisional IRA* and the latter the *Official IRA*.

The Official IRA, though initially stronger, gradually lost support throughout Northern Ireland as the Provisional IRA campaign developed. The Official IRA was forced to conduct a "defensive" campaign against the British until May 1972, when it called a cease-fire in order to gain the release of its interned members. From then on the only violence engaged in by the Officials (locally referred to as "the Stickies") has been feuding between it and other factions and bank robberies for money needed to fund their frequent and largely unsuccessful election efforts. Another split from the Officials came in late 1974 with the formation of the *Irish Republican Socialist Party* by Official members who were discontented with the increasingly moderate policies being pushed by the Dublin leadership.

In the meantime the Provisional IRA (the "Provos") became the main nationalist guerrilla group in Ireland. Starting out under the leadership of Sean MacStiofain as an amalgam of rather conservative 1940s IRA leaders with a following of mainly Belfast supporters from the poor Catholic ghettos, it quickly developed into a widespread, formidable force commanding considerable support both in Northern Ireland and in the Irish Republic. The Provisional leadership went through several political aberrations, espousing in the mid-1970s a sort of Ulster nationalism, only to develop in the direction of militant leftish ideology. By 1980 the movement was in the hands of young Belfast left-wing leaders determined to fight a long war of attrition in the classic guerrilla mold.

IRISH REPUBLICAN SOCIALIST PARTY. Formed in late 1974 by members of the Official IRA and Official Sinn Fein who became concerned at what they considered the lack of militancy in the leadership and the failure of the movement to emphasize the question of partition. The Irish Republican Socialist Party (IRSP) sought to combine a strong Marxist analysis of the Irish problem with an uncompromising stance on the national question. Their armed wing, the *Irish National Liberation Army* (INLA), is made up of ex-Official IRA men who wanted to end the Officials' cease-fire and, when unable to do so, launched their own guerrilla group, which became involved in a bloody feud with their former comrades. The INLA murdered Airey Neave, the leading Conservative Party spokesman on Northern Ireland, in March 1979. It has since kept up a sporadic campaign of attacks on British soldiers, policemen, and prison officers throughout Northern Ireland. It is regarded by the security forces as small but dangerous, with a hard core of veteran guerrillas.

NATIONALIST PARTY. The antipartition party of Northern Ireland founded in 1921. It vacillated from attempts at being Stormont's loyal opposition to periods of complete abstention from parliament. Dominated by middle-class Catholics, it never grew into a force capable of winning any concessions from the Unionist government, which either patronized or openly despised it. The party became irrevelant after the formation of the Social Democratic and Labour Party in 1970.

NORTHERN IRELAND CIVIL RIGHTS ASSOCIATION. Founded in 1967 by diverse elements, including republicans, in order to draw attention to discrimination in housing allocation and job opportunities against Catholics by the Unionist regime. A series of well-publicized protest marches was met by violent opposition from the government and loyalist groups and set off a chain reaction which brought Northern Ireland to the verge of civil war in August 1969. From the early 1970s the Northern Ireland Civil Rights Association (NICRA) has been under the influence of the Official republican movement, gradually losing support and relevance as the Provisionals' guerrilla war developed.

NORTHERN IRELAND LABOUR PARTY. A trade union–based labor party dating from 1924. Except for brief periods in the mid-1960s, it has achieved no widespread support among either Catholic or Protestant working classes, both of which suspect its attitudes on the partition issue. Its position on partition has varied over the last sixty years but is now identical with that of the loyalist-Unionist political bloc.

ORANGE ORDER. Regarded as one of the great bastions of pro-British, Unionist ideology, it grew originally from sectarian struggles in the late eighteenth century to become the cultural-religious-political partner of the Unionist Party hegemony in Northern Ireland. Its membership overlapped with that of the Unionist Party, and its shrill anti-Catholic rhetoric complemented the sectarian policies of that party. No Catholic was allowed to join the Orange Order. Its rituals were celebrated every July 12th with marches, banner waving, and bonfires to proclaim Protestant supremacy. Since the mid-1970s, however, it has been declining in importance, as Protestant paramilitary groups such as the Ulster Defence Association have stolen its militancy and since the Unionist Party itself has split into factions.

PEOPLE'S DEMOCRACY. A student-based organization founded in 1968 and active in the civil rights campaigns, it was responsible for conducting what many regarded as provocative marches, such as that in January 1969, which took place in Protestant countryside and led to violence. As the civil rights organization NICRA became more moderate, the People's Democracy (PD) adopted an ever more left-wing and pro-Provisional IRA stance. It is now a small group wrecked by factions and splits, making little impact on the Irish political scene.

ROYAL ULSTER CONSTABULARY. Founded as the Northern Ireland police force in 1922, it was a paramilitary force with mostly Protestant membership. (Catholics only made up 10 percent of the RUC at most.) Its function was not so much that of a civil police body as a defender of the Unionist government and the territory of Northern Ireland. Reformed in 1969 and again, though less drastically, in the mid-1970s as part of the British government's policy of "Ulsterization," the RUC has been regaining its importance as the primary security force in Northern Ireland, in spite of many controversies created because of its documented violations of prisoners' rights.

SINN FEIN. The nationalist party founded in 1907 which went on to become the political wing of the IRA. It swept the Irish polls during the 1918 Westminster general election and went on to set up its own Irish parliament, or "Dail," which was outlawed by the British. Pursuing an abstentionist role after partition, refusing to recognize either the Dublin or Belfast regimes, it dwindled in power throughout the 1920s and 1930s. With the formation and success of Fianna Fail, it grew closer to the IRA. After the latter split in late 1969, Sinn Fein followed suit with the formation of *Provisional* and *Official Sinn Fein* organizations. Since then neither faction has exercised much political influence in Ireland, where they remain essentially rump parties.

ULSTER DEFENCE ASSOCIATION. The largest of the Protestant paramilitary organizations and the one responsible for most of the sectarian violence in Northern Ireland. Founded first in 1969 as a loose collection of vigilante groups, it was taken over in 1971 by extremist elements who transformed it into a militia with a hard core of assassins. It reached its peak strength in 1972—with the deteriorating security situation and the abolition of Stormont, many confused and angry Protestants joined its ranks. Support fell away in 1973, but has remained at a sufficient level to enable the UDA to control loyalist ghettos in Belfast. In 1973 the UDA assassins started calling themselves the *Ulster Freedom Fighters,* and issued statements claiming responsibility for sectarian murders under that name. Though the UFF as such does not exist, being only a term of convenience, the British proceeded to ban it, while the UDA itself remains quite legal. Since mid-1973 its chairman has been Andy Tyrie. Its actions have remained at a sectarian level, responding to the IRA campaigns. In 1977 it temporarily abandoned violence and pursued the idea of an independent Ulster as a solution to the crisis. But two years later it resumed its sectarian campaign, which it seems capable of conducting for the foreseeable future.

ULSTER DEFENCE REGIMENT. Formed by the British government in April 1970 to replace the abolished B-Specials, the Ulster Defence Regiment (UDR) is a locally recruited unit of the British army. It is made up of part-time and full-time members whose duties range from guarding power installations to regular patrolling and manning checkpoints. In its early years there was a concerted attempt to recruit Catholics into the regiment and prevent it from developing into a sectarian force like the B-Specials. However, the Provisionals conducted a ruthless campaign of assassination against the UDR, choosing as their special targets Catholic members. The vast majority of UDR men are Protestants. An alarmingly high number of members and ex-members of the UDR have been involved in sectarian crimes, and many have associations with the UDA and UVF. In spite of the suspicion in which Catholics hold the regiment, the British have been (as part of their "Ulsterization" policy) giving it more and more security responsibilities. Its strength is now almost 8,000 members, of whom an estimated 2 percent are Catholics.

ULSTER PROTESTANT VOLUNTEERS. Formed in the mid-1960s by the Reverend Ian Paisley, the Ulster Protestant Volunteers (UPV) was a paramilitary body attached to the Free Presbyterian Church. In the late 1960s several of its members were involved in terrorist bombings that helped oust liberal Unionist Prime Minister Terence O'Neill from power. The UPV disappeared from the scene after 1969 with the rise of more overtly violent loyalist groups.

ULSTER UNIONIST PARTY. For many years the leading loyalist party in Northern Ireland, committed to opposing Irish unity. Formed at the turn of the century as the Ulster Unionist Council; with the setting up of Northern Ireland in 1921, it became the Unionist Party, the party of government, until Stormont was suspended in 1972. From the beginning it had strong links with the British Conservative Party. Its policies were consistently right-wing and most of its leading members were landowners, industrialists, and businessmen. With the Orange Order, the Unionist Party formed a powerful political-social-cultural-religious monolith, dominating all aspects of life in Northern Ireland for fifty years. However, during the 1970s its unity was disrupted by the political crisis. It fragmented into several parties, the main ones being the *Vanguard Unionist Party* of William Craig, at one time strongly in favor of Ulster Independence; the *Unionist Party of Northern Ireland,* set up by the late Brian Faulkner to pursue more moderate, pro–power-sharing policies. After these splits the Unionist Party became known as the *Official Unionist Party,* which remains the strongest, most basic tendency of the loyalist cause, while the others have withered. Within the last few years, however, it has been challenged by Paisley's party, the more militant Democratic Unionist Party, which has been growing rapidly in support among Protestants.

ULSTER VOLUNTEER FORCE (1). A Protestant militia formed in 1912 to oppose home rule for Ireland. It was recruited almost en masse into the British army, where it formed a separate division and suffered heavy casualties during the First World War. The Ulster Volunteer Force (UVF) became a hallowed symbol for loyalists of their intransigent opposition to Republican-Catholic struggles for an independent Ireland.

ULSTER VOLUNTEER FORCE (2). A paramilitary group created by Gusty Spence in the mid-1960s, using the emotive initials "UVF" and determined to oppose what its members perceived as the threat of IRA subversion. The organization conducted a clumsy but brutal sectarian terror campaign from 1965 until—after it killed three people—the police rounded up the leaders in the summer of 1966. It was declared an illegal organization. Regrouping in the early 1970s, the UVF went on to conduct a sectarian campaign of great ferocity until once more its ranks were thinned by arrests. To date it is still active, but much less so than the UDA.

ULSTER WORKERS COUNCIL. A body of loyalist trade unionists that came together under the aegis of the UDA to coordinate industrial actions against the power-sharing executive of Brian Faulkner and Gerry Fitt in early 1974. Its actions resulted in the closing down of Northern Ireland's power stations, which was instrumental in bringing down the power-sharing government.

Index

(Italicized numbers indicate references to photo captions)